The Financial Storm V

Jeff Camarda · Steven James Lee · Jerusha Lee

The Financial Storm Warning for Investors

How to Prepare and Protect Your Wealth from Tax Hikes and Market Crashes

palgrave
macmillan

Jeff Camarda
Family Wealth Education Institute
Jacksonville, FL, USA

Steven James Lee
California State Polytechnic University
Pomona, CA, USA

Jerusha Lee
Claremont Graduate University
Claremont, CA, USA

ISBN 978-3-030-77270-3   ISBN 978-3-030-77271-0   (eBook)
https://doi.org/10.1007/978-3-030-77271-0

This Palgrave Macmillan imprint is published by the registered company Springer Nature Switzerland AG
The registered company address is: Gewerbestrasse 11, 6330 Cham, Switzerland

Important Disclosure Information

Among other things, Jeff Camarda PhD, EA, CFA is the founder and Chief Executive Officer of Camarda Wealth Advisory Group ("CWAG"), an investment adviser registered with the United States Securities and Exchange Commission, located in Fleming Island, FL. The book content is for information purposes only, and does not provide any personalized investment or securities advice from the author to the reader that is based upon the reader's specific situation or objectives. To the contrary, no reader should assume that this book serves as the receipt of, or a substitute for, personalized investment or securities advice from the investment and/or other professionals of his/her choosing. The author is not a lawyer, accountant, or commission insurance agent. Given this author's lack of familiarity with individual readers' situations, no portion of the content serves as *personalized* legal, accounting, tax or insurance advice. Please remember that different types of investments involve varying degrees of risk. Therefore, it should not be assumed that future performance of any specific investment or investment strategy (including the investments and/or investment strategies referenced and/or recommended in the book), or any non-investment related content (including regulated financial planning topics), will be profitable, equal any historical performance levels, be suitable for a reader's individual situation, or prove correct. Certain portions of the book may reflect positions and/or recommendations as of a specific prior date, and may no longer be reflective of current positions, recommendations, or laws. **Please Note: Limitations**. Neither rankings and/or recognitions by unaffiliated rating services, publications, media, or other organizations, nor the achievement of any professional designation, certification, degree, or license, membership in any professional organization, or any amount of prior experience or success, should be construed by any client or prospective client as a guarantee that he/she will experience a certain level of results if CWAG is engaged, or continues to be engaged, to provide investment advisory services. Rankings published by magazines, and others, generally base their selections exclusively on information prepared and/or submitted by the recognized adviser. Rankings are generally limited to participating advisers (participation criteria/methodology available at www.camarda.com). No ranking or recognition should be construed as a current or past endorsement of CWAG by any of its clients.

Contents

List of Figures

The Social Security and Medicare Crisis

The Government Debt Crisis

Investment Strategies to Prosper in the Storm

List of Tables

The Problem

The Coming Wealth Storm—The Many Risks You Face and Why You Need This Book

This will be a short but unpleasant chapter. The best thing about it is its brevity. But I must do all in my power to get your attention, so you may protect your wealth for you and your family.

When I say wealth, I don't mean some abstract, greed-driven fantasy of King Midas or Gordon Gekko.

Greed is good, but not how Gordon meant it. I am talking about your family wealth. The engine that fuels your life, your lifestyle, your ability to stay healthy, live longer, help your kids and grandkids get educated and in other ways. Your fuel to enjoy a long and comfortable retirement, free from worries of scrimping or even running out.

Your money is your life. It is the tool that gives you freedom and choices. It is the bedrock of civilized comfort.

Just think, for a moment, what your future would look like if your wealth was taxed to a thin shadow of its current value, if government benefits like Social Security disappeared or were cut way down because you are not poor enough, or if the stock and bond markets began a years-long crash you could not live long enough to recover from.

Do I have your attention?

Because there is a medium to high risk that some of these—or all of these and then some—may come home to roost in the very near future.

Am I sure of this? Of course not.

Am I really worried about it?

You betcha.

© The Author(s), under exclusive license to Springer Nature
Switzerland AG 2021
J. Camarda et al., *The Financial Storm Warning for Investors*,
https://doi.org/10.1007/978-3-030-77271-0_1

Who am I to say this? Why should you listen?

Without tooting my horn too awful loud, I'll give you a little background.

The short of it is I've made a lifelong study of wealth, for pushing a half-century.

I began as a stockbroker in New York and managed brokerage branches there, in DC, and in Florida before I lost my stomach for it. I completed the Certified Financial Planner (CFP®—financial planning), Chartered Financial Consultant (ChFC®—financial planning), and Chartered Life Underwriter (CLU®—insurance, estate planning & tax) designations. I also completed the Chartered Financial Analyst (CFA®—investments—by far the hardest one I've done), Certified Funds Specialist (CFS® investments) designations, and became Board Certified in Mutual Funds (BCM™).

But wait, there's more.

I know I promised a short chapter, and I will stick to that.

I got an EA Federal tax license, giving me unlimited IRS practice rights, like CPAs and attorneys, to basically practice tax law when representing clients before IRS. I got a Master's degree in Financial Planning, and a PhD in Financial and Retirement Planning, and am fortunate to be an award-winning academic researcher, specializing in financial advisor education and professionalism (or frequent lack thereof, I am sad to say). And I am currently admitted to graduate study at Georgetown Law, taking a Master's of Science in Tax Law (what they call the LLM for non-JDs).

Just a couple more, then back to all those unpleasant risks you face.

I was early in becoming a no-commission fiduciary advisor, a pioneer, really, back in the 1990s. I am proud to have founded many firms and other organizations, including the Family Wealth Education Institute, devoted to teaching you-know-what. I've been blessed to have been named a "top advisor" by *Barron's, Forbes, Bloomberg* and others and to have been repeatedly featured in *Barron's* and the *Wall Street Journal*. I've been a published wealth author for decades and have been a wealth contributor to *Forbes* for years.

Whew! Glad that's over. As I hope you can tell from my writing style, I'm also a regular guy. I learned all this stuff out of a burning desire to build and keep wealth for my own family, and I worry a lot about yours. I bore you with all this background on me for only one reason: to try to convince you of the quality of information I am about to share, and the depth of my expertise and considered opinion on the risks I'm about to share.

This truly could be the most important book you ever read, in terms of keeping your life on the track you hope and dream for it.

So back to the dangers that have surrounded you, probably without your noticing. In my many decades of wealth study and professional practice, I have never seen so many dark forces line up or ever before been inclined to forecast the potential for an investors' perfect storm.

So hear this!

Wealth warning! The COVID-induced global (economic) chilling—short-lived though we hope it will be!—is forecast to unleash profound economic distortions that could prove highly hazardous to your wealth and upend your financial goals!

Is an investors' perfect storm about to hit? Evil forces are gathering that could derail or completely destroy your wealth and retirement plan. Could you run out of money? Those at or near the magic retirement years should take heed, as should all those concerned with retirement income. Those affected extend well beyond baby boomers.

The impact of this storm could affect income streams even for the youngest savers who have little hope of living off fixed income doled out by the future Social Security Administration.

Will the COVID crisis, piled on top of the new cold war with China, brewing civil unrest, and increasingly contentious political discord trigger an economic cataclysm?

What about the out-of-the-park record levels of national debt, the looming bankruptcies of Social Security and Medicare, and the high risk that the Fed's round-the-clock money printing will launch the next period of high or hyperinflation?

Could all these dark forces trigger an economic cataclysm or even another Depression? Could they, on top of the frothiest, most overvalued stock market in decades, trigger the mother of all long-term bear markets? Could these conditions swallow your financial plan, eviscerate your investments, and destroy your retirement?

I surely hope not, but consider some of these threats facing today's investors:

1. Mega-market crash: Stock market valuations are flying too high, completely divorced from economic reality. Even *Barron's* and the *Wall Street Journal* have branded this market a tech-stock-driven "bubble." Bubbles always end badly, with huge losses and devastated dreams. The recent pounding tech stocks have taken could just be the initial tremors. Consider: In the last tech bubble, stocks peaked in March of 2000 before plunging by more than 80% in the months to come…and it took over sixteen years to recover those losses. If that happened again, could you wait a decade and a half to break even?

2. Hyperinflation: The United States hasn't seen serious inflation in decades, but conditions are ripening to see this return with a vengeance. The Federal Reserve has pulled out all the stops to drive interest rates down, juice the economy with cash, and implement a long-term easy money policy. These are perfect conditions for a plunging dollar, huge losses on investment bonds, the loss of purchasing power, and massive losses on "inflation-ignorant" investments. Mid-2020 has already seen the worst inflation since 1991, and it's probably going to get much, much worse—even as the Fed keeps rates in the sub-basement for an extended period. Consider: If your nest egg were to keep shrinking at the same time prices for what you need are shooting up, where does that leave your life and retirement? Double-danger warning: Such conditions spell doom for the bond market and may put severe cracks in the credit ratings of the revered US Government Bond. And don't forget the potential impact of run-away inflation on critical needs like health care!

3. Massive tax hikes are inevitable. Even before COVID-19, the US Federal Deficit was barreling toward unsustainable levels. Now, government debt is projected to actually exceed gross domestic product in short order. This is a huge deal. This is a massive debt load never before seen, even higher than after World War II. And from here, economic prospects look far drearier than in post-war America, arguably our country's finest hour. On top of that, Social Security and Medicare will go upside down shortly thereafter. This will be a massive bust. This crushing debt load can only be addressed one way—by raising taxes on the minority of voters who've accumulated wealth….and by "monetizing the debt"—basically letting inflation run rampant and paying the debt off "pennies-on-the-dollar-wise" with shrinking dollars. As this juggernaut rolls down the pike, neither the Trump tax cuts nor the proposed Joe Biden tax plan will make much difference.

This trifecta of disasters could result in unbridled misery for those who don't find ways to avoid them.

Consider: What could a sixteen-year nosedive in the value of your investments do if you are in or approaching retirement? At the same time taxes are gobbling ever-great shares of your incredibly shrinking dollars?

Let's look at some simple math that maybe your financial planner has not done or shared with you.

Say the market tumbles 80% or so like it did in the last tech crash.

And if you think you're not exposed to tech, better check and think again. Unlike on the last go-round for the tech bubble, indexes like the S&P 500 are increasingly dominated by pie-in-the-sky-valued tech. For instance, just 5 names—Apple, Microsoft, Google, Facebook, and Amazon—recently represented pushing 30% of the S&P 500! That does not leave much room for the other 495 names, and that's before we consider "lesser" tech, like Adobe, Advanced Micro, and pure-tech-siblings like FLIR, commutations, biotech, and other stealth tech bets that heighten the concentration of tech in the index.

Back to the 80% tumble. That would take a respectable $2M nest egg down to $400K—ouch!

And if you are pulling and spending—like out of an IRA—that's before we look at taxes and inflation.

So if your nest egg tracks the last 16-year climb from tech crash to breakeven, your nominal return—before inflation—would be about 10.6% a year. Sounds good until you remember you're digging out from an 80% loss!

If we adjust for not the mega-inflation I fear but just the 5% annualized from the recent reading, the actual return—before taxes!—is about 5.5% (for you nerds, from real return = $(1+ \text{nominal return})/(1+ \text{inflation}) -1$ which is near enough return minus inflation rate for most of us!).

If we then take that nest egg with that real return and assume you pay today's highest income tax rate of 37%—which is before any state income tax and I think much lower than future rates on "fat cats" like those interested in reading this book—we get some ugly news.

If someone did that at 65, and say, lived to 85, and spent both return and principal, leaving nothing for the kids or even a surviving spouse, here's what the annual "pension" number would look like:

$31,726 before taxes.

$19,987 after taxes. That's a year, not a month, by the way.

Jiminy Cricket, that's scary!

I bet even five times that amount would leave you scrimping!

Surely, I hope that I am wrong. And I have exaggerated and simplified more than a bit to get your attention.

But in all my decades studying and practicing wealth management, I have never, ever seen the sky so dark.

My solutions?

Here's just a couple of the wealth rescue themes we'll explore in the book.

Embrace the sort of tactical trading ethos that could enable you to not only skirt the devastation, but actually prosper through the carnage. Most advisors and securities analysts are clueless on this skill set, but in my view your asset allocation needs entirely new thinking to get you through this storm.

We'll tell you why the hold and pray textbook approach is so much Kool-Aid, and give you the methodology to make money in any market, and have more than a fair shot at beating it!

Study and accumulate the sort of assets that are likely to withstand and grow through inflation. And please, don't knee-jerk yourself punch-drunk by saying real estate. That's so 1970s, and COVID-19 has Zoomed much of the real estate pantheon into the same barn where they keep the buggy whips. We will show you more enlightened paths to inflation-proofing your assets.

Master your tax profile! Taxes are indeed the master wealth skill, and the reason that as a PhD—where I thought to finish my 40 years of higher education—I am now getting a Masters in Tax Law from Georgetown Law in my early 60s. There is no bigger club in the wealth toolbox than tax. I have made a lifelong study of it, and even I feel compelled to sharpen the saw. Showing you how to protect your wealth from the acid of tax—and you will be amazed at what you learn and how valuable it is!—is probably the most important thing the book will teach you. I mean, rocket-fuel important!

This gathering triumvirate of dark lords—market bubble, hyperinflation, and confiscatory taxes—is so killer-dangerous, and critically urgent, that you much take proactive steps to protect your wealth for you and your family. Many fortunes will be swept away. But yours, gentle reader, will be safe and sheltered from the storm. It will grow—you will prosper, even—by applying the many gems that will tumble out of this book as you go through it.

I am so excited for you and your family. I hope you enjoy reading this as much as I enjoyed writing it.

This book is very focused on a few key areas. There is so much more to smart wealth than what we cover here. For this reason, I founded the Family Wealth Education Institute. We call it FWEI (fee-wee) for short. FEWI offers a bunch of online courses—mostly taught by me—on lots of important wealth concepts. The course catalog is large and ever-expanding. I try very hard to make the classes fun, entertaining, and to communicate complex material in a way that is clear and useful. You don't need to be able to engineer a Ferrari to enjoy driving the car. These classes are online and open to readers of this book at no cost. I invite you to register. To sign up and unlock your personal treasure education chest, go to www.fweibook.org.

The Social Security and Medicare Crisis

These retirement safety net programs present a double threat.

First, they may not be there for you when you really need them. Both are on the verge of bankruptcy and will have to undergo pretty massive changes and cuts if they are to survive at all. That means benefit cuts, reduced payouts, and more cost-sharing on Medicare health costs. It also means stealthier cuts for many Americans, in the way of taxes on benefits. Once upon a time, Social Security benefits were tax free: "Since a pair of 1938 Treasury Department Tax Rulings, and another in 1941, Social Security benefits have been explicitly excluded from federal income taxation. (A revision was issued in 1970, but it made no changes in the existing policy.) This changed for the first time with the passage of the 1983 Amendments to the Social Security Act. Beginning in 1984, a portion of Social Security benefits have been subject to federal income taxes."[1] Since the 1980s, the IRS has steadily chipped away at this tax-free nature, and more and more has become taxable over time. The net effect? You only keep part of the benefit. If you get $1,000 but IRS imposes a 30% tax, you only keep $700, which is the net benefit. The tax math is way more complicated than this simple example, but you get the point.

Second, with the programs about to go belly-up, massive tax hikes will be needed to keep them even partially afloat. And float they must, since it is both socially unthinkable and politically impossible, to ditch them. Hark, those who read this book! The brunt of these taxes will be borne by those who have accumulated some private wealth of their own. The richer you are, the more you will pay for others' benefits, and the less you will get yourself.

© The Author(s), under exclusive license to Springer Nature Switzerland AG 2021
J. Camarda et al., *The Financial Storm Warning for Investors*,
https://doi.org/10.1007/978-3-030-77271-0_2

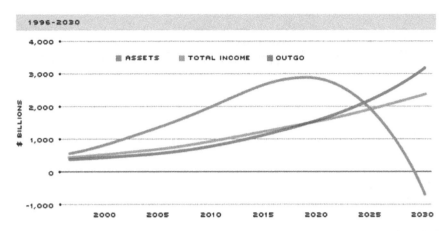

Fig. 1 Social security income, outgo and assets (*Source* Neely, Michelle Clark. "Shaking the Third Rail: Reforming Social Security." Federal Reserve Bank of St. Louis, October 1, 1996. https://www.stlouisfed.org/publications/regional-economist/october-1996/shaking-the-third-rail-reforming-social-security)

It's not like this is breaking news, though it may seem new to you. It doesn't get nearly the press it deserves. The crisis has been forecast for decades. I remember studying it as an undergrad circa 1980 and as a young financial professional in the 1990s. But little has been done to address it. Long known as "the third rail of American politics—touch it and you will die," this has been kicked down the road so long it's a miracle there's any metal left on it. Here what the picture looked like way back in 1996, from an old Federal Reserve Bank report (Fig. 1).[2]

The belly-up crossover point is around 2025 on that old graph. As we will see in a bit, it's probably gotten far, far worse than predicted back then.

The problem is pretty easy to understand if you think about it. First of all, we need to remember that Social Security is a "pay as you go" system. That means they spent the money you may have thought you contributed to "your" Social Security "retirement account" long, long ago. A 50-year-old's Social Security "contribution" is instantly converted into a 70-year-old's payment; it does not go into some individual account for the 50-year-old.

The reality is Social Security is and has always been a tax-based system. They tax workers and take the tax money and pay it to retirees. When it's your turn, they collect taxes from younger workers and give some to you. These taxes are bundled into so-called payroll taxes, which are different from income taxes but come out of employees' paychecks just the same, shaving the "take home." The part that funds Social Security and Medicare is called FICA—Federal Insurance Contributions Act.

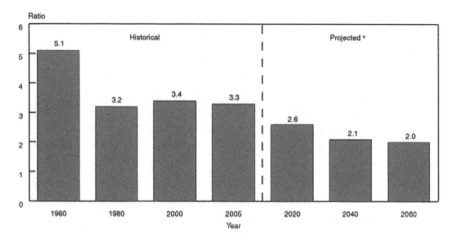

Fig. 2 Worker to beneficiary ratio, selected years 1960–2060 (*Source* Reznik, Gayle L., Dave Shoffner, and David A. Weaver. "Coping with the Demographic Challenge: Fewer Children and Living Longer." *Social Security Bulletin*, 66, no. 4 (2005/2006). https://www.ssa.gov/policy/docs/ssb/v66n4/v66n4p37.html)

The big problem, now, is there's lots more old folks than workers to pay them, and those old folks are living lots longer then ever imagined when the Old-Age, Survivors, and Disability Income program (this is the official name for Social Security[3]) was conceived way back in FDR's time.

Back in the 1930s, when Social Security was founded, demographic trends and life expectancies were very different. As designed, Social Security provides a lifetime pension beginning at age 65. I should not have to tell you, but that was pretty old, way back then. In 1930, the life expectancy for men was 58 and women 62. Lots of folks did not make it to 65. Those that did could be expected to live into their 70s.[4] Life expectancies have gotten far longer, even before we consider the Med Tech effect we'll get to in another chapter.

Besides retirees living and needing inflation-adjusted checks for longer, the number of Social Security tax-paying workers has steadily declined since the golden days of radio back in the 1930s and is forecast to get far worse. Look at the worker-to-beneficiary ratio graph below.[5] This report from the Social Security Administration in the 1990s is a little old, but you get the picture. Fewer and fewer workers, and more and more old folks on the dole, living far longer than ever dreamt of while the Great Depression was raging and World War II was brewing. Population-wise, America was young, and the baby boom produced a bulge of workers with plenty of payroll to tax for the new Social Security program. Now it is old, the baby boom generation is mostly retired, and the calculus has flipped (Fig. 2).

Way back when this report was written, the prognosis was already clearly dire. "Due to demographic changes, the U.S. Social Security system will face financial challenges in the near future. Declining fertility rates and increasing life expectancies are causing the U.S. population to age…at the same time, the working-age population is shrinking …consequently, the Social Security system is experiencing a declining worker-to-beneficiary ratio, which will fall from 3.3 in 2005 to 2.1 in 2040 (the year in which the Social Security trust fund is projected to be exhausted). [*It is now predicted to go bust way sooner— Jeff*]. This presents a significant challenge to policymakers. One policy option that could help keep the Social Security system solvent is to reduce retirement benefits, either by raising the normal retirement age or through life expectancy indexing, to reflect the fact that people are living longer. However, these reductions in benefits have the potential to harm economically vulnerable retirees. Other options, such as progressive price indexing proposals, explicitly protect the retirement benefits of low lifetime earners. Still other options would seek to raise additional revenue for the system… it is important to encourage older workers to delay retirement…." Translation? Cut benefits. Raise the retirement age. Implement means-testing, or protect the poor but cut benefits for the fat cats likely to be reading this book. And, oh, yeah; raise taxes!

Those options haven't changed much. While an extremely knotty problem, the math is not rocket science. We simply can't afford Social Security and Medicare as they are, and something's gotta give. If you're not careful, it will be your family's wealth that, er, "gives."

So where are we now? According to the Social Security Administration's 2020 report,[6] "Social Security and Medicare both face long-term financing shortfalls under currently scheduled benefits and financing. Both programs will experience cost growth substantially in excess GDP growth during through the mid-2030s due to rapid population aging….the Old-Age and Survivors Insurance (OASI) Trust Fund, which pays retirement and survivors benefits, will be able to pay scheduled benefits on a timely basis until 2034…at that time, the fund's reserves will become depleted…."

Beyond the decaying finances, it's important to appreciate how gargantuan these programs are. From the same report: "Social Security and Medicare together accounted for 41 percent of total federal expenditures in fiscal year 2019. … any drawdown of trust fund balances, as well as general fund transfers into Medicare's SMI fund, increases financial pressure on the unified budget." In other words, continuing to pay benefits will play havoc with the general Federal budget, which is already close to hitting the fan in a big way without this massive problem, as we explore in another chapter.

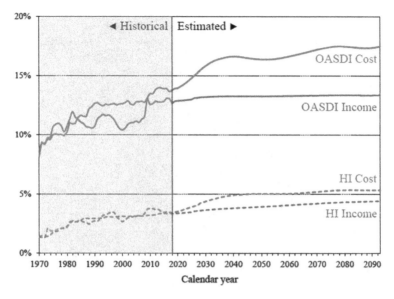

Fig. 3 OASDI and HI income and cost as percentages of their respective taxable payrolls (*Source* "A Summary of the 2020 Annual Reports." Social Security Administration. Accessed January 11, 2021. https://www.ssa.gov/oact/TRSUM/)

Some other graphs are gloominating:

As you can see, the costs of the program far exceed the take on payroll taxes, and have since early in the century (Fig. 3).

Looking down the road from today, we can see the crushing weight of promised benefits, far exceeding not only program revenues, but the gray-area massive transfusions from general government reserves that themselves are fast approaching depletion (Fig. 4).

One final graphic from this report. HI is Medicare's Hospital Insurance, and OASI, of course, is Social Security retirement income benefits. The zero% line is flat-out, belly-up broke. As I write this in the days before Christmas of 2020, we are already past the gray historical zone. As incredibly bad as this looks, the reality is probably even worse (Fig. 5).

As has long been the case for hands-sitting politicians, "lawmakers have many policy options that would reduce or eliminate the long-term financing shortfalls in Social Security and Medicare. Lawmakers should address these financial challenges as soon as possible. Taking action sooner rather than later will permit consideration of a broader range of solutions and provide more time to phase in changes so that the public has adequate time to prepare…the projections and analysis in these reports do not reflect the potential effects of the COVID-19 pandemic on the Social Security and Medicare programs.

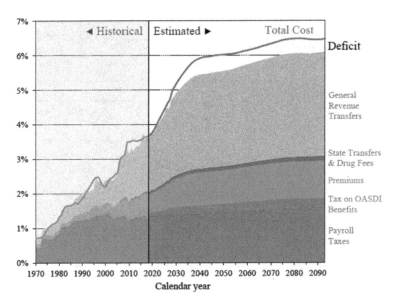

Fig. 4 Medicare cost and non-interest income by source as a percentage of GDP (*Source* "A Summary of the 2020 Annual Reports." Social Security Administration. Accessed January 11, 2021. https://www.ssa.gov/oact/TRSUM/)

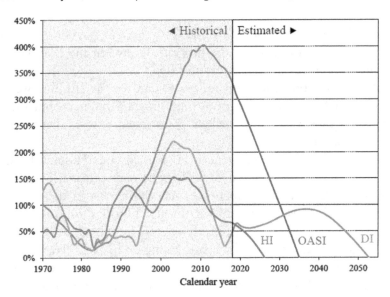

Fig. 5 OASI, DI, and HI, trust fund ratios [Asset reserves as a percentage of annual cost] (*Source* "A Summary of the 2020 Annual Reports." Social Security Administration. Accessed January 11, 2021. https://www.ssa.gov/oact/TRSUM/)

Given the uncertainty associated with these impacts…it is not possible to adjust their estimates accurately at this time."

Shortly after this report was issued, *the New York Times* had this[7] to say: "According to the report, the cost of Social Security, the federal retirement program, will exceed its income in 2020 for the first time since 1982. The program's reserve fund is projected to be depleted in 16 years, at which time recipients will get smaller payments than they are scheduled to receive if Congress does not act.

Meanwhile, Medicare's hospital insurance fund is expected to be depleted in 2026—the same date that was projected a year ago. At that point, doctors, hospitals, and nursing homes would not receive their full compensation from the program and patients could face more of the financial burden. Fiscal watchdog groups said on Monday that the new figures underscored the need for changes to the programs. 'That fact that we now can't guarantee full benefits to current retirees is completely unacceptable, and it should be cause enough for every policymaker to rally around solutions to restore solvency to those programs.. we need solutions.' That appears unlikely in the near term. The weight of Social Security and Medicare on the economy is projected only to grow."

While the government may not officially opine on the fix COVID's twisted an already-dire situation into, the media has.

According to The Motley Fool,[8] the essence of the report is "Social Security's combined trust funds will run dry in 2035. Once that happens, the program will no longer have the financial means to continue paying benefits as scheduled. Rather, Social Security will be forced to implement benefit cuts that hurt current and future recipients." But wait, there's more. The Fool goes on to say "prediction of a 2035 trust fund depletion date was made prior to the worst of the COVID-19 crisis, so it's fair to say that if current economic conditions persist well into 2021, Social Security is going to have a major problem on its hands sooner than anyone would like…" and (gulp)…"if current economic conditions persist, *we may see Social Security deplete its trust funds prior to 2030,* thereby causing untold harm for beneficiaries sooner than expected." COVID is unquestionably pushing the needle on this. Unemployment hit the worst levels since the Great Depression—the Great bloody Depression!—early in 2020,[9] and despite the promise of multiple miracle vaccines (thanks goodness!), it may get worse before it gets better. Early 2021 was saddled with a double dip recession, hopefully not to 2020 lows but that may be overly optimistic. Economic damage from COVID has been deep, widespread, and savage, and it will take years to be healed, assuming we lick the virus fast, and that remains a long bet even in late 2021.

So why have lawmakers been so blindly deer-in-the headlights on this? Why is this frog lingering in the pot long past the boiling point? It's all about the political economics. Politicians get paid in votes, and those that cut benefits starve and get replaced by those that sing a popular song.

Even before COVID, the go-bust date for Social Security was inching down from the early 2030s to the 2020s—yikes that's the decade we're in! I have little confidence Washington will make the painful, fair, and logical choices to shore up the system. I have some ideas on that but since I think donkeys will fly before that happens, I won't waste your time.

Instead, I see massive tax hikes ahead for those that have decent incomes and have acquired some wealth. Both FICA and regular income taxes will go up, big time, plus others we talk about elsewhere in the book. If you're interested enough in managing your wealth to be reading this, assume you are honored to be targeted within this "fat cat" group. FICA will go up and apply to more and more of your income. The Social Security part of FICA— by far the biggest piece—will rise "3.7% to $142,800, from $137,700 in 2020."[10] Proposals are already on the table to hike that more, and I look for them to tax your whole enchilada before long, about the same time you learn your own Social Security benefits will be taxed to smithereens, or be yanked entirely because you're too rich to meet the means test. To be clear on what that is: "In its simplest form, means-testing would look at the annual income of Social Security beneficiaries and determine, based on that income, whether they'd receive a reduced benefit check, or no benefit check at all….the idea of means-testing is to ensure that Social Security benefits are going to people who really need them, which is how the program was designed in the mid-1930s." A noble aim, but since this is *your* money we are talking about, you may feel differently.

No? then consider how hard it will be to suffer steep tax hikes and at the same time try to scrape by without Social Security payments to supplement your income and without the jewel of Medicare to pay for the care needed to comfort you and maybe extend your life.

If you are rational—and I know there's a rational economic actor in there somewhere, you rascal!—you will seek to minimize your tax burden and at the same time increase your personal dole from the fading Social Security system.

Fortunately, the solution—clever taxable income and tax management— kills both (to be politically correct, let's call them virtual and angry) birds with the same stone.

We get to cookbook detail in the solutions/countermeasures Part 2 of the book.

But, please, try to quell yourself from jumping ahead. I know it's tempting! And I truly wish the challenges facing you as a wealth holder were limited to Social Security and Medicare. Unfortunately, the sky is far darker, and I think you will do best to get fully briefed on the many crises you may have to navigate, before plotting your course.

And remember, as a reader of this book you have free access to a wealth of wealth education classes from FWEI, you just need to register at www.fweibook.org.

Notes

1. DeWitt, Larry. "Research Note #12: Taxation of Social Security Benefits." Social Security Administration, February 2001. https://www.ssa.gov/history/taxationofbenefits.html#:~:text=Since%20a%20pair%20of%201938,changes%20in%20the%20existing%20policy.
2. Neely, Michelle Clark. "Shaking the Third Rail: Reforming Social Security." Federal Reserve Bank of St. Louis, October 1, 1996. https://www.stlouisfed.org/publications/regional-economist/october-1996/shaking-the-third-rail-reforming-social-security.
3. Kagan, Julia. "Old-Age, Survivors, and Disability Insurance (OASDI) Program." Investopedia, December 28, 2020. https://www.investopedia.com/terms/o/oasdi.asp.
4. "Life Expectancy for Social Security." Social Security Administration. https://www.ssa.gov/history/lifeexpect.html#:~:text=Life%20expectancy%20at%20birth%20in,and%20paid%20into%20Social%20Security.
5. Reznik, Gayle L., Dave Shoffner, and David A. Weaver. "Coping with the Demographic Challenge: Fewer Children and Living Longer." *Social Security Bulletin*, 66, no. 4 (2005/2006). https://www.ssa.gov/policy/docs/ssb/v66n4/v66n4p37.html.
6. "A Summary of the 2020 Annual Reports." Social Security Administration. Accessed January 11, 2021. https://www.ssa.gov/oact/TRSUM/.
7. Rappeport, Alan. "Social Security and Medicare Funds Face Insolvency, Report Finds." *The New York Times*, April 22, 2019. https://www.nytimes.com/2019/04/22/us/politics/social-security-medicare-insolvency.html.
8. Backman, Maurie. "Could Social Security Be Pushed Into Insolvency Before 2030?" *The Motley Fool*, May 20, 2020. https://www.fool.com/retirement/2020/05/20/could-social-security-be-pushed-into-insolvency-be.aspx.
9. Backman, Maurie. "Unemployment Is at Its Worst Since the Great Depression." *The Motley Fool*, May 9, 2020. https://www.fool.com/careers/2020/05/09/unemployment-is-at-its-worst-since-the-great-depre.aspx.
10. Ebeling, Ashlea. "Maximum Social Security Taxes Will Increase 3.7% While Benefits Will Rise 1.3% In 2021." *Forbes*, October 13, 2020. https://www.forbes.com/sites/ashleaebeling/2020/10/13/maximum-social-security-taxes-will-increase-37-while-benefits-will-rise-13-in-2021/?sh=5dcfa25e22f1.

The Government Debt Crisis

As we explore in detail in an upcoming chapter, colossal tax hikes are inevitable, and probably coming down the pike in short order.

Even before the global COVID pandemic, US Federal red ink was gushing to *The Shining* proportions, already unsustainable and barreling toward breakdown levels.

In COVID's wake, government debt is now projected to actually exceed gross domestic product in the very near term order.

This is a very, very big deal. This is a crushing debt load, far beyond anything seen before in America. Bigger than even the huge bill paid to finance World War II, back when the country was young, fertile, and the US demographic picture was much more amenable to paying it off.

Nearly a century later, economic prospects look far gloomier than in Post-War America. As we saw in the Social Security chapter, Social Security and Medicare will go upside down very soon.

There is a massive bust brewing. There are very few options to address this crushing debt load. One is by raising taxes on the minority of voters who've accumulated wealth, like you, dear reader. The other is by "monetizing the debt"—basically by printing and devaluating money, letting inflation run rampant, and paying the debt down with incredibly shrinking dollars. As this juggernaut rolls down the pike, neither the Trump-era tax cuts nor the gathering tax hike legislation will make much difference in the face of this mega-black hole of debt.

© The Author(s), under exclusive license to Springer Nature
Switzerland AG 2021
J. Camarda et al., *The Financial Storm Warning for Investors*,
https://doi.org/10.1007/978-3-030-77271-0_3

Before we really get into this, it's helpful to get a sense of the ebbs and flows of US Federal dollars. Let's start with the income side. The below graphics and background come from the Congressional Budget Office, from a 2020 report[1] based on 2019 data. It's ironic the graphs take the shape of a bullseye, and it may be helpful to think of the first one being plastered on your back.

Why? If we add up the payroll taxes (mostly FICA—96% of payroll taxes!—which are perennially burnt to a crisp on the alter of Social Security and Medicare benefits) and income taxes, we get to about 83% of total Federal income, coming entirely off the backs of individual taxpayers. Even more, when we consider things like the excise taxes you pay, as well as estate and gift taxes, which we'll develop more in the solutions part of the book. You may be surprised to see that less than 7% of total Federal funding comes from corporate taxes, even from behemoths like Amazon, Tesla, Google, Facebook, and so on. For instance, CNBC reported[2] that Amazon paid zero in Federal income taxes for 2017 and 2018, despite making billions of dollars. "In 2018, Amazon posted income of more than $11 billion, but the company paid $0 in federal taxes. In fact, thanks to tax credits and deductions, Amazon actually received a federal tax refund of $129 million. That was a year after Amazon received a $137 million refund from the federal government for 2017." For 2019, did pay $162,000,000—which was still only 1.2% of the $13,900,000,000 it made.

One reason for this is the massive effort and resources poured into tax control and avoidance by smart corporate players, far more, sadly, than the effort most smart individuals put into avoiding tax. Hopefully, this book will help to change your mindset on that and inspire you to preserve your wealth while there's still time. In the Part II of the book, we'll share proven techniques you can use to convert wasted tax dollars into personal wealth and family fortune growth, just like Bezos and Amazon.

This is important. Not only do individuals carry almost the entire crushing load of Federal tax and debt, fat cats like you pay a shockingly disproportionate share. According to a recent Tax Foundation's analysis of IRS data[3] "half of taxpayers pay 97 percent of all income taxes." The bottom 50% of taxpayers in terms of income paid at an average tax rate of 4% and paid only 3% of all Federal income taxes. By contrast, the top 1% "accounted for more income taxes paid than the bottom 90% combined." They earned 21% of the income but paid about 40% of the taxes. The reason for this is we have a "progressive" income tax code, which is a nice word for meaning the more you make, the bigger the chunk of your income the government takes. That's what tax brackets are all about. For 2020, the individual Federal tax brackets are 0%, 10%, 12%, 22%, 24%, 32%, 35%, and 37% for individuals. The corporate tax bracket is a simple, flat 21% (one more good reason to be or own a company, as we will discuss in the solutions part of the book). These individual brackets are in addition to payroll taxes, excise taxes, applicable state, local, estate, gift, property, and you-name-it taxes. The major point is with progressive tax brackets, the higher you climb on the taxable income ladders, the more of your income ain't yours anymore.

Take a look at Table 1, courtesy of the Tax Foundation.

If you are reading this book, you may not be in the top 1% of earners, but you are probably deep in the upper 50%...who pay nearly 100% of the taxes. The bottom 50% pays 3.1% of taxes at an average rate of 4%. If you are reading this, you are almost for sure in the higher brackets. And you are at the greatest risk of increasing income redistribution, where wealth is transferred from your pocket to fund programs—like decaying Social Security that you probably won't get much benefit from—for those bottom 50% who pay nearly no taxes at all.

We will be striking this theme frequently as we go through the book. My intent, by the way, is not to opine on social justice. There are many very strong and valid arguments for income redistribution, and I agree with many of them. But we are not here to make moral judgments. My mission is to show you the landscape and empower you to better get from Point A to Point B if you so choose. Personally, I'd rather be rich enough to do good how and to whom I choose, instead of seeing my wealth confiscated and wastefully redirected at the whims of a semi-mindless bureaucracy. I'll never forget my dad's story about Hurricane Andrew's devastation of the Miami metro area. At the time, he worked for the State of Florida on the disaster management team and complained about some politician's speech about rebuilding, that went something like "it's not *our* money we're spending....these are *Federal* dollars...." No, knucklehead, this is *our* money, our sweat we are talking about, not magic money from heaven created from nothing! This kind of political mindset—that the money belongs to the government, not the people—is, in my view, a major contributor to waste compounding the many problems we face in the now-middling twenty-first century (Fig. 1). Anyway, off my soapbox, and on with the program!

Now, let's look at where it goes. From the CBO graph below, we see that the lion's share is spent on the social entitlement programs of Social Security, Medicare, and Medicaid (which if you don't know is a healthcare program for poor people who can't otherwise afford medical treatment). When we add in "other" mandatory category—unemployment compensation, federal non-Social Security retirement programs, and welfare programs like food assistance and the earned income tax credit—entitlements soak up about

Table 1 Summary Federal income tax data, 2017

	Top 1%	Top 5%	Top 10%	Top 25%	Top 50%	Bottom 50%	All taxpayers
Number of returns	1,432,952	7,164,758	14,329,516	35,823,790	71,647,580	71,647,580	143,295,160
Adjusted Gross Income ($ millions)	$2,301,449	$3,995,037	$5,220,949	$7,561,368	$9,706,054	$1,230,446	$10,936,500
Share of Total Adjusted Gross Income	21.0%	36.5%	47.7%	69.1%	88.7%	11.3%	100.0%
Income Taxes Paid ($ millions)	$615,979	$946,954	$1,122,158	$1,378,757	$1,551,537	$49,772	$1,601,309
Share of Total Income Taxes Paid	38.5%	59.1%	70.1%	86.1%	96.9%	3.1%	100.0%
Income Split Point	$515.371	$208.053	$145,135	$83,682	$41,740	$41,740	
Average Tax Rate	26.8%	23.7%	21.5%	18.2%	16.0%	4.0%	14.6%

Source York, Erica. "Summary of the Latest Federal Income Tax Data, February 2020 Update." Tax Foundation, February 25, 2020. https://files.taxfoundation.org/20200225110058/Summary-of-the-Latest-Federal-Income-Tax-Data-2020-Update.pdf

Fig. 1 Federal Revenues of the U.S. Government, Fiscal Year 2019 (*Source* Congressional Budget Office. "The Federal Budget in 2019: An Infographic." April 15, 2020. https://www.cbo.gov/publication/56324)

61% of Federal spending. And when we peek at "nondefense," we find yet more entitlement-type benefits, including for education, health, and housing assistance. Finally, the net interest wedge—a tiny slice of tasty pie at today's low! low! rates!—is a truly a monster lurking under the basement stairs, just waiting to drag the whole mess into the pit of hell, as we'll examine when we get into inflation risk (Fig. 2).

If you're like most folks, this primer on where the money comes from (you! all you!) and where it goes—mostly entitlement payouts—is a bit of a shocker. I see a lot more stress on this overbaked pie in the fairly near term, as Social Security/Medicare implodes (at least for those of us with some milk in our udders to "share"), and the socialism fashion which has swept most of the Western world takes firmer, and more expensive, root in the United States.

Before looking at the kinks the road ahead may hold, let's take a straight-shot extrapolation from where we are to the very near future. The numbers above, based on the 2020 report, are actually from 2017. They've been getting

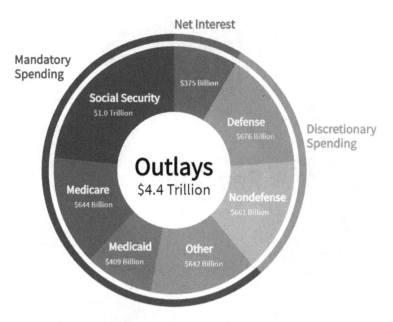

Fig. 2 Federal Outlays of the U.S. Government, Fiscal Year 2019 (*Source* Congressional Budget Office. "The Federal Budget in 2019: An Infographic." April 15, 2020. https://www.cbo.gov/publication/56324)

steadily worse, and COVID's taken a madman's axe to an already troubling trend.

So now, a tale from Grimm.

Let's consult our old friend, the Congressional Budget Office. If we want the straight, un-sugarcoated dope, Congress is the place, right? Quoting from the September 2020 report[4], "By the end of 2020, federal debt held by the public is projected to equal 98 percent of GDP. The projected budget deficits would boost federal debt to 104 percent of GDP in 2021, to ***107 percent of GDP (the highest amount in the nation's history) in 2023***, and to 195 percent of GDP by 2050."

Those are record levels in two years, assuming (and I don't!) that Congress gets it right, accurately assessed the COIVD spin (or death spiral, I should say) and does not try to put the lipstick, er, happy face, on the pig. But wait, there's more! You note the stat references "federal debt held by the public...." The public don't hold it all. Guess "who" has a huge chunk? Social Security and the bloody government itself! From Pew Research[5] way back in July of 2019 pre-COVID la la land: "26.5% of the debt (about $5.83 trillion) is owed to another arm of the federal government itself as of the end of June. The single biggest creditor, in fact, is Social Security: The program's retirement and disability trust funds together held more than $2.9 trillion in

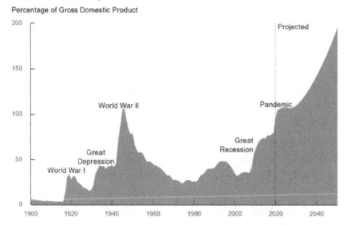

Fig. 3 The 2020 long-term budget outlook *Source* Congressional Budget Office. "The 2020 Long-Term Budget Outlook," September 30, 2020. https://www.cbo. gov/publication/56598#:~:text=In%20CBO's%20projections%2C%20federal%20d ebt,time%20as%20the%20economy%20expands)

special non-traded Treasury securities, or 13.3% of the total debt Another big holder is the Federal Reserve System, which as of mid-July collectively held nearly $2.1 trillion worth of Treasuries, or 9.5% of the total debt." (The Fed's holdings are included in the 'debt held by public' category.)

When we include this double-dippin', house of mirrors accounting, government debt already passed 100% of GDP—that's the entire annual economic output of the biggest economy in the world—a couple years ago. It also means the government owes Social Security a tidy $3 trillion it doesn't have, which can only hasten the doom of your retirement checks and Medicare payments.

And wither we go, sage Congressional Budget Office? A picture paints a thousand words, so gander this (Fig. 3):

As mentioned, we are already where we were in the 1940s, paying the colossal cost of the biggest war of all time. Also as mentioned we are in a much worse spot, population-wise, to pay for it, with much of America retired, and thousands more fixin' to every day.

CBO notes "high and rising federal debt makes the economy more vulnerable to rising interest rates and…rising inflation…(it) raises borrowing costs, slowing the growth of the economy and…increases the risk of a fiscal crisis…." Looking forward, CBO acknowledges the gross underfunding of Social Security and Medicare, and adds "spending as a percentage of GDP rises in CBO's projections. With growing debt and higher interest rates, net spending for interest nearly quadruples in relation to the size of the economy over the long term, accounting for most of the growth in total deficits."

This bit is utterly predictable but truly scary: "net spending for interest nearly quadruples..." glance again at the Outlays chart above, where interest is $375B. Quadrupling takes it to about $1.5T—and the biggest wedge on the graph. The implications for tax hikes, hyperinflation, a tanking dollar, budget squeezes, and US debt ratings sinking to Third World status are frightening.

The United States may be unique in facing this problem, at least on this scale. While due to COVID, " debt has risen in most advanced economies, the U.S. is the only country whose debt-to-GDP ratio is expected to continue rising after 2021, according to the International Monetary Fund's Fiscal Monitor Report. It is also expected to record the biggest jump in debt-to-GDP this year among advanced economies, including Germany, France, Italy and the U.K." In fact, "the U.S. (now) has the third highest debt-to-GDP ratio in the world," right behind Italy. Mama mia! That's a sobering thought.

Before leaving the cheery topic of a federal government careening toward possible insolvency, one more downer. The above does not address the very sorry—and worsening!—state of many state and local governments, for whom the Feds are the bailers of last resort. Even before COVID, per the *Wall Street Journal*: "state and local governments haven't been setting aside enough to fund the increasingly expensive costs of pensions. That will compound their problems now that sales and income taxes have plummeted. Many state and local governments have already cut services and furloughed workers....some states with heavy liabilities have taken loans tied to specific streams of revenue, like sales tax, to keep borrowing costs down, which will now be even harder to pay off." Lots of states' and municipal governments are in deep, deep trouble. Besides a warning that municipal bond investors might get stiffed, the bigger worry is a strangulation of state budgets, curtaining benefits and services and exacerbating misery, and increasing the pressure on Washington to perhaps unsustainable levels.

All this before the rising tide of popular socialism. Don't forget that votes matter, and that the top 25% of taxpayers that pay 86% of the taxes are woefully outgunned at the polls.

Again, the problem is thorny but the solutions are simple.

Raise taxes. Devalue the dollar. Either or both of which could drive you and your family out of the rich, or at least comfortable, category, unless you effectively adopt the solutions we will present in Part II of the book.

To paraphrase Willie Sutton, who after all was talking about robbing banks: "why do you soak the rich so hard? That's where the money is...." Here's some wisdom from a few of my other favorite tax quotes, to tide you over until next chapter. As Ten Years After had it, "tax the rich, feed the poor/'till there are no rich no more," excessive taxation risks universal poverty, and the loss of the productive engine that expands prosperity. That did not stop the Beatles singing, even as they lamented Britain's then-top 95% bracket in the song Taxman: "here's one for you, nineteen for me /should 5% appear too small, be thankful I don't take it all." Of course, politically driven social engineering is a prime tax policy motivator, often couched as shining altruism. FDR's New Deal was swaddled with his anthems like "...as new conditions and problems arise beyond the power of men and women to meet as individuals, it becomes the duty of the Government itself to find new remedies with which to meet them." The reality, as Robert A. Heinlein noted, is that "taxes are not levied for the benefit of the taxed," and that "a government which robs Peter to pay Paul can always depend on the support of Paul" as George Bernard Shaw pithily postulated. In the end, let us never forget the timeless wisdom of Prime Minister Margaret Thatcher: "the problem with socialism, is that you eventually run out of other people's money."

In the months and years ahead, the money will run out in bloody gushers and geysers. Let's hope they don't run out of yours! Let's be sure the bleeding passes over you, and your family! Partake deeply of the medicine in Part II…and get ahead of the curve by taking a free class or two at www.fweibook.org.

Notes

1. Congressional Budget Office. "The Federal Budget in 2019: An Infographic." April 15, 2020. https://www.cbo.gov/publication/56324.
2. Huddleston Jr., Tom. "Amazon Had to Pay Federal Income Taxes for the First Time Since 2016—Here's How Much." *CNBC*, February 4, 2020. https://www.cnbc.com/2020/02/04/amazon-had-to-pay-federal-income-taxes-for-the-first-time-since-2016.html.
3. York, Erica. "Summary of the Latest Federal Income Tax Data, February 2020 Update." Tax Foundation, February 25, 2020. https://files.taxfoundation.org/20200225110058/Summary-of-the-Latest-Federal-Income-Tax-Data-2020-Update.pdf.
4. Congressional Budget Office. "The 2020 Long-Term Budget Outlook." September 30, 2020. https://www.cbo.gov/publication/56598#:~:text=In%20CBO's%20projections%2C%20federal%20debt,time%20as%20the%20economy%20expands.
5. Desilver, Drew. "5 facts about the National Debt." Pew Research Center, July 24, 2019. https://www.pewresearch.org/fact-tank/2019/07/24/facts-about-the-national-debt/#:~:text=The%20single%20biggest%20creditor%2C%20in,13.3%25%20of%20the%20total%20debt.

The Coming Tax Storm—Will There Be Massive Tax Hikes on Wealth Holders

As explored in other chapters, there's good reason to believe taxes will skyrocket in the years to come, especially so for the readers of this book.

For one thing, the Federal and states' governments are getting awfully short on cash, as the COVID Depression unwinds, and Social Security and Medicare crumble into a sinkhole of diminution and transformation. For another, the "socialism-ization" of Western civilization takes ever-deeper root on our shores and is expensive to nourish. For third but not last among many, many things, the tech-driven reinvention of the labor market will spawn a lot of losers from the social ranks least able to afford the changes.

Rich people are easy to tax. For one thing, they have the money. For another, they are vastly outnumbered by millions on millions of voters easily rallied with cries of "just a one-penny tax" or "everyone needs to pay their fair share," whatever that is.

If I Google "wealth distribution in America," I get hits like "wealth inequality in the United States" from Wikipedia[1] which tells me "the bottom 50% of households had $1.67 trillion, or 1.6% of the net worth, versus $74.5 trillion, or 70% for the top 10%." Yikes! Seems pretty unfair, even to capitalist-spider-me, and a great battle cry for the campaign stump.

As you read this, I bet you feel pretty ordinary. That's part of the human condition. If your net worth—including your house, cars, investment accounts, and so on—is over $1 million, I bet you don't feel particularly rich. I used to say "one million is the new one-hundred-thousand," and before that, showing my age, that "one hundred thousand is the new ten-thousand."

J. Camarda et al., *The Financial Storm Warning for Investors*,
https://doi.org/10.1007/978-3-030-77271-0_4

Back in the *Beverly Hillbillies* days, a million was real money. Now most millionaires I know feel pretty poor.

So it might surprise you, dear and gentle reader, to discover just how special and elite you really, truly are.

One study[2] shows "11.8 million households which have a net worth of $1 million" in the U.S." Ah ha, Camarda! You see! There are lots of us poor shmoos! Well, I am afraid you are woefully outvoted. That same study makes the number of millionaires "equal to 3% of the United States entire population." That's a tiny, tiny fraction. The *NY Post* echoes[3] this, but *Kiplinger's* math is a little different, but still puts the percentage at under 7%.[4] No matter the differences in small change, fat cats like you are pretty rare, easily outvoted, and easily taxed. And as any child should know, votes are the currency of politics, the very mothers' milk, and politicians, by gosh, go where the "money" is.

We see in other chapters why taxes must go up. Let's take a look at some of the ways how, so you may be on your guard. We promise a squadron of countermeasures when we talk about solutions in Part II of the book, but I need to convince you to put on your armor!

As I have said many times before, I call tax the "master wealth skill"—the cutting edge of wealth leadership—because the stakes to grow or bleed wealth are perhaps higher for tax than any other area. I stress that most readers' tax advisors may not be even aware of—or believe possible—the many legitimate techniques to build real wealth via tax control. For one thing, tax law is so complex it requires deep study to master. This is hard work. I've been studying taxes since running my first businesses in my 20s, and here I am admitted to Georgetown Law in my 60s taking a Masters in Tax Law—my third graduate degree—to sharpen an already keen saw. Taxes matter *that* much.

A "yougottapay" stance requires less effort than constant strategic vigilance. I sadly report this seems to be the default state of the tax-prep/advisory industry.

Beyond deep and constant education, one needs a hungry attitude of tax aversion and a true desire to avoid legitimately avoidable taxes. In my experience, many tax advisors lack this attitude, either by disposition or from inertia. Finally, I think the advent of tax prep software has dulled the edge of many advisors, who may myopically follow the bouncing software ball instead of actually thinking about what's happening. In the old days with paper forms, instructions, and calculator in hand, one became immersed in the math and logical relationships of how the schedules were connected and what they meant. This if nothing else spurred the quest for opportunity, as one puzzled the relationships and pondered the possible. These days, it can be far too easy to miss checking a box—or misinterpret the dumbed-down software guidance of what the box means and does—and so generate lots of missed tax savings opportunities. For instance, we see millions in wasted deductions for real estate investors whose preparers just don't hit the right software field. Software—buggy and with hard coded tax code errors as it can often be—is an incredible tool for the tax advisor, but is no substitute for study and thought.

All this was true before the COVID crisis started supercharging the dark forces pointing to massive tax hikes. The winds have been gathering for years and really started to whistle during the 2020 election cycle.

As the *Wall Street Journal*[5] noted just before the election, the Biden tax plan is "focused squarely at the top of the income distribution that the U.S. can expand government programs without imposing a burden on most voters..." and that "there are trillions of dollars in potential tax revenue from... high-income households. That room for tax increases at the top...leaves Democrats defending direct tax increases only on a small share of the population."

In other words, most voters will love it!

Some of the ideas on the Biden table?[6] Boosting the top income tax rate—before payroll taxes like FICA for Social Security—back up to about 40%, while at the same time cutting deductions for high-income folks, which is essentially a stealth tax hike above 40%. That's before eliminating the cap on FICA for high earners, about another 15.3% (including both employee and employer ends) on top of the 40% rate on most of their income. These pieces add up to over 50% before any state or local taxes.

What else? Boosting the capital gains rate for high earners to the same top rate as income, about 40%, plus the Obamacare tax. That is a big deal and a big change. Plus eliminating the "step up" forgiveness at death of capital gains taxes, so they would be due on top of any estate taxes. These provisions are only for the top of the wealth stack, but better watch out if you are up there. And also watch for downward creep from the really rich to the merely rich. According to analysis by the Tax Policy Center[7] "The top 1% of households would pay 74% of the additional taxes and they would see their after-tax income drop by 17% in 2021." The *Journal* article also noted this plan affects only 1.8% of households, those projected to earn 24.8% of adjusted gross income n 2021, that "the top 0.1% of households would see ... tax rates jump to 38.4% from 27.8%" in order to raise "between $3 trillion and $4 trillion in tax increases."

As this book is written, these are proposals only, dancing in the political wind. Depending on how it blows, even stiffer hikes may be in the offing.

So the first big tax risk is higher income taxes. There are lots of levers the government can pull to hit more of a jackpot from you. Besides the obvious lever of raising rates, there's the complex math shell game of tax accounting, like what rate is applied to what kind of income. Boosting the top capital gains rate from 20% to 40% (rounded)—higher if you consider the Net Investment Income Tax[8] (an Obamacare tax) applicable to many fat cats— is an obvious example. Less so are the funhouse rules that already apply to the taxation of Social Security, which I expect to get lots worse. Remember that taxable income is a function of gross income less allowable deductions. The deduction part is very easy to mess with to yield what I call stealth tax increases, because they increase taxable income in a sneaky way.

Here are some examples from the 2017 Tax Cut and Jobs Act. Miscellaneous deductions including employee business expenses were been pretty much eliminated. Employees—as contrasted to independent contractors and business owners—have traditionally been shortchanged on write-offs. What little there was left is now gone, and W2 folks now have no write-offs related to business. Also gone were moving expenses, brokerage, IRA and investment advisory fees, post-tax-reform alimony, and most casualty losses. If you were affected by these categories, your taxes went up, probably without you knowing it. You gave your CPA your numbers, he or she shrugged, ran the software, and let Uncle Sam reach a little deeper into your pants. Making it worse, personal exemptions were also eliminated. Exemptions were effectively a "free" deduction based on the size of a taxpayer's eligible family and were available whether you itemized deductions or not. Been around since even I was a child, now gone, unlikely to come back even as tax rates rise. You in high-income tax states did probably notice the $10,000 SALT cap on the total of deductions for income taxes, real estate taxes, and sales taxes now in place. The so-called kiddie tax now taxes kids more in arcane ways, such that income attributable to kids will get taxed at steeper and faster rates than the case for their parents. As a last example, IRA/ROTH conversion became more dicey. Since lower stock prices mean more shares converted for a given tax cost, getting the timing right on conversions can save a bunch of tax. Up until TCJA, taxpayers could get do-overs if better conditions appeared since conversions could be undone up until October 15th of the next tax year. Now, you get one shot that can't be undone.

All these little tweaks add up to billions of additional taxes, grabbed in ways many folks don't notice, and ways many tax preparers don't know or care to take countermeasures for. Remember and beware them! It's not just the ostensible tax rate that matters—it's also the taxable income that it is applied to. Just for grins, below is the IRS table from 1945, the last time US government debt was as high as it *just* is now. Remember it's going much higher, right quick. Of course, it's in 1945 dollars, so the income levels seem tiny. But the important thing to remember is how much more, progressively, they take of each taxable income dollar the more you make. The top rate in 1945—94% (gee willikers!) marched steadily up from 25% in 1930 as the Great Depression was starting. Have I mentioned anywhere that the COIVD recession was the worst since then? (Table 1).

Let's talk estate tax, which some call the death tax because it applies to the value of all your stuff when you die, if you are exposed. Well, not all; the deductions and stealth taxes here can be as mind-blowing as for income taxes.

The estate tax is dead! Long live the estate tax! I say that because this tax is even more of a political football than income tax, and because it applies only to that tiny fraction of the population—you?—with enough scratch to have a taxable estate, it's really easy to target the tiny part of the electorate with the money to pay their "fair share." By the way, and because I won't get into it much here, the estate tax is part of the Unified Transfer Tax which includes gift tax. The short of that if you try to give it away before you die, you pay the same rates, plus some nasty extra stealth taxes in many cases. You can't win! (Oh yes you can! See Part II).

Per TCJA, the estate tax-free amount was increased to $11,180,000 per person, double that for a married couple. It's worth noting that the estate tax bar is now far higher than before, meaning only the richest families are exposed—at least in the short term. This should make fewer estates taxable, but watch out, as things can change rapidly. Unless extended, the exemptions drop back to the old level in 2026.

Extension is unlikely. Quite the opposite. From our friends at the Tax Foundation and used with their kindly permission: "Biden is proposing two major tax increases on accumulated wealth. First, he would tax unrealized capital gains at death for taxpayers with incomes above $400,000. For a (deceased) taxpayer who earned more than $400,000 but less than $1 million, this would subject those unrealized gains to the current capital gains rate of 20 percent, plus the 3.8 percent Net Investment Income Tax (NIIT), for a total of 23.8 percent. This is before the assets might be subject to the estate tax (more on that below).

However, Biden also wants to tax the capital gains of millionaires at ordinary income tax rates, which would be levied at his proposed top marginal rate of 39.6 percent. Added to the NIIT, this would mean a total tax rate on capital gains of 43.4 percent. As the accompanying table illustrates, for

Table 1

Nominal			1945								
Married Filling Jointly			Married Filling Jointly			Single			Head of Household		
Marginal tax rate	Tax brackets		Marginal tax rate	Tax brackets		Marginal tax rate	Tax brackets		Marginal tax rate	Tax brackets	
	Over	But not over		Over	But not over		Over	But not over		Over	But not over
23.0%	$0	$2,000	Listed tax rates and brackets apply to all taxpayers			Listed tax rates and brackets apply to all taxpayers			Listed tax rates and brackets apply to all taxpayers		
25.0%	$2,000	$4,000									
29.0%	$4,000	$6,000									
33.0%	$6,000	$8,000									
37.0%	$8,000	$10,000									
41.0%	$10,000	$12,000									
46.0%	$12,000	$14,000									
50.0%	$14,000	$16,000									
53.0%	$16,000	$18,000									
56.0%	$18,000	$20,000									
59.0%	$20,000	$22,000									
62.0%	$22,000	$26,000									
65.0%	$26,000	$32,000									
68.0%	$32,000	$38,000									
72.0%	$38,000	$44,000									
75.0%	$44,000	$50,000									
78.0%	$50,000	$60,000									

Nominal

1945

Married Filling Jointly			Single			Head of Household		
Marginal tax rate	Tax brackets		Marginal tax rate	Tax brackets		Marginal tax rate	Tax brackets	
	Over	But not over		Over	But not over		Over	But not over
81.0%	$60,000	$70,000						
84.0%	$70,000	$80,000						
87.0%	$80,000	$90,000						
90.0%	$90,000	$100,000						
92.0%	$100,000	$150,000						
93.0%	$150,000	$200,000						
94.0%	$200,000							

Source: Tax Foundation. "Federal Individual Income Tax Rates History." Accessed January 11, 2021. https://files.taxfoundation.org/legacy/docs/fed_individual_rate_history_nominal.pdf

an asset worth $100 million (all of which is a capital gain for the sake of simplicity), this would mean an immediate tax of $43.4 million at the time of death.

It appears that Biden does not believe these assets had been taxed enough because he is also proposing to turn back the clock on the estate tax to 2009, when the top rate was 45 percent (compared to 40 percent today), and the exemption level for single taxpayers was $3.5 million (as opposed to $11.58 million today)."[9]

If enacted—and there are far more confiscatory proposals floating to soak the rich—that would be quite a jump from today's rates while the TCJA law lasts. All the more reason to get tax wise fast and implement the solutions I'll share in Part II of the book.

Before TCJA, *couples'* tax-free amount—the exemption or estate value under which no tax is imposed—was $11,180,000, two times the individual exemption amount, of course! While it lasts—until 2026 unless cut by Congress—it is now $22,360,000 (unmarrieds get half this of course). Take note: Even if you think you are comfortably under the taxable level now, investment success and estate growth may eventually put you there. It should be noted that this is an area where expensive advice often falls short. A good example is James "Tony Soprano" Gandalfini's $30 million estate tax bill which was completely avoidable had he gotten good tax advice.

Like a Phoenix flaming on the political wind, only to extinguish, then burst anew, this now-you-see-me, now-you-don't tax is overlooked only at the peril of lasting prosperity. For exposed families, the estate tax can be a devastating blow to generational wealth, from which fortunes never recover. Recent changes in tax treatment have induced a false sense of immunity in many families and their advisors, to the point where a healthy respect for the ravages the estate tax might visit on family wealth has waned, if not disappeared.

This can be a huge mistake for several reasons.

It is true that the expansion of the tax-free amount to about $11 million ($22 million for married couples) might seem to give endless breathing room to all but the richest families, but it is important to remember that these lofty exemptions have a short fuse and will drop to half (about $5.5M per individual or about $11M per married couple) for those who have the misfortune to survive past 2025, when the temporary exemption levels sunset. This sudden shrinkage in the tax-free amount may catch many families unawares, and what seems like an immune estate now—say $8 million—with modest growth (7%) can grow to a taxable sum of almost $16M in a mere 10 years. In 25 years, an estate on the order of $35M is reasonably forecast, with a lurking tax due of some $10M under current law—and more under Biden's and others' proposals.

Worse, nothing is so certain in tax as change, and there is no reason to believe that new Congresses may not change to far more oppressive policy—perhaps to stoke the populist "soak the rich" mantra and keep extended office—in the years ahead and possibly before 2025, even. With COVID and the other risks shown in this book, that risk has never been higher. Those protective of their purse strings would be wise to recall that the estate tax was initially enacted, back in the original Robber Barron days, not to raise Federal revenue, but to throttle the perpetuation of vast family fortunes (and the political influence they might enable). In other words, to punish and control the affluent. Could such a theme return a century later? The answer may be blowin' in the populist wind. Even absent a redistribution bent, mere fiscal pressures—forget not the soaring deficits, and the looming Social Security/Medicare train-wrecks (to say nothing of labor displacement at the "hands" of robots and AI)—could well drive Washington into revenue-scramble mode, and a tax that will impact only a small fraction of the electorate, like youse (this is the N.Y. version of y'all, y'all) fat cats reading this book.

To appreciate what a blow such a turn might deal to your legacy, reflect that not so long ago the individual tax-free amount was a mere $600,000, and that without jumping through some arcane hoops (the old "A/B" trust hustle, now obsolete), married couples did not automatically get two exemptions as in the examples for current law above, but just one! The law actually required that if the spouse was the primary beneficiary (as she darn well better be!), half of the tax break was forgone.

One might suggest that the perennial reports of the estate tax's demise—or relative toothlessness—are greatly exaggerated, at least for those expecting to draw breath for more than a few short years. Sadly the tonic, such as using relatively simple devices such as Family Bank Ongoing Trusts (F-Bots—explained in detail in Part II), can reasonably render many otherwise taxable estates tax free for generations, without unreasonably burdening ma and pa who might wish to use their dough to make merry and live well for a long, long time. Such devices, while simple, are often not employed by even high-dollar advisors to the well-heeled, but that is grist for another chapter.

And let's not forget that socialist wind a'blowin' through the polls that the Bernie Sanders crowd is fanning. We all love free stuff, but let's also remember "the trouble with Socialism is you eventually run out of other people's money" wisdom, even as progressive politicians beat the drum of Robin Hood-like wealth redistribution. Robin's mandate, as readers will recall, was to "take from the rich and give to the poor," but as Thatcher (and Ten Years After) noted, under such a scheme eventually only the poor remain. Redistributionist socialism's carnage has a long and tattered history, with the steaming carcass of Venezuela as the current period's most spectacular and tragic example. Could it work in the United States? Seems to me like economic voodoo, but the jury's out, and free stuff is cool. Still, the historical record ain't good.

Again, this is not a political statement! There is much good in the objectives of progressives, and I am sympathetic to many of them. But this is a book about money, and my mission is to advise you on how to effectively keep it. Please bear this in mind.

So what's that to you, my still-merry 1%-ish men (and bonnie maids?) It may be time to batten down the hatches afore your wealth sub is flooded and its hull plunges to the "till there ain't no rich no more" bottom of universal impoverishment. Regardless of which way your political tail wags, you may want to steel yourself against some of the transformative tax changes lately running up the flagpole. Here are some of the soak-the-rich ideas floating around lately, and a few derivatives likely to pop up as political transformation unfolds over the home of the brave, as it sinks deeper in debt.

Estate Tax "reform." It was not so long ago that the estate tax began for many families at the $600K mark, including life insurance proceeds. While the current threshold is a lofty $22M or so (back to $11M in 2026), this could change in a heartbeat. Mr. Biden has already proposed dropping this to some $3M, and he probably isn't done, plus the other stealth taxes discussed above. Others have proposed raising the top estate tax rate to 77% from the current 40%. This author believes sharply higher estate tax exposure for many if not most readers to be extremely likely in the years to come, and that proactive tax control measures should be taken. Also proposed by Mr. Biden and others is the elimination of the step up in basis, under which capital gains taxes are essentially waived at death. With the step up gone, affected families would face the double whammy of both estate and capital gains taxes. Gee, could they add up to more than 100%? Depends on the dark tax math. And that's before considering the possibility that capital gains favorable rates—already chipped away at in recent years—might be curtailed or eliminated entirely. Heavens, one Biden proposal[10] would impose capital gains tax at death even if the asset is not sold! Such a stealth tax really just layers on and increases the estate tax rate, already about half the value of a taxable estate and maybe reaching for the sky going forward.

Millionaire Taxes. This magnanimous notion would subject those above a subjective wealth bar—$5M in income has been recently bandied about in NY—to extra taxes. It is noteworthy that the last time NY did this—the current "millionaires' tax"—the bar was eventually lowered to some $300K in forming existing law. Quite a drop! That was before COVID and NY was knocked into the sewer. Recent proposals in NY include a special additional property tax on second "luxury" residences, as well as an additional closing "fee" on real estate transactions over $3M. The stated use is for the subway (yeah, right, and we promise to remove the toll booths once the bridge is paid for!). Note the hourly rate for NYC subway borers is some $120 (which surpasses even Germany's) though they still can't seem to get the darn thing done.

Property Taxes Kissin' cousin to NY's millionaire taxes these, as most landowners know, are nearly unavoidable, and inescapable for the reason you can't flee to a lower tax jurisdiction, at least not with your real estate. Worse, Mother State has a perpetual, first claim lien on the dirt, and is quite wont to foreclose and redistribute for unpaid taxes. They kinda got you by the short hairs here, and it's easy to see how such a tax could quickly get soak-the-rich progressive while sparing the dear voting class. Benefits-rich, deficit-doomed states like Alaska are prime candidates for such a shift, and it looks like NY was already halfway there before COVID. Of course, the net economic effect of increasing expenses without offsetting benefits would be to suppress values, wasting wealth sunk in real estate that might never return. It's like a growing mortgage that never gets paid off. Think about that, and consider selling real estate in high-risk areas. You can't take it with you (if you change states) never rang truer!

Stealth Corporate Taxes designed to chill stock buybacks which generally are used to juice stockholder returns similar to dividend payments. Bernie Sanders opined in the NY Times that buybacks unfairly enrich shareholders—that they are the owners of the companies notwithstanding—at the expense of other stakeholders. Past proposed legislation would prohibit buybacks, and possibly dividend payments, unless all workers are paid at least $15/hour regardless of the job or the labor market valuation of it. Beyond this stealth minimum wage boost, such policy would divert erstwhile owners' profits to the workers' paradise of higher wages, expanded company-paid training, and richer benefits. Such an expansion of the stakeholder model at the expense of shareholders seems likely to divert capital to less productive and accountable ends and would certainly shave stock values to levels commensurate with the truncated returns. This de facto bump in labor costs, especially during times of economic stress, could put some companies over the edge.

Higher FICA/ Payroll Taxes to "save" Social Security and expand benefits to recipients beyond Uncle Sam's current $1,000,000,000,000 (i.e., a big $1T and growing like a beanstalk) annual nut. As discussed above, this salvation would be "paid for" by hiking the current FICA tax from about 12% to almost 15%—a 25% rise!—and subjecting those earning over a certain threshold to the full FICA tax, instead of the present $133K cutoff for the Social Security part (which is by far the biggest piece). A supremely progressive proposal, taxes would also be cut for those below a certain means, large in number, voting power, and aggregate taxes paid, but low in fat cat income. Still, as we see in the Social Security and Medicare Crisis chapter, all this—while it may cost *you* a lot, gentle reader—is mere public-spin window dressing, good for votes but hopeless to save a pretty doomed system from collapse.

Wealth Taxes. These have become very popular proposals, a darling of Senator Warren and many of her mind. These would be kind of like an annual estate tax levied on the entirety of an affected family's assets, from stocks to real estate to business to livestock. Since only the dastardly rich are targets, you'd have to have a lot of cattle to get in this game, which seems only fair given the volume of milking hoped to be at hand. A good way to visualize the concept is to contrast a sales tax (one time) with a personal property tax (like paying sales taxes over and over as if you were buying the *same car* every year) or real estate taxes. In other words, you pay a percentage tax on your net worth *each year.* Such a tax would be a real compliance bear given the complexities of annual valuations in complicated, squishy things like businesses. Just figuring your net worth to government standards could cost a ton in CPA fees—each year! On top of enormous tax prep costs, such a tax could be a real rich-soaker, for sure. While for now, anyway, most strains of wealth tax proposals only target the mega-rich, it wouldn't take much of a political nudge to expand that to soak the entire still-tiny millionaire class, which would still leave 97% of the electorate[11] to rally around a "you deserve it!" campaign trail cry. Shoot, you could even soak the top 10%—going well below the millionaire level—and still have plenty of electoral hay left to roll the rich around in. Think this is pure never-happen fantasy? Try this *Wall Street Journal* headline from late 2020 on for size: "A California Plan to Chase Away the Rich, Then Keep Stalking Them. A proposed wealth tax would apply for a decade to anyone who spends 60 days in the state in a single year." The pending bill "proposes calculating the wealth tax based on current world-wide net worth each Dec. 31…." This tax would hit Mark Zuckerberg of Facebook to the tune of $400 million…the first year! No wonder Musk hit the road. It is especially audacious in that it would also tax visitors spending only 60 days or more. Thank goodness, for them, "the tax would be proportionate based on their number of days in California...." Another pending bill there would raise the top *State* income tax bracket to about 17% (on top of FICA, Federal income tax, excise taxes, etc.).[12]

I hope I got your attention with this chapter. It was long, but deadly important. Nothing is so constant in tax policy as change. While many or most of the changes discussed here may not or may come to pass, one never knows, do one, and the wise would be carefully ready with plans B. Tax policy is a political football, and the right vs. left game is on with a vehemence perhaps not seen since the old New Deal was young. Unfortunately, as explored throughout Part I of this book, the United States may be in an even tighter spot than during the Great Depression, though the chickens are still flocking far from roost.

The time to prepare tax battle plans to protect your family's wealth is NOW. We will give you plenty of ammo, and clear tactics, when we get into solutions in Part II. We also teach plenty tax stuff at www.fweibook.org.

Notes

1. Wikipedia. "Wealth Inequality in the United States." Accessed January 11, 2021. https://en.wikipedia.org/wiki/Wealth_inequality_in_the_United_States.
2. Lynkova, Darina. "27 Millionaire Statistics: What Percentages of Americans Are Millionaires?" *Spendmenot*, December 15, 2020. https://spendmenot.com/blog/what-percentage-of-americans-are-millionaires/#:~:text=How%20m any%20US%20millionaire%20households%20are%20there%3F&text=A%20new%20survey%20has%20found,country%20with%20the%20most%20m illionaires.
3. Bowden, Ebony. "The US Has more Millionaires Than Greece Has People." *New York Post*, March 14, 2019. https://nypost.com/2019/03/14/the-us-has-more-millionaires-than-greece-has-people/.
4. Burrows, Dan. "Millionaires in America: All 50 States Ranked." *Kiplinger*, May 28, 2020. https://www.kiplinger.com/slideshow/investing/t006-s001-mil lionaires-america-all-50-states-ranked/index.html.
5. Rubin, Richard. "Why Biden Would Start Tax Increases at $400,000 a Year." *The Wall Street Journal*, October 3, 2020. https://www.wsj.com/articles/why-biden-would-start-tax-increases-at-400-000-a-year-11601730000.
6. Rubin, Richard. "Biden Tax Plan Targeting Top Earners Would Raise $4 Trillion in 10 Years, Study Says." *The Wall Street Journal*, March 5, 2020. https://www.wsj.com/articles/biden-tax-plan-targeting-top-earners-would-raise-4-trillion-in-10-years-study-says-11583429764?mod=article_inline.

7. Mermin, Gordon B., Surachai Khitatrakun, Chenxi Lu, Thornton Matheson, and Jeffrey Rohaly. "An Analysis of Former Vice President Biden's Tax Proposals." Tax Policy Center, March 5, 2020. https://www.taxpolicycenter.org/publications/analysis-former-vice-president-bidens-tax-proposals.

8. Internal Revenue Service. "Questions and Answers on the Net Investment Income Tax." News. Accessed January 11, 2021. https://www.irs.gov/newsroom/questions-and-answers-on-the-net-investment-income-tax.

9. Hodge, Scott A. "Joe Biden's 67 Percent Tax on Wealth." Tax Foundation, October 28, 2020. https://taxfoundation.org/joe-biden-estate-tax-wealth-tax/.

10. Mercado, Darla. "This Is How Joe Biden Will Tax Generational Wealth Transfer." *CNBC*, March 13, 2020. https://www.cnbc.com/2020/03/13/this-is-how-joe-biden-will-tax-generational-wealth-transfer.html.

11. Bowden, Ebony. "The US has more millionaires than Greece has people." *New York Post*, March 14, 2019. https://nypost.com/2019/03/14/the-us-has-more-millionaires-than-greece-has-people/.

12. Adler, Hank. "*A California Plan to Chase Away the Rich, Then Keep Stalking Them.*" *The Wall Street Journal*, December 18, 2020. https://www.wsj.com/articles/a-california-plan-to-chase-away-the-rich-then-keep-stalking-them-11608331448.

The Changing World Crisis

The Shifting Geopolitical Sands

Once upon a time, in the dim past as I was coming of age and getting interested in newspapers, I remember asking my father (a lifelong history teacher) about the world situation and just how dangerous and horrible it was, to the point where it seemed to me that it could not go on.

His only response? "Same old world, son."

Throughout history, both splendor and horrors and dangers have abounded. So I don't want to get too melodramatic here. But that said, the world constantly changes, nothing (not even Rome) lasts forever, and there are several other trends that are ringing alarm bells in my mind.

Probably the loudest come from the increasingly belligerent rise of Great China. Make no mistake, I have great respect for Chinese culture—I practice Chi Kung every day—and love for its people. Its government is another matter. I think at this point I will surprise no one by saying China seems intent on worldwide economic domination, as well as geopolitical/military supremacy, if not domination. While Russia (whose people I also love—my sister-in-law is from the real St. Petersburg, as is a Russian PhD on our tax team) is clearly problematic, China has for the first time figured out how to merge capitalist wealth alchemy with totalitarian control in a way that makes them enormously formidable. They know how to make money. Lots and lots of money, to fund and execute their agendas. And they have long-duration leadership that, for better or worse, enables very long-term strategic planning

© The Author(s), under exclusive license to Springer Nature
Switzerland AG 2021
J. Camarda et al., *The Financial Storm Warning for Investors*,
https://doi.org/10.1007/978-3-030-77271-0_5

and actual (by gosh!) execution, something which seems impossible in the United States.

A good example of this is the so-called Belt and Road Initiative, the "road" being an allusion to the Silk Road of historical Chinese export grandeur. Announced in 2013, it has a 37-year timeline. "Costing between \$4–8 trillion and affecting 65 countries, China's ambitious One Belt, One Road (OBOR) initiative is the granddaddy of all megaprojects. By the time of its estimated completion in 2049, OBOR will stretch from the edge of East Asia all the way to East Africa and Central Europe, and it will impact a lengthy list of countries that account for 62% of the world's population and 40% of its economic output."[1] While ostensibly intended to foster economic development and global prosperity, many suggest more sinister motives, including political influence and even hegemonic dominance. One criticism is that it ensnares candidate satellite states by "engaging in 'debt trap diplomacy' by extending excessive credit to countries that will struggle to pay it back."[2]

Per the *Wall Street Journal*,[3] the Obama-era US assessment that China was committed to stable ties with America and better global geopolitical integration "was one of the biggest strategic miscalculations of the post-Cold War era." Its current leader, Xi Jinping, "has pursued an expansive, hypernationalistic vision of China's future…drawing comparisons to Mao Zedong, he has crushed critics and potential rivals, revitalized the Communist Party and even scrapped presidential term limits so he can, if he chooses, rule for life." China scholar Jiang Shigong observed the current party-state system is key to the "China solution" whose ultimate goal was "creating a new order for human civilization."[4] From the *Journal*, again: "now, with Covid-19 under control in China but still widespread across the U.S., he is promoting his self-styled, tech-enhanced update of Marxism as a superior alternative to free-market democracy—a 'China solution' to global problems."

Ironically, the Trump-era efforts to isolate China may have backfired, presenting a rare opportunity for it to divide and conquer Western allies. Despite COVID and Trump, late 2020 saw new deals with Europe to "position (China) as an indispensable global leader," *the New York Times* reported,[5] which represented "a geopolitical coup for China" demonstrating "once again that it pays little or no diplomatic cost for abuses that violate European values" and that China's already "vast economic and diplomatic influence…means that countries feel they have little choice but to engage with it, regardless of…Mr. Xi's hard-line rule…Chinese leadership is concerned about a trans-Atlantic front, a multinational front, against it (and has figured out how) to bring the Europeans on board…They've been very smart about this."

So what clouds do I see on the China front? My eyes blur, but here's a few.

The Trump-era hardline policy has excluded the United States from multi-national economic cooperation agreements, while at the same time partially closing markets, choking trade through tariffs, hampered supply and acted to raise the costs of the cheap Chinese imports Americans have become quite accustomed to. Regardless of your feelings for how harsh the treatment China deserves—which I think is justified but devilishly difficult to execute—the potential inflationary consequences are inescapable. Interrupted supply chains increase costs and prices. Tariffs/import bans/closed markets increase prices and can spur inflation. The isolation of America while most of the rest of the world cooperates on trade can't be good for America. If China seeks to displace the United States as global leader—and who can doubt that it does?—the recent several years have played nicely into its hands, with our bungling of COVID-control icing on its cake.

China's efforts to legitimatize its currency—the yuan or renminbi (renminbi is the generic name meaning "people's currency", but the currency is denominated in yuan)—and even displace the US dollar as the global standard are not news. Despite playful references to the yuan as "redbacks," China has a long way to go before making much of an impact.[6] The yuan is still a yawn. Still, it is certain it will keep grinding away, and were this to occur the consequences—none good for the United States—would be monumental. For one thing, America's ability to influence and control global commerce—and enforce sanctions as a policy tool—would fade significantly. For another, the inflationary impact could be fierce as trillions are dumped by non-US central banks in favor of a replacement: Dollar supply goes up, price goes down (hopefully we could count on the Fed to burn such dollars as fast as they are currently printing them!). And, of course, China's ability to influence and control global commerce—including our own!—would grow substantially.

Beyond this, the need to project military power to Asia to counter an increasingly formidable China is expensive and will exacerbate already skyrocketing US deficits and national debt. China has engaged in progressively provocative acts as it seeks to dominate its region, with the "invasion" of strategically important international shipping lanes perhaps the most obvious act. While the "U.K., France and Germany are…rejecting Beijing's extensive claims in the South China Sea…," Europe continues to play economic pattycake with China, even while complaining its claims "do not comply with international law" and have "no legal ground…."[7] US Navy ships and warplanes have engaged in repeated close encounters in the disputed region, most recently in December of 2020,[8] and it is perhaps only a matter of time before an incident goes hot. China has been repeatedly accused of firing military lasers at American planes in the Pacific,[9] in Africa (where pilots took casualties),[10] and elsewhere. After the recent crackdown in Hong Kong, action on Taiwan may be looming, a line the United States may feel it can't let China cross without military reprisal. And let's also not forget the nuclear wildcard of North Korea, clearly a Chinese satellite state, and its longtime enmity toward US allies Japan and South Korea. The North has been in recent habit of lobbing nuclear-capable missiles (which have for years been able to reach the entire United States, by the way[11]) at South Korea and Japan. Japan, in response to these threats, has renounced its three-quarter-century renunciation of militarism and is arming itself to the teeth once again,[12] an ominous sign in a historically volatile region.

This is a thorny, long-term, and expensive problem. Besides the economic stresses, incidents or threats of a shooting war can rattle or upend markets. Remember how wildly optimistic and overvalued the stock market was as COVID raged, and how easy the switch flips from greed to fear, sending the herd stampeding for the exits.

I have similar, though less profound, concerns about other major adversaries, Russia and Iran principal among them.

There is no question Iran is dedicated to regional, occasionally global, mischief, and the fact that it was able to, even allowed to, blatantly attack Saudi Arabia in the months before COVID made news is surprising and disturbing. Israel has the bomb, Iran will soon, and other regional players will no doubt follow suit, if their nuclear ships have not already come in from the fission arms mongers in Pakistan or North Korea.

Russia plays its cards closer, but few doubt Putin is quietly rebuilding the Soviet empire to the extent of his considerable ability. Its recent, expansive but unknowably deep attack on US computer infrastructure[13] is provocative and chilling. We may never know how deep they went or what they can now control, in civilian, government, and possibly even military systems. Affecting election results may be the least of it. What if they can—or when they do? —turn off electric power to cities or regions? Or launch a US missile at China? And make no mistake, this threat is by no means limited to Russia. Everyone is doing this, including of course the United States. But after the recent Russian attack news, I fear for how well up to it we are. This brings to mind a line from one of my favorite movies, the 1960s *Lion in Winter*, when Katherine Hepburn as the queen, in fear, says "we're jungle creatures, Henry, and the dark is all around us. See them…in the corners? You can see the eyes." To which Peter O'Toole as the king replies "And they can see *ours*. I'm a match for anything…."

Let's hope we still are.

One final thought before leaving this theme. Throughout the twentieth century, the dictatorial central planning governance model failed dismally, with the most spectacular examples being Soviet Russia and Mao-era China; countries like Venezuela and Cuba continue the struggle while their people starve.

Failure of the central planning model largely changed with the out-of-park success of Singapore, closely watched and emulated by modern China,[14] at least. This sort of planning is not something the fractal US democratic system is very good at, where projects of even a few years morph, lose support and funding, and die. NASA got lost in space—I mean government short-sightedness—years ago. Seems we can't even finish a pipeline anymore.

To better compete in a fast-changing world where effective government is evolving, we might do well to ponder how to expand our planning horizons. To the extend we don't, our economic and other prospects dim.

The COVID Depression Crisis

COVID has been said to have sparked the worst economic recession since the Great Depression of the 1930s, which did not end until the massive spending needed to fund World War II turned the tide. The social welfare programs of FDR's New Deal—many of which remain today—are also credited with helping to restore prosperity. But in the end, it was the massive fiscal stimulus—read unbridled government spending—that snapped us back from the brink.

That is the reason we're seeing stimulus of that scale now. Pre 2021, it was mostly monetary—the Fed printing money and otherwise expanding the money supply—but fiscal programs like the CARES act and other subsidies to companies and citizens have made an impact. Fed Chair Powell had throughout 2020 lamented the lack of more robust fiscal life support under the Trump administration, but this is likely to change under Biden as Congress accommodates his desire to scale spending to juice the economy to pursue his social and economic agenda. The 2021 multi-trillion dollar infrastructure package is just a beginning, funded nearly entirely by new government debt, by the way.

And make no mistake—despite the stock market euphoria, parts of the economy still hurtle down the hall on an I.C.U. gurney, festooned with IV needles.

Immediately prior to the breakout of the COVID virus in the United States, things were doing decently well. The world economies in 2019 were strong. We even had a peak in monthly economic activity for what turned out to be the rest of 2020. Unfortunately, it also marked the end of the longest recorded US expansion since records began to be tracked in the 1940s. The expansion had begun in June of 2009 but ended abruptly when the pandemic hit the United States and we went into lockdown.[15] The plummet happened very quickly. Many businesses were forced to shut down from their loss of income. By April of 2020, the COVID-related job loss totaling 20.5 million ended a 113 straight month job growth streak.

The second quarter of 2020 fared no better. The United States had a record drop of economic output of 9.1% (prior to this quarter, the highest drop on record was 3%[15]). COVID also caused retail sales to decline. Part of this was from companies being closed, part was people not wanting to leave their homes, and part was the overall uncertainty people were starting to feel from the global pandemic. From February to March of 2020, retail sales fell by 8.7% (another record), as it was the largest month-to-month decrease since data began to be collected on those statistics[15]. Small businesses suffered the most. Their revenue from January to September of 2020 was down 20%[15]. With already small profit margins, the economic shock from the pandemic hit these enterprises particularly hard. From January to April of 2020, the number of labor force participants that were not at work quadrupled in the United States[15].

Not surprisingly, things got very bad in the United States for many citizens. The number of families having difficulty getting food increased greatly. So has the number of people unable to pay their rent or mortgage or even cover their household expenses.[16] This has wide-reaching implications for the economy. First, the number of people that were unable to pay for food caused a huge increase of people on the Food Stamp (SNAP) program. Additionally, the high number of people that lost their jobs caused a similar increase in people who qualify for state-funded medical care. This high influx of citizens and others on welfare programs caused even more of a burden on the already-strained economy. Second, it is not just the people that have lost their jobs and can't afford their mortgages that got hurt. Landlords, who for long periods could not evict anyone due to the COVID rules, must pay their mortgages without revenue from tenants. With the passage of several huge coronavirus relief bills that helped support business owners, gave people under a specified yearly income direct payments, and greatly increased unemployment benefits to those who lost some or all employment, the United States has increased its deficit more than ever before. This has also led to widespread fraud that cost the government $36 billion.[17] The hit on the economy will be felt for years to come especially as the blue wave of 2021 across the White House and Congress suggests even more payouts, and likely other entitlements, are on the horizon.

Job loss has been felt by more than just the poor and reached into the lower middle class. From April to May of 2020, 12% of the people that made above $60,000 became unemployed.[18] The repeated tightening and loosening of restrictions caused the recovery of the economy to look more like a jagged mountainside than a smooth slope[18]. Parts of the US economy doubtlessly remain in trouble…trouble that may persist long past the vaccine rollout. Between April and June of 2020, the economy shrank by an annually projected rate of 32.9%.[19] This was the largest decline the United States had ever seen (the prior record was 10% in 1958[19]). Of course, it isn't just the United States suffering economically. This is a worldwide disaster. In 2020, global growth also fell in an unprecedented fashion. It is unlikely things will improve anytime soon. It will take years and years to get back to where we were in 2019. Yes, uncountable green shoots are appearing, and the numbers and activity are encouraging. But the hole blown by the COVID thermonuclear recession is deep indeed, and it will take a long, long time to get back to ground zero.

Things got bad. They won't heal overnight. Even with the truly miraculous advent of the hi-tech vaccines in late 2020, it will take months and years to restore the economic mojo to 2019 happy days levels. For one thing, vaccine manufacture and distribution present a nettlesome global bottleneck. The vaccines take time to make, global demand still far exceeds supply, and some require extraordinary care in transport and storage. Distribution and inoculation planning—for which American embarrassingly had many months to prepare—remains ad hoc and abysmal in early 2021, hampering and delaying the process. As the vaccination rollout stretches, mutant variants breed that impede true herd immunity. The hole will get deeper before it heals, and some businesses already on life support will continue to suffer and fail before Americans resume normal consumption patterns. COVID- "friendly" industries like tech will continue to prosper, but many won't. While the West lingers—and Europe has not handled COIVD much better than the United States—the recoveries of more "disciplined" nations like China will continue to pull ahead. When the COVID dust settles in a few years—and I think it will be the mid-2020s before things are back to normal—the world economic order may have changed considerably, possibly with America and Europe in far worse positions than previously.

The Rise of Western Socialism Risk

At the turn of the twenty-first century, the United States began to embrace European-style social welfare to a degree never before seen in America. Endemic to Europe for over a century, it has thrived in countries such as Austria, Denmark, Finland, Ireland, the Netherlands, and the UK where total annual benefits across four broad categories of social welfare—social assistance, housing, family and child benefits, and tax credits—exceeded $24,456 (inflation-adjusted) even way back in 1900.[20, 21]

From 1900 to 1940, public assistance originated within corporations who grew weary of strikes that resulted in the destruction of property, lowered productivity, and reductions in shareholder wealth.[22] Any notions of welfare prior to this point were thought as ad hoc, temporary, and insufficient to address large-scale economic shocks. Despite these admirable efforts by employers to improve living conditions of individuals, they lacked consistency across industries with the widest gap at the public–private sector divide. Franklin Roosevelt sought to remedy this discrepancy with his New Deal.

Fast forward to the twenty-first century. Today, we have social welfare or "entitlement programs" at both the Federal and state/local levels. The vast majority of US taxpayers—96% to be exact—will notice with each and every paycheck the Old Age Survivor and Disability Insurance (OASDI) and Medicare reductions to pay to the tune of 15.2% to a certain threshold. If you are a W-2 employee, your employer pays half; if self-employed, you carry the full burden. In 1996, the US government paid out $343.2 billion in Social Security benefits (paid for by your generous OASDI bi-monthly contributions).[23] In 2019, that number jumped to an astonishing $1.1 *trillion*.[24] Even if you remove waste, mismanagement, corruption, and other inefficiencies from the equation, the mere fact that 10,000 Baby Boomers are retiring *daily* over the next two decades has created a top-heavy effect where the ratio of workers-to-retirees is shrinking. This is bad because there are fewer workers to tax in order to pay for retiree benefits. In 2019, Medicare spending grew to about $800 billion. Combined, annual expenses for Social Security and Medicare total nearly $2 trillion.[25] That's nearly 10% of our country's estimated GDP last year![26] The annual cost is also nearly 1.0% of the national debt.[27] Countless other entitlements exist on the Federal level such as the National School Lunch Program (NSLP),[28] Pell Grants,[29] mobile phone subsidies (LifeLine),[30] and women, infants, and children program (WIC).[31]

Welfare spending has also substantially increased over time at the state and local levels. In 1977, state and local governments in the United States spent $140 billion on public welfare. In 2017, they spent $673 billion.[32]

The percentage increase of state and local budgets devoted to public welfare increased from 13% in 1977 to 22% in 2017. As the lingering damage from COIVD squeezes state budgets more and more this situation will become even more dire.

For a glimpse of where the new socialism trend may carry the United States, let's have a look at the trend-setting state of California. California leads the nation in terms of total public welfare spending at $98.5 billion.[33] Proponents of socialist benefits have long had sway over the state legislature in California.[34] Over the decades, they've rolled-out a robust entitlements program for California residents, including cash aid, job training, and child-care (CalWORKs), food stamps (CalFresh), government-subsidized housing assistance (Sect. 8 Program), cash assistance program for immigrants (CAPI), kingship guardianship assistance payment program (Kin-GAP), California assistance dog special allowance program (ADSA), and Medi-Cal—the state's robust public medical insurance program that encapsulates Medicare benefits, dental and vision benefits, and coverage for mothers and newborns (AIM). Each program has different eligibility conditions, many of which are tied to poverty metrics. In California, the average poverty line (since it's calcu-lated by county) was $25,500 for a family of four in 2018.[35] California also uses a separate metric—the California Poverty Measure or CPM—valued at $34,200 the same year. Respectively, 12.8% and 17.6% of Californians fell beneath these measures. Despite the largess of these programs, nearly one-third of Californians are living in or near poverty. Several of these entitle-ments are wrapped together into a single program. Moreover, note that a large portion of California residents are on some form of assistance and remain eligible for lengthy periods of time. In terms of caseload, the California Department of Social Services (CDSS) estimates public welfare programs assist 6.6 million of the 39.5 million (or nearly 17%) Californians living in the state.[36] That's nearly one in five people who are on some form of social welfare. As far as eligibility goes, adults can receive monthly cash aid from CalWORKs for up to 48 months. However, children, those with disabili-ties who are ineligible for Social Security Insurance (SSI), those who care for disabled persons, those who are pregnant, are over 59 years old, are younger than 19, are a victim of domestic abuse, or reside within Indian territory with an unemployment rate of at least 50%, can continue to receive aid beyond the four-year mark.[37] For many of these programs, eligibility thresholds are fairly easy to meet. For CalWORKs, one need only claim emergency need assis-tance for housing, medical, utilities, or clothing. Any resident of California who possesses low income is unemployed or has little resources is eligible. CDSS and other state agencies commonly define *resident* as, "someone who lives in California and plans to stay there, or someone who is working or looking for work in the state."[38] Medi-Cal requires residency, but CalFresh (food stamps) only requires recipients to live with their children who are under 18 years, or to receive disability benefits or assistance.

While California tends toward the bleeding edge of US States in terms of socialistic welfare, the trend toward increasing socialism-style benefits is undeniable—and one widely embraced by the Democrat party now fully in power in Washington D.C.

The basic danger of public welfare in this country is twofold. One, we as a population are aging, living longer, and having fewer children than previous generations, creating a top-heavy effect when it comes to supporting the elderly and retired before considering other welfare recipients. Second, more and more people are turning to government at all levels to provide basic necessities, creating a bottom-heavy effect. Together, these are squeezing the fiscal integrity of our nation and those in the middle who are working, employing workers, and paying taxes to fund these entitlement programs.

The reality is that social welfare is not some pipe dream in a faraway land. The Federal government and the State of California's influence are spreading. This time around, it is being presented by some under the label *Democratic Socialism*. Some worry this political philosophy is less about empowering big government in fiscal matters and more about sheering the power off of large corporations (and their owners) who own sizeable amounts of wealth in the United States.[39] Democratic Socialists push the concept of majority rule over private enterprise. Stakeholder theory—where the interests of non-owners can trump those of business owners—has taken firm root. Proponents believe democratic political principles should be extended to fiscal matters such as smoothing the burden of unattractive work (such as trash collection) over the greatest number of people. On this view, power and wealth should be redistributed from powerful conglomerates to the masses.

It's not just some in our country's political leadership touting Democratic Socialism as the next panacea. Younger generations in America as well as those situated on the lower end of the socioeconomic spectrum have grown up with an affinity for public assistance. Recent movements such as Occupy Wall Street and the Fight for $15 have deeply resonated with this segment of America.[40] Combined with low job and economic growth as well as sharp political divides largely fostered by social media, Americans and their factions have drifted apart, failing to civilly discuss difficult issues.

The forgoing sounds like political drum beating, but it is not. The authors of this book cleave to one party—capitalism. But hopefully, we have got your attention. Regardless of your feelings about income redistribution and social welfare, there is no question but that it is expensive and can put a very big dent in your net worth. If you wish to have some say in protecting yours—or at least redistributing in a manner consistent with your own values and moral compass—hark to the solutions in Part II, and the classes you can access at fweibook.org.

Notes

1. Desjardins, Jeff. "MAPPED: China's Most Ambitious Megaproject—The New Silk Road." *Business Insider*, March 18, 2018. https://www.businessinsider.com/chinas-most-ambitious-megaproject-the-new-silk-road-mapped-2018-3.
2. Clarke, Michael. "Why Is There so much Furore over China's Belt and Road Initiative?" *The Conversation*, May 28, 2020. https://theconversation.com/why-is-there-so-much-furore-over-chinas-belt-and-road-initiative-139461.
3. Page, Jeremy. "How the U.S. Misread China's Xi: Hoping for a Globalist, It Got an Autocrat." *The Wall Street Journal*, December 23, 2020. https://www.wsj.com/articles/xi-jinping-globalist-autocrat-misread-11608735769.
4. Veg, Sebastian. "The 'Restructuring' of Hong Kong and the Rise of Neostatism." *Toqueville 21*, June 27, 2020. https://tocqueville21.com/le-club/the-restructuring-of-hong-kong-and-the-rise-of-neostatism/.
5. Myers, Steven Lee. "With Concessions and Deals, China's Leader Tries to Box Out Biden." *The New York Times*, January 3, 2021. https://www.nytimes.com/2021/01/03/world/asia/china-eu-investment-biden.html.
6. Rapoza, Kenneth. "China Is Nowhere Near Replacing the Dollar." *Forbes*, April 23, 2020. https://www.forbes.com/sites/kenrapoza/2020/04/23/china-is-nowhere-near-replacing-the-dollar/?sh=528832914dfd.
7. Jibiki, Koya. "Rejection of China's 'Nine-dash Line' Spreads from Asia to Europe." *Nikkei Asia*, December 1, 2020. https://asia.nikkei.com/Politics/International-relations/South-China-Sea/Rejection-of-China-s-nine-dash-line-spreads-from-Asia-to-Europe.
8. Ziezulewicz, Geoff. "U.S. Navy Warship Steams Near Contested South China Sea Islands. *Navy Times*, December 22, 2020. https://www.navytimes.com/news/your-navy/2020/12/22/us-navy-warship-steams-near-contested-south-china-sea-islands/.
9. "China Disputes Report it Fired Laser at US Navy Plane." *The Associated Press*, March 7, 2020. https://www.navytimes.com/news/your-navy/2020/03/07/china-disputes-report-it-fired-laser-at-us-navy-plane/.
10. Browne, Ryan. "Chinese Lasers Injure US Military Pilots in Africa, Pentagon Says." *CNN*, May 4, 2018. https://www.cnn.com/2018/05/03/politics/chinese-lasers-us-military-pilots-africa/index.html.
11. Cohen, Zachary, Ryan Browne, Nicole Gaouette, and Taehoon Lee. "New Missile Test Shows North Korea Capable of Hitting All of US Mainland."

CNN, November 30, 2017. https://www.cnn.com/2017/11/28/politics/north-korea-missile-launch/index.html.

12. Detsch, Jack. "On V-J Day, U.S. Pushes for a Stronger Japanese Military." *Foreign Policy*, August 15, 2020. https://foreignpolicy.com/2020/08/15/v-j-day-japan-world-war-2-surrender-victory-trump-military/.

13. Ibid.

14. Ortmann, Stephan, and Mark R. Thompson. "China and the 'Singapore Model'." *Journal of Democracy* 27, no. 1 (January 2016): 39–48. https://journalofdemocracy.org/articles/china-and-the-singapore-model/.

15. Bauer, Lauren, Kristen E. Broady, Wendy Edelberg, and Jimmy O'Donnell. "Ten Facts about COVID-19 and the U.S. Economy." *Brookings,* September 17, 2020. https://www.brookings.edu/research/ten-facts-about-covid-19-and-the-u-s-economy/.

16. "Tracking the COVID-19 Recession's Effects on Food, Housing, and Employment Hardships." Center on Budget and Policy Priorities, January 28, 2021. https://www.cbpp.org/research/poverty-and-inequality/tracking-the-covid-19-recessions-effects-on-food-housing.

17. Iacurci, Greg. "Scammers Have Taken $36 Billion in Fraudulent Unemployment Payments from American Workers." *CNBC,* January 5, 2021. https://www.cnbc.com/2021/01/05/scammers-have-taken-36-billion-in-fraudulent-unemployment-payments-.html.

18. Iacurci, Greg. "Coronavirus Recession Ends for the Rich But Is Far from over for Lower Income Communities." *CNBC,* September 20, 2020. https://www.cnbc.com/2020/09/20/coronavirus-recession-ends-for-rich-crisis-persists-for-others.html.

19. "Coronavirus: US Economy Sees Sharpest Contraction in Decades." *BBC News*, July 30, 2020. https://www.bbc.com/news/business-53574953.

20. Tanner, Michael D., and Charles Hughes. "The Work-Vs-Welfare Trade-Off." CATO Institute, October 7, 2015. https://www.cato.org/publications/commentary/work-vs-welfare-trade.

21. "British Pound to US Dollar Spot Exchange Rates for 2015." ExchangeRates.com, January 2, 2021. https://www.exchangerates.org.uk/GBP-USD-spot-exchange-rates-history-2015.html.

22. Berkowitz, Edward, and Kim McQuaid. "Businessman and Bureaucrat: The Evolution of the American Social Welfare System, 1900–1940." *The Journal of Economic History* 38, no. 1 (March 1978): 120–142. https://www.jstor.org/stable/2119319?seq=1.

23. "Social Insurance Programs." Social Security Administration. Accessed January 11, 2021. https://www.ssa.gov/policy/docs/progdesc/sspus/oasdi.pdf.

24. "Fiscal Year 2019 Budget Overview." Social Security Administration. Accessed January 11, 2021. https://www.ssa.gov/budget/FY19Files/2019BO.pdf.

25. "NHE Fact Sheet." Centers for Medicare & Medicaid Services. Updated December 16, 2020. https://www.cms.gov/Research-Statistics-Data-and-Sys

tems/Statistics-Trends-and-Reports/NationalHealthExpendData/NHE-Fact-Sheet.

26. "Gross Domestic Product." Federal Reserve Bank of St. Louis. Updated January 28, 2021. https://fred.stlouisfed.org/series/GDP.

27. https://www.usdebtclock.org/.

28. "National School Lunch Program: Feeding the Future with Healthy School Lunches." U.S. Department of Agriculture Food and Nutrition Service. Accessed January 11, 2021. https://www.fns.usda.gov/nslp.

29. "Federal Pell Grants Are Usually Awarded only to Undergraduate Students." Federal Student Aid. Accessed January 11, 2021. https://studentaid.gov/unders tand-aid/types/grants/pell.

30. "Lifeline Program for Low-Income Consumers." Federal Communications Commission. Updated January 29, 2021. https://www.fcc.gov/general/lifeline-program-low-income-consumers.

31. "Special Supplemental Nutrition Program for Women, Infants, and Children (WIC)." U.S. Department of Agriculture Food and Nutrition Service. Accessed January 11, 2021. https://www.fns.usda.gov/wic.

32. "Public Welfare Expenditures." Urban Institute. Accessed January 11, 2021. https://www.urban.org/policy-centers/cross-center-initiatives/state-and-local-fin ance-initiative/state-and-local-backgrounders/public-welfare-expenditures#Que stion1Welfare.

33. Olya, Gabrielle. "States That Spend the Most and Least on Welfare." *Yahoo! Finance,* March 10, 2019. https://finance.yahoo.com/news/10-states-spend-most-least-090000541.html.

34. "Partisan Composition of State Legislatures 1978–1988." National Conference of State Legislatures. Accessed January 11, 2021. https://www.ncsl.org/docume nts/statevote/legiscontrol_1978_1988.pdf.

35. "Poverty in California." Public Policy Institute of California. Accessed January 11, 2021. https://www.ppic.org/publication/poverty-in-california/.

36. "2020 May Revision Executive Summary." California Department of Social Services, May 14, 2020. https://www.cdss.ca.gov/Portals/9/Additi onal-Resources/Fiscal-and-Financial-Information/LOcal-Assistance-Estimates/ 2020%20May%20Revise%20Executive%20Summary.pdf?ver=2020-05-18-073110-207.

37. "CalWORKS: FAQs." World Institute on Disability. Updated December 31, 2020. https://ca.db101.org/ca/programs/income_support/calworks/faqs.htm.

38. Johnson, Ann. "How Long Do You Have to Live in California to Get Welfare?" *Pocket Sense.* Updated July 2 7, 2017. https://pocketsense.com/long-do-live-cal ifornia-welfare-8627026.html.

39. "What Is Democratic Socialism?" Democratic Socialists of America. Accessed January 11, 2021. https://www.dsausa.org/about-us/what-is-democratic-social ism/.

40. Meyerson, Harold. "Why Are There Suddenly Millions of Socialists in America?" *The Guardian*, February 29, 2016. https://www.theguardian.com/ commentisfree/2016/feb/29/why-are-there-suddenly-millions-of-socialists-in-america.

The Bernie Madoff/Bad Advisor Risk

At this point, you are probably saying to yourself, "Wow, there are a lot of things in this world that want to separate me from my money. Good thing I have a financial advisor to help me navigate these landmines!".

Yes and no. Assume you find the "right" advisor—someone you connect with, have good chemistry, share your points of view on politics, the market, taxes, and other issues…I could go on and on. There is still what us puffed-up academics like to call *counterparty risk*. This is the risk that the person with whom you are doing business turns out not to have your best interests at heart. That they're looking out for themselves, drat them, instead of us. What's particularly frustrating about counterparty risk in the case of advisors is that this asymmetry could be conscious or subconscious. In other words, your advisor means well, but other forces at work intercept their ability to serve you to the best of their ability: employer pressures, burdensome regulation, vendor dynamics, third party policy shifts…pretty much anyone with whom your advisor interacts can rain on your money-making parade (directly or indirectly). But let's assume for the moment that none of this exists (it does exist in pretty much all advisor engagements, but setting this aside briefly). One excruciatingly painful reality you may be facing now is that your advisor is a bad actor.

Maybe not as bad as the too good to be true Bernard Madoff. He duped investors for decades. Because he had served as the chairman of NASDAQ prior to being discovered for fraud, he remained above suspicion in the eyes

J. Camarda et al., *The Financial Storm Warning for Investors*, https://doi.org/10.1007/978-3-030-77271-0_6

of regulators (despite being warned on an annual basis that Madoff's so-called returns were impossible). Madoff's silver-tongued tactics resulted in $65 billion in losses to investment funds, wealthy individuals, and even charities. In the case of Madoff, there was no investment program; he simply stole the money, printed fictitious statements, and kept on selling investors to invest with him. This was not a case of forgetting to include material information or failing to adequately explain an investment to the client—it was straight-up textbook fraud.

Fraud is a slippery concept in both academic and practical spheres. Different people and agencies define the term differently, but it basically means to induce you, through deception, to make a financial decision based on inaccurate information. Those who defraud you knowingly make false statements to coax you into giving over your money when they know those statements aren't true. As a result, you rely on those statements thinking things will turn out well when the schemer has other plans. The problem with fraud is that, unlike other crimes where the phrase "should have known" or "is likely to" appears, it doesn't apply when it comes to fraud. Here are two definitions each regarding a separate crime from Black's Law Dictionary—the bible from which lawyers learn definitions while still in law school:

- Indecent exposure— "The crime of deliberately showing one's sex organs in a place where this action is likely to offend people."[1]
- Fraud—"A knowing misrepresentation or knowing concealment of a material fact made to induce another to act to his or her detriment."[2]

In the case of fraud, the offender must know the material fact is false. With indecent exposure, the perpetrator need not know that the action would offend others. You may think, "This is a good thing because it creates a clearer standard for fraud offenses, right?" Except that, in this case, if your advisor is misinformed or otherwise doesn't know the information they tell you is false or misleading, then there's no fraud. This doesn't mean you can't bring the matter to arbitration or possibly to a court of law, but as far as crimes go, you would think fraud would be easier to prove and carry a harsher punishment. Proving intent is notoriously difficult. Most often, it's the reverse. And when it comes to counterparty risk and advisor fraud, definitions are the least of your problems.

Problem #1 You don't have an anti-fraud police squad. Corporations—at least the major ones—generate plenty of revenue to adopt and implement anti-fraud measures and internal controls into their infrastructure. They hire employees specifically to look for irregular financial activities within the company. Corporations also hire external auditors, who in turn hire fraud examiners and forensic accountants, both of whom have received specialized training to detect, report, and deter fraud. Corporations also have the capital to purchase insurance to defray costs or completely transfer the risk of fraud to someone else. If that weren't enough, corporations can also rely on law enforcement and regulators to conduct investigations when it believes shadiness is afoot.

You, on the other hand, probably don't have these resources. Your capital, though perhaps substantial, is limited by comparison. Even if it was on your radar, you would be hard-pressed to fund all of the aforementioned safeguards against fraud and still manage a comfortable retirement, college for your children, and your current lifestyle. Even if you could afford your own anti-fraud taskforce, you would still be limited by the lack of information and resources available to individuals when compared to corporations. Much of the academic literature on fraud is geared toward corporate accounting, for instance. Also, while entire institutions and membership organizations are devoted to the study and prevention of fraud, individuals only get a smattering of academic papers and a few government web pages containing fraud prevention tips.

Problem #2 You're a juicy target. You have plenty of assets that have varying degrees of protection. Your bank accounts probably have linked credit cards, which are protected by the financial institution's fraud and identity theft insurance. The deposits themselves are protected by FDIC. Your investment and retirement accounts—assuming they are managed by registered companies—have SIPC insurance, which protects up to $500,000 ($250,000 of which can be cash) from failed brokerage firms, and many firms buy additional insurance into the millions. But it's important to realize that SIPC only protects against loss on the custodial side of your account—not on the investment management side.[3] And when we say loss, we mean against "misplacing" the securities not losses from a decline in value. Or if your broker lends them to a short seller (for a fee they don't share with you or even tell you about!) who sells them, and then the broker goes belly up with your shares gone. If a bank fails, FDIC replaces the dollars, up to FDIC limits. With SIPC, if a broker fails, SIPC makes sure you eventually get your stock or bond or what-have-you certificates—even if they are worthless.

Another danger today, particularly within corporate retirement accounts, is that the same company often fulfills custodial obligations and manages the money. In other words, the investment advisor/salesperson works for the same company in charge of auditing accounts and making sure your money is not only invested as it should be, but is where it should be. If there is any fraud, it is less likely to be brought to light because the same company is left to essentially police itself. By contrast, many other platforms like independent registered investment advisors maintain separate custodians and investment managers. Any illegal or ethically dubious activity at one has a higher chance to trigger suspicion (and therefore action) by the other. Admittedly, when it comes to retirement accounts, there are extra duties placed upon those who operate in a professional capacity by the Employee Retirement Income Security Act (ERISA) of 1974 such as stringent reporting requirements both to plan participants and the Internal Revenue Service. But, as we will discuss momentarily, possessing a duty does not guarantee the professional will behave professionally, and there's still lots of abuse in qualified plans like 401ks. And, sadly, the tough rules of ERISA don't apply to IRAs.

Returning to your $500,000 of SIPC insurance: It essentially only covers failures on the custodial side of the ledger. If a broker-dealer (B/D) becomes insolvent, up to $500,000 of your money held in separate capacity at the firm will be covered. What does "separate capacity" mean? It basically means you can't create multiple accounts like you can at a bank just to get more insurance. At an FDIC institution, if you cross the $250,000 threshold, you can simply create another account and move some of the money over. Not so with SIPC insurance. You would have to open a separate type of retirement account, a joint account, an account owned by an irrevocable trust, or one owned by a corporation; You cannot simply open five brokerage accounts (well you can, but they will be combined into a single account for the purpose of SIPC insurance). In short, you are limited both in dollar amount *and* in scope when it comes to this type of insurance. Again, lots of brokers buy up this coverage, but you have to be careful.

It's also worth noting that SIPC does not specifically cover losses from fraudulent activity. If your accounts were targeted for unauthorized trading or theft, SIPC will step in, particularly if there was a failure on the part of the custodian (whose job is to guard against these types of events). However, normal market loss and fraud on the part of your advisor will not trigger SIPC recovery. Breaking this last distinction down even further: If your advisor simply takes money out of your account, transfers it into their personal account, and buys a boat, that's theft (not fraud), and should be covered by SIPC…theoretically. Trading excessively in your account for the sake of generating commissions, specifically without your input or approval, is called churning and unauthorized trading can produce losses not covered by SIPC; for instance, "SIPC does not protect against the decline in value of your securities. SIPC does not protect individuals who are sold worthless stocks and other securities. SIPC does not protect claims against a broker for bad invest-ment advice, or for recommending inappropriate investments."[4] Promising you x% return on your money by placing your funds into ABC investment and then failing to deliver on that promise is fraud and is *not* covered by SIPC. Again, this does not mean there's no road to recovery, but that road is fraught with uncomfortable conversations with the advisor, redirection over the phone or via email by a supervisor or registered principal, stonewalling by the firm's compliance officer, and eventually, playing hardball courtesy of the firm's counsel.

Remember when you opened your accounts with that brokerage firm? There's a 99% chance you signed a mandatory arbitration agreement, which means you must drag the advisor and/or their firm into FINRA arbitration instead of filing a lawsuit, and you should know the arbitration proceedings work differently than a court of law. For example, it is almost unheard of for an arbitration panel to award the client who has been wronged by a financial advisor punitive damages. Not impossible—just *extremely unlikely*. The best part is, your (probably) three-member arbitration panel will likely consist of all public members (those who have never been affiliated with the securities industry).[5] This is both good and bad. It's good in that it prevents any sort of perceived insider collusion among FINRA members, but it's also bad because public members have no expertise in financial services. They are trained in conducting themselves ethically and professionally as arbitrators for FINRA, that's it. Beyond that, they could be botanists, not economists. They do not receive special legal or financial training. In fact, you and your attorney are solely responsible for bringing legal statutes and past rulings to the panel's attention. Otherwise, out of sight, out of mind. Like members of a jury, FINRA arbitrators are prohibited from conducting their own outside research to determine the merits of a claim. It is *your* responsibility to support your position.

Problem #3 Your quest for returns. In a capitalist, democratic society, we are rewarded for taking risks. Particularly early in our adult lives, it behooves us to be risk-takers. We end up being accepted by better schools, landing better careers, and ultimately making more money because we took risks, whether as star employees or entrepreneurs. Unfortunately, taking risk is only beneficial as long as you are rewarded for doing so. Fraudsters punish you for being risky. They prey on your knowledge that return increases with risk, and on your desire for return. If you found yourself in a world full of fraudsters (assuming no other criminals), your best bet would be to stuff all your money in your mattress. Fortunately, we don't live in that world, yet fraudsters still abound.

Every player's performance within the investing world is measured as a function of risk. That is, by risk-adjusted rates of return.

Fraud undermines all of this theory because you receive no return in exchange for absorbing all the risk. Fraudsters prey upon those who are risk-seeking because those people think they will be fairly rewarded for taking that risk. Those who are extremely risk-averse (who place all their investible assets in things like certificates of deposit and government treasuries) are more stalwart against fraud because they are so reluctant to part with their money. And even these are duped by false promises of guarantees and security. But if you are in the former category, risk-seeking, you are more likely to be approached by scammers than those who are risk-averse.

Fraud Victim Characteristics

In addition to risk-seeking behavior, victims share several other notable qualities.[6] Those who report fraud victimization tend to be male. Also, they usually have education beyond high school and are between the ages of 50 and 70 (coincidentally, when they have the greatest amount of retirement assets). Moreover, they tend to be less irresponsible when it comes to spending behaviors. Specifically, they may consume windfalls such as inheritance or lottery winnings over a shorter period of time.

It should be noted that just because you are risk-seeking doesn't mean you are irresponsible. You can be smart and perform adequate due diligence on financial opportunities and still be willing to take risks.

How Fraud Affects Your Investments

When it comes to investing, one of your top financial goals is probably retirement. After all, you can obtain a loan for nearly all of your financial needs—purchasing a home or car, funding your or your child's education, or starting a business. But you can't obtain a loan for retirement. You can use retirement assets to margin or leverage, take out reverse mortgages, or buy income real estate but nobody is going to loan you a million dollars that you can and don't intend to pay back (because you'll be dead and penniless). Once you retire, you will begin withdrawing funds from your account, and you expect there to be enough to last until you pass away, regardless of how the market behaves. Good financial planners—and they are hard to come by!—can help you calculate your odds of retirement success, but you still have to be careful. When you introduce fraud into the equation, your odds of retirement success could drop by a lot, even to zero, depending on how much, and how often, you are taken for. Only If you experience fraud at any point during retirement, that chance will drop. If you are defrauded again, it will drop yet again. For serial fraud (where fraud occurs intermittently or regularly every year in retirement—either by a family member taking advantage of the retiree or an advisor defrauding the client), the chance of successful retirement, across every scenario, drops big time. In fact, the highest chance of success is a meager 58%.

Even without the worry of fraud—and that's a big worry!—finding quality financial advice is lots harder than you probably think. For one thing, the educational bar is unbelievably low to obtain a financial advisor license. It has been said it's harder to get a license to cut hair than to advise on investments, and that seems to be true. In Florida, for instance, barbers must complete at least 1000 hours of study before taking the exam in order to be licensed.[7] The advisor's exam only requires a passing grade,[8] which someone smart can achieve with little study in a short time. I once knew a brokerage manager who did not study at all for the supervisors' license exam—he just took the test repeatedly until he passed. Even convicted felons can get investment sales licenses,[9] and even those found cheating on license exams are not necessarily barred from becoming licensed.[10] Likewise, in California, the only state to license "professional fiduciaries" (like trustees, guardians, conservators, and those operating under powers of attorney), applicants must satisfy education, experience, and exam requirements, all of which are more robust than the securities commission sales or advisory licence exams.[11] When Steve first began the process for securities licensure, he recalls studying for one of the exams over Memorial Day weekend; he obtained the study materials on Friday, then walked into the testing center, and passed the exam on Tuesday. There is no way a hairdresser, plumber, or car mechanic could do this in their respective professions. But your financial advisor can! And note this bar—low to the ground that it is!—is not unique to California...it is true across the United States.

What's worse, relying on "professional" badges like CFP® (Certified Financial Planner) is not enough to let your guard down—our academic research has demonstrated that CFP®s often have worse records of misconduct than "ordinary" advisors, and the *Wall Street Journal* said of CFP® listed as clean on the CFP Board find-a-planner site "thousands...(with) customer complaints...criminal or regulatory problems—often directly related to their work with clients... for bankruptcy within the past decade...website says they haven't disclosed such an event in the last 10 years...more than 5,000 have faced formal complaints from their clients over investment recommendations or sales practices, and hundreds have been disciplined by financial regulators or left brokerage firms amid allegations of misconduct. At least 140 faced or currently face felony charges, including one who pleaded no contest to a charge of possessing child pornography...."[12] And these are CFP®s, the ones the ads say set "...the standard of excellence in financial planning. CFP® professionals meet rigorous education, training and ethical standards, and are committed to serving their clients' best interests ...."[13]

When it comes to advisors, as Jimmy Buffett said in *Fruitcakes*, "it's a jungle out there, kiddies...have a very fruitful day." Dangers abound, far beyond the pitfalls we've highlighted in this chapter. You have to be very, very careful! Fortunately, when we get to the solutions part of the book, we'll share some "inside secrets" and give detailed instructions on how to sort the good from the bad, and what to look for in a needle-in-the-haystack exceptional advisor.

Notes

1. Black's Law Dictionary Abridged Tenth ed. (2015), s.v. "Indecent exposure." (Toronto: Thomson Reuters), 645.
2. Ibid., 560.
3. "What SIPC Protects." Securities Investor Protection Corporation. Accessed January 11, 2021. https://www.sipc.org/for-investors/what-sipc-protects.
4. Ibid.
5. "FINRA Rule 12,403: Cases with Three Arbitrators. Financial Industry Regulatory Authority." Accessed January 11, 2021. https://www.finra.org/rules-gui dance/rulebooks/finra-rules/12403.
6. Lee, Steven James, Benjamin F. Cummings, and Jason Martin. "Victim Characteristics of Investment Fraud." *Social Sciences Research Network*, February 3, 2019. https://papers.ssrn.com/sol3/papers.cfm?abstract_id=3258084.
7. "Barber Licenses By Examination." Florida Department of Business & Professional Regulation. Accessed January 11, 2021. https://www.myflorida license.com/CheckListDetail.asp?SID=&xactCode=1010&clientCode=0301& XACT_DEFN_ID=5060.
8. "Series 65—Uniform Investment Adviser Law Exam." Financial Industry Regulatory Authority. Accessed January 11, 2021. https://wwwfinra.org/registration-exams-ce/qualification-exams/series65.
9. "General Information on FINRA's Eligibility Requirements." Financial Industry Regulatory Authority. Accessed January 11, 2021. https://www.finraorg/rules-guidance/guidance/eligibility-requirements.

10. Hopper, Jessica. "Working on the Front Lines of Investor Protec-tion—Test Cheaters Beware." Financial Industry Regulatory Authority, September 14, 2020. https://www.finra.org/media-center/blog/working-front-lines-investor-protection-test-cheaters-beware.

11. "Pre-Licensing Education Information." Department of Consumer Affairs Professional Fiduciaries Bureau of California. Accessed January 11, 2021. https://www.fiduciary.ca.gov/forms_pubs/prelicreq.shtml.

12. Zweig, Jason, and Andrea Fuller. "Looking for a Financial Planner? The Go-To Website Often Omits Red Flags." *The Wall Street Journal*, July 30, 2019. https://www.wsj.com/articles/looking-for-a-financial-planner-the-go-to-website-often-omits-red-flags-11564428708.

13. "The Standard of Excellence." Certified Financial Planner Board of Standards. https://www.cfp.net/.

The AI Displacement Risk

Please read the following very short story. No, I've not gone bonkers. This is about money. Your money!

But I need to make an important point so you get it in your bones.

This is the quickest way. So… read?

* * *

"If you're tired of being single in New York, here's a list of the best single bars in the city where you can get your next first date. Whether for the person you prefer or a place where you can spend the night, we have you covered with our lists of the best single bar in our city.

This cheerful Brazilian bar combines bumpin 'forros and music to ensure that the dance floor remains sweaty and full until it's time to close at 4am. Quench your thirst with expensive cocktails and stroll through the bar to rub shoulders with the all-too-willing to mix crowd. After you have completed the first round, go to the back, where they offer food served in a seedy place where people come to get blotto and mingle….

The largest bar is Tropicalia, whose centerpiece is likely to be a popular meeting place for couples following the lifting of COVID-19 restrictions. The perfect place to bring friends ready to dance the night away. Tropicalia has a live DJ set that usually replaces hip-hop and top 40 jams. On one wall is a framed sketch of the Star Wars universe, on the other side are Luke and Leia, as well as a picture of Darth Vader."

© The Author(s), under exclusive license to Springer Nature
Switzerland AG 2021
J. Camarda et al., *The Financial Storm Warning for Investors*,
https://doi.org/10.1007/978-3-030-77271-0_7

* * *

Yes, blah, blah blah. How nice, Dr. Camarda! What the....finance? Can I get off the bloody couch now?

Sure. In a second. But don't get up just yet.

The really amazing thing about that story is that it was written....by a computer.

Totally from scratch. I just plugged "singles bar love story" into the free story-writer box at ai-writer.com, that popped out in about 2.5 minutes.

I bet you couldn't tell. Maybe you even wanted to hit that bar and mingle in that seedy place...

Crap, when I read a recent AI article[1] in *The New York Times* and saw a similar story, I knew it was written by a machine before I started, and I still couldn't tell!

It doesn't quite satisfy the Turing Test—where a human can't tell if it's interacting with a machine or another human—but it's getting there.

What does this have to do with your money, you ask. Could be, lots. This will be an extremely short chapter, I promise you. But it contains an extremely important stone to fill in your mosaic of what the future may be shaping up to be.

AI—artificial intelligence, machine learning, etc.—is developing very rapidly and promises to be a quantum transformative force. It will change the world and holds the promise of incalculable benefits for humanity—if the machines don't decide to snuff us and take over, that is! But that's the stuff of a different book!

For this book, I don't want to talk about all the ways it might make your life easier, longer, and filled with inexpensive riches beyond your wildest dreams. These are awesome prospects, but, as with most in life, there is a downside.

I want to talk about the profound risk that machines may put you, your kids, and billions of others out of work. As the *Times* article says, "This is a great time to be alive. The only problem is that, in the next five years, A.I. will replace millions of jobs."

Five years. Can you imagine, at the blazing speed of tech advance, how many jobs will be lost in the next ten and fifteen years?

Robots on auto assembly lines have been commonplace for decades and in recent years have made big inroads everywhere from warehouses to home vacuums and lawnmowers. Of course, we typically don't think of such machines as "intelligent," but it's a slippery slope, indeed. Recently, an MIT economist reported[2] "We find fairly major negative employment effects... negative wage effects, that workers are losing in terms of real wages in more affected areas, because robots are pretty good at competing against them." His team noted that so far the effect is most pronounced among workers with the least reemployment options—those that are not trained or otherwise suited to jump career tracks. This is at the crux of the risk I highlight in this chapter, though I forecast the effect will spread, like ripples in a pond, to wider and more complex segments of the labor and professional pools. *Time* magazine reported[3] that COVID seems to have accelerated this trend, noting "This replacement of humans with machines may pick up more speed in coming months as companies move from survival mode to figuring out how to operate while the pandemic drags on. Robots could replace as many as 2 million more workers in manufacturing alone by 2025...." The article noted that many firms closed call centers, replacing humans with chatbot software, and that COVID just seems to have accelerated "what was going to happen anyway...." And those ripples? They may be spreading wider than you think. AI is getting much better at tasks once though beyond it, "making it harder for humans to stay ahead of machines. JPMorgan says it now has AI reviewing commercial-loan agreements, completing in seconds what used to take 360,000 hours of lawyers' time over the course of a year. In May, amid plunging advertising revenue, Microsoft laid off dozens of journalists at MSN and its Microsoft News service, replacing them with AI."

OK, so you don't worry (most of you) about the lawyers. But what about everyone else?

So, clearly, the economic risk is 1) your lost income and 2) utter transformation of economic activity. I have no idea what a machine economy might look like, but the same sword that will make stuff way cheaper and better is poised to bleed your income, maybe. And in you own a business, maybe impoverish your customers.

What jobs are at risk, when? I think this will go by order of complexity. It will be easier to write reliable algorithms to replace Uber drivers (though Musk is finding this far more nettelseome than he proclaimed) than brain surgeons, brilliant lawyers, and guys who think they're pretty sharp financial advisors, like me.

But it's coming and faster than you think. The key is expert systems, like I design in my business to render sophisticated tax and estate planning advice. Most cases are already solved by the detailed rules I've created. Only the most complex require me to sit, ponder, test, confer, and cogitate. And even cases like these are reducible to complex rules, given sufficient effort and resources. And if you can write rules, you can code them. And as the machine becomes more integrated, nuanced, and enabled, they'll soon be able to generate rules even better, gosh, than guys like me.

Here's—jeepers!—the story ai-writer.com wrote for me when I plugged in "financial advisors being replaced by computers," again in less than three minutes:

"Artificial intelligence (AI) is at the cutting edge of financial services, with machines that can learn and adapt independently. This technology has the potential to disrupt and change more than financial services, and is spreading to almost all industries. Most of the AI used today is for Wall Street professionals, but industry analysts predict it will soon be used in other industries as well."

But just because technological advances like robo-advisers won't crowd out human financial advisers right away, that doesn't mean they can sit back and relax. Robots may not be doing their jobs, but other financial advisers using the latest and most powerful technology are likely to dominate. With a predetermined equation based on certain assumptions, robo-advisers can create an investment plan that will prepare you for your long-term goals. They bring empirical methods to financial advice and also offer lower fees than human consultants. Financial advisers and planners are already being replaced by programs and chatbots that manage money and wealth. Together, they manage nearly half a trillion dollars, according to *Business Insider*. "Using algorithms and customer information, robo-advisers make recommendations on financial allocations and investments, and in some cases make transactions on behalf of the customer. Technology, algorithm, and artificial intelligence can do much more than just manage your money for you, but also process huge amounts of data at a speed that humans will never reach. So will robo-planners like Viviplan take over the market and replace human financial advisers once and for all? While we are still working to develop the technology and automate the process more, we hope that consumers will eventually be able to play with their data and forecasts themselves, with a little less involvement from financial planners, and take planning into their own hands...."

As Jimmy Buffett once said, "thank you, robot!".

I am not so kind. Scat and begone, freaking terminator! Where's the darn plug....

As AI transforms and replaces jobs—likely beginning with the least fortunate among us—there is a very high risk of income disruption. This factor will exacerbate other trends we discuss in the book, like higher taxes, income redistribution, the demise of Social Security, and more. The cold equation? More people out of work or making less, relying on an already-strained government whose only recourse is to squeeze more out of those folks who've managed to hang on to some wealth and income, like those probably interested in reading this book.

I promised a short chapter, and it's time to wrap this one up. As Forrest Gump said, "that's all I have to say about that." I just wanted to make sure this risk, this massive change force, was on your radar. It will sneak up on you like warming water in a pot full of frog. It may be time to consider the likely AI trajectory of your own occupation, and perhaps tweak your course to target a better-protected outcome. Ditto for your kids and those you care about.

Like so many of the other risk factors in this book, this one argues for you to make more off your occupation and investments faster, better protect them, and structure your tax profile so as to keep more of your wealth in your hands, and out of the government's.

Gather ye wealth-buds whilst you may, children of man!

Notes

1. Metz, Cade. "When A.I. Falls in Love." *The New York Times,* November 24, 2020. https://www.nytimes.com/2020/11/24/science/artificial-intelligence-gpt3-writing-love.html.
2. Dizikes, Peter. "How Many Jobs Do Robots Really Replace?" *MIT News*, May 4, 2020. https://news.mit.edu/2020/how-many-jobs-robots-replace-0504.
3. Semuels, Alana. "Millions of Americans Have Lost Jobs in the Pandemic—And Robots and AI Are Replacing Them Faster Than Ever." *Time*, August 6, 2020. https://time.com/5876604/machines-jobs-coronavirus/.

The Hyperinflation Risk & Inflationary Storm Crisis

Inflation has been quiescent for so long that most of us have forgotten what it means, in real terms, and how it can drive behavior and blast our wealth.

Back when I was coming up in the 70s, the US dollar was dropping in value so fast people would rush out to spend their money before prices went up. And prices went up with clockwork regularity. Interest rates were in the teens—I remember seeing 20%+ briefly—but money in the bank still lost value because the dollar dropped at a rate faster even than those crazy interest rates….and don't forget that taxes had to be paid on the interest, a double whammy to the decimation of consumer purchasing power.

That was a hard time to be a wealth holder. Many investments—like bonds!—dropped like stones in value, stocks seemed stuck in endless bear mode, and it was very, very hard to get ahead. Unless, of course, you tuned your investment dial to things that benefited from inflation, as we will explore in Part II.

Since then, inflation has grown so calm most of us don't think about it at all. We don't factor it into investment or purchase decision making, and, if anything, we worry more about deflation than inflation. Deflation, by the way, is where a currency increases in value, and prices for goods drop because the currency becomes more and more valuable.

In all fairness, there are many solid reasons to believe this time is really different, and inflation is gone for long, if not good. It certainly has not been a problem in the United States, nor in most major economies. No one really knows why this is, though there are many theories.

© The Author(s), under exclusive license to Springer Nature Switzerland AG 2021
J. Camarda et al., *The Financial Storm Warning for Investors*,
https://doi.org/10.1007/978-3-030-77271-0_8

Globalization—the interconnectedness of economies around the world—has leveled the playing field, reducing prices to the lowest common denominator. A simple example of this is labor costs. If a shirt can be cut and stitched in Asia for under a dollar in pay, compared perhaps to $10 in the United States, prices stay down. That's bad for US worker wages, but good for US worker consumption since it keeps prices lower. Globalization also levels the costs of resources to the cheapest worldwide (shipped) price. A similar issue is the decline of unionization and the ability of labor to demand inflationary wage hikes. The world de-globalized to a major extent post COVID, but we will have to see if that sticks. Major supply bottlenecks stemming from breakdowns in just-in-time inventory, shortages as countries horded health supplies made in Asia, and other reasons have caused many to call for local production, even at higher (inflationary) cost.

The march of tech is a big factor in finding ways to do and make things faster, cheaper, and better. TVs are a great example. Prices plummet, quality soars. A huge TV nearly smart enough to make me waffles sells for way less than those 1970s-era good-as-it-got 25″ floor model console TVs—remember those hulking horrors of four-legged wavering pixilation?

Many suspect that government measures of inflation are understated, and that the official CPI—which affects Social Security increases and other government payments—belies actual cost increases in the markets. This is an oft-opined suspicion. Recently, *the New York Times* noted "Inflation Is Higher Than the Numbers Say; While government statistics say inflation is low, the reality is that the cost of living has risen during the pandemic…"[1]

Another theory holds that increases in worldwide wealth and savings rates have altered the supply/demand curve for capital, with a greater supply and more competition for interest payments keeping rates low and hence inflationary pressures down.

Like I said, no one really knows, least of all your humble author. So please bear all this in mind as we explore the potential inflationary risk going forward. While current conditions are such to spark the mother of all hyper-inflationary cycles from a traditional perspective, there may be an invisible fire hose, to badly misquote Adam Smith, keeping the fires at bay in the modern world.

Before I get into my hyperinflationary concerns—which have bothered me since early in the COVID crisis—let me give you a late-2020 pundits check and share what some others are saying.

Just before New Years of '21, my fellow *Forbes* contributor Mike O'Sullivan commented that "Inflation Might Be The Most Important Market Factor In 2021."[2] Bloomberg noted "the set up for faster inflation is better than it has been for decades. But don't expect the Federal Reserve to tighten monetary policy next year in response – even if inflation comes in higher than central bankers are forecasting."[3] CNBC? "2021 may mark the first inflation comeback in a generation, market researcher Jim Bianco warns," saying "'you could have a burst of economic activity that could produce higher inflation for the first time in a generation…that's the big worry I have for 2021…if interest rates are going up because of inflation, historically risk markets like the equity market don't take well to that…'".[4]

Talk about your stealth taxes, inflation is the sneakiest of all, a real frog-in-the-hot-pot problem, where you don't realize the danger until your goose is cooked. It is insidious. The average inflation rate in the 1940s and 1970s was about 7%.[5] Many of you reading this will be as concerned with the cost of health care as much as the cost of bread, so look at it this way. In 2020, the average cost of a heart bypass was about $135K.[6] At 7% price inflation, that cost jumps to $270K in ten years and $525K in 20 years. That's before all the ancillary prep and get better costs, mind you. Pretty stiff, doubly so when you look at the tax and Medicare disruption concerns discussed elsewhere in Part I.

What forces presage big inflation ahead? For one thing, the Fed is stimulating the economy like mad to keep COVID from slipping us into another Great Recession. The printing press is whirling around the clock. Bond buying by the Fed to trump up demand and suppress interest rates is 2008-crash collossal. Free money—near zero interest rates, government payments to millions of citizens, programs like the Payroll Protection Plan (I&II), the massive Biden stimulus train barreling down the fiscal tracks, the list goes on—creates a couple big problems. First, the dollars become less valuable as the supply expands—hopes of Modern Monetary Theory's magic wand notwithstanding—and will have to be repaid or officially devalued at some point. These are not gold-backed dollars, mind you. They are paper money created out of thin air. The second is they expand an already-crushing national debt. How bad is that again?

Well, Again, from our friends at the Congressional Budget Office.[7] "By the end of 2020, federal debt held by the public is projected to equal 98 percent of GDP. *The projected budget deficits would boost federal debt to 104 percent of GDP in 2021, to 107 percent of GDP (the highest amount in the nation's history) in 2023,* and to 195 percent of GDP by 2050. *High and rising federal debt makes the economy more vulnerable to rising interest rates and, depending on how that debt is financed, rising inflation. The growing debt burden also raises borrowing costs, slowing the growth of the economy and national income, and it increases the risk of a fiscal crisis or a gradual decline in the value of Trea-sury securities"* (my *emphasis*). As noted, the Fed is also printing money to buy government bonds—basically enabling more borrowing and spending with magic-wand money—pretty big time as another way to hold rates down and expand the easy money supply. What the Fed does, by the way, is called monetary stimulus, since the main tool is the money supply. Past Fed Chair Ben Bernanke was called "helicopter Ben" because of his reference to drop-ping money via helicopter to support the economy. These days, the monetary skies are so black with helicopters that nary a scrap of blue's to be seen.

At the same time, the Federal government—read Congress with POTUS pen partner—is borrowing and spending like mad in what is called fiscal stimulus, ratcheting up debt faster than a slot machine spins. Like the Fed's actions, this is absolutely necessary to keep our economic wagon from sliding off the cliff. But both are creating one heck of a mess when the aftermath hits. And lots of pork-barrel social welfare stuff inevitably slips into the legisla-tive shaping tug of way. Beyond this, with the Federal government already knocking on the poorhouse door, states and smaller governments across the nation are nearly belly-up from COVID budgetary pressures, increasing the pressure on Washington as the bailout window of last resort.

So how do we get out of this mess? As I lament in other chapters, taxes are going to be nightmarish for those that still have a few bucks. At the end of the day, taxes are the only real source of government wealth. Borrowing is not forever, and printing money does not create real wealth. Besides taxes, there are only two other "options," both inflationary.

The government can default on its debt. Stiff those who invest (like the dwindling Social Security fund!) in Treasury bonds and such. The United States flirted with losing the top bond credit rating in the last recession and may likely lose it this time. Besides pressuring credit ratings—and lower ratings mean higher interest costs, another inflation factor—a bout of infla-tion would drive down the value of the dollar on world markets as well as in the United States, boosting the costs of imports (even from cheap China) and further driving the inflationary spiral.

The government could also seek to monetize the debt, basically printing money to pay debt off. Make sense? This is the banana republic solu-tion. You remember those! Here's what one professor wrote about one of Venezuela's many recent devaluations: "Venezuela recently announced one of the most dramatic currency reforms in history in a move that essen-tially devalues the bolivar by about 95 percent. Its ironically named bolivar fuerte, meaning 'strong,' first introduced 10 years ago, will be replaced by a new 'sovereign' version at a conversion rate of 100,000 to one sovereign."

Presto! One hundred thousand dollars is now worth…one dollar! Good luck buying a hamburger with it. That would let a government pay off a $100,000 bond with one new dollar, fresh off the printing press. Professor Cohen also noted "in today's Venezuela, domestic prices are rising at an annualized rate of 108,000 percent. And economists at the International Monetary Fund estimate that by the end of the year the rate could top 1 million percent – imagine the price of milk tripling every minute."[8] That was 2018. They did it again in 2019.

Now, of course, we are no Venezuela, and that is a very extreme case, but I hope it makes the point. Such periods of hyperinflation are actually pretty common in the modern age. You may remember Weimer Germany from grade school, all those wheelbarrows of near-worthless money? While I trust the US Federal Reserve to act far more carefully and effectively than these two outlier examples, some things are beyond its control, like the unforeseen consequences of juicing a depressed economy to unprecedented (for the US) levels. Congress's restraint on runaway borrowing and spending I have less confidence in. Lots less.

In some quarters of the dismal science, it has been expressed that the government can both print and borrow without restraint, and without fear of inflation. This miraculous alchemy goes by the name of Modern Monetary Theory (MMT). While initially developed in the 1970s by American economist Warren Mosler,[9] MMT has been making headlines lately due to a book by Stephanie Kelton entitled *The Deficit Myth* as well as popularity with many progressive politicians, including Alexandria Ocasio-Cortez and Bernie Sanders.[10] The premise of MMT is that the government does not need to worry about its debt or reign in its spending or even balance its books because it has the ability to print any amount of new money it needs. The theory is that provided that the government controls inflation, there is no problem with just creating new money. On this theory, national debt is not actually debt, it is just money that has been injected into the economy and not yet regained through taxes.[11] Where is the inflation control dial? Tax increases![12]

Former Fed Chairs Alan Greenspan and Ben Bernanke have lent credence to MMT theory by stating things about printing money instead of borrowing due to our weak economy and about how there is nothing stopping the government from printing whatever money they want and nothing bad will happen.

The main idea of the cycle of money is that the government prints as much currency as the country needs. This then is spent by the government and flows into circulation. This causes demand for the goods and service to increase because the citizens have more money in their hands to spend. Jobs likewise increase because companies will create more positions to keep up with the demand. As we near 100% employment prices will stabilize, enabling society to fund programs like the Green New Deal, universal free college, universal basic income, and many more programs that other more socialized countries already provide their citizens.

Proponents state that there have been successful implementations of MMT already, such as in Japan. Japan runs a deficit of 240% of GDP and has no inflation, in fact their economy has experienced bouts of deflation for some time. While deflation often signals low-to-no economic growth, proponents of MMT point to the government to right the ship under such circumstances. When Ben Bernanke added $1 trillion dollars to the economy, the US Fed lowered interest rates to almost zero to halt deflation. This recent example, MMTers hold, underscores the fact that hyperinflation is not a concern so long as there are goods and services in the country on which to spend the newly printed money and employment does not reach 100%.

Despite the benefits propounded by MMT enthusiasts, in our view the theory contains many unwarranted assumptions and implies severe problematic consequences. First, printing money can suggest a reduced need to borrow it, or worse, enable irresponsible Congressional borrowing. Remember, the Fed controls monetary policy including money printing, while Congress oversees borrowing and spending money. These forces are not always on the same page.

Another concern is that excessive money printing could radically distort capital markets.

Governments have tried doing this before, to little avail. Back to Wiemar Germany during World War I. When Germany created more money in order to finance military expenditures and war reparations, it devalued the mark from 4.2-to-one vs the US dollar to 4.2 *trillion*-to-one. The government sponsored 130 printing companies to create new currency. Prices were changing twice per hour, and workers had to collect their wages in wheelbarrows. At that point, many people used tangible assets to barter for goods and services because they could not keep up with the amount of money being injected into the economy, let alone carry enough to buy stuff!

Zimbabwe also tried printing money with impunity in the early 2000s to finance its military conflict with the Democratic Republic of Congo. Despite the fact that Zimbabwe had suffered a drop in food production and their banking sector had all but collapsed, they continued to print, and the country's currency spiraled into hyperinflation. Similar failures plagued Greece in 1944, Hungary in 1946, Yugoslavia in 1994 and, again, most recently Venezuela over the past few years.[13] Many of these examples involved highly corrupt governments, far more reckless than even own. Still, it is helpful to remember that many of our elected officials have been trained as lawyers—not economists. The past history of MMT has not stopped some politicians like Bernie Sanders or Alexandria Ocassio-Cortez from proposing legislation that will require the generation of massive government revenues to offset the onslaught of freshly printed dollars. MMTers believe that unbridled money printing is easily controlled by tax hikes (on you know who!) to avoid hyperinflation. Importantly, this is theoretical only and has never been demonstrated to work. Real world examples, like the many above, indicated very dire consequences. We think it's playing with fire, but we fear it may be tried in the United States in the near future.

With as deep a fix as we are already in as explored here and throughout Part I, can you imagine the consequences of relying on MMT—with its tax-hike mandate—to finance yet more government spending on top of our already-record levels of national debt? Proposals to fund the Green New Deal, free college for all, universal free income payments (why work?) and job guarantees, and more have been seriously proposed by many recently. These proposals won't go away anytime soon and could become even more popular. Government handouts are widely blamed for labor shortages in 2021, driving up the cost of labor and prices in affected industries.

For many reasons, and even without MMT, the risks of a return of damaging inflation have become extremely pronounced. Such inflation poses deadly risks to investors and retirees. Bonds—and the US dollar—would plunge in value, as would fixed incomes like pensions, annuity payments, and what's left of Social Security. Some asset classes—which we explore in detail in Part II—should pace inflation, and even benefit from it. Please pay careful attention when we turn to solutions and countermeasures later in the book. While the inflationary path forward is far from certain, the unwary risk a devastating sinkhole from which they and their wealth might never recover.

Notes

1. Wolfers, Justin. "Inflation Is Higher Than the Numbers Say." *The New York Times*, September 2, 2020. https://www.nytimes.com/2020/09/02/business/inflation-worse-pandemic-coronavirus.html.
2. O'Sullivan, Mike. "Inflation Might Be The Most Important Market Factor in 2021." *Forbes*, December 29, 2020. https://www.forbes.com/sites/mikeosullivan/2021/12/29/inflation-might-be-the-most-important-market-factor-in-2021/?sh=5a809889d51d.

3. Duy, Tim. "How the Fed Will Respond to the Coming Inflation Scare." *Yahoo! Finance*, December 30, 2020. https://finance.yahoo.com/news/fed-res pond-coming-inflation-scare-110020820.html.

4. Landsman, Stephanie. "2021 May Mark the First Inflation Comeback in a Generation, Market Researcher Jim Bianco Warns." *CNBC*, December 30, 2020. https://www.cnbc.com/2020/12/29/2021-may-mark-first-inflation-comeback-in-generation-jim-bianco-warns.html.

5. Hall, Robert E. *Inflation: Causes and Effects*. Chicago: University of Chicago Press, 1982. https://www.nber.org/books-and-chapters/inflation-causes-and-eff ects.

6. Costhelperhealth. "How Much Does Heart Bypass Surgery Cost?" Accessed January 11, 2021. https://health.costhelper.com/bypass.html#:~:text=Heart% 20bypass%20surgery%20typically%20is%20covered%20by%20health.

7. Congressional Budget Office. "The 2020 Long-Term Budget Outlook." Accessed January 11, 2021. https://www.cbo.gov/publication/56598#:~:text= In%20CBO's%20projections%2C%20federal%20debt.time%20as%20the% 20economy%20expands.

8. Cohen, Benjamin J. "Venezuela's 'Desperate' Currency Devaluation Won't Save Its Economy from Collapse." *The Conversation*, August 22, 2018. https://the conversation.com/venezuelas-desperate-currency-devaluation-wont-save-its-eco nomy-from-collapse-101939#:~:text=Venezuela%20recently%20announced% 20one%20of.bolivar%20by%20about%2095%20percent.&text=At%20the% 20same%20time%20the.per%20dollar%20to%206%20million.

9. D'Souza, Deborah. "Modern Monetary Theory." Investopedia, December 29, 2020. https://www.investopedia.com/modern-monetary-theory-mmt-458 8060#:~:text=Origins%20of%20MMT.as%20a%20Wall%20Street%20trader.

10. Edwards, Jim, and Theron Mohamed. "MMT: Here's a Plain-English Guide to 'Modern Monetary Theory' and Why It's Interesting." *Business Insider,* March 2, 2020. https://www.businessinsider.com/modern-monetary-theory-mmt-exp lained-aoc-2019-3.

11. King, Stephen. "MMT: The Case Against Modern Monetary Theory." *Financial Times*, October 21, 2020. https://www.ft.com/content/bcb523c3-7448-4cd6-a2d2-69b8f13be8f3.

12. "An MMT Response on What Causes Inflation." *Financial Times* , March 1, 2019. https://www.ft.com/content/539618f8-b88c-3125-8031-cf46ca197c64.

13. McKibbin, Warwick J. "Is Modern Monetary Theory Too Good to Be True?" *Brookings*, March 12, 2019. https://www.brookings.edu/opinions/is-modern-monetary-theory-too-good-to-be-true/.

The COVID Stock Bubble: Is a Mother of All Stock Bubbles Brewing?

Let's start with a gut check.

The COVID recession is widely reported to be the worst economic crisis since the Great Depression.

But the market's partying like it's 1999. You may recall that was the year before the year of one of the biggest stock market crashes in history. Then, as now, many tech stocks were soaring out of all proportion to even any wisp of profitability, only to crash so hard it would take sixteen years to breakeven. I'll repeat that a few times, as it bears (no pun!) repeating.

Except for a brief gut punch in March of 2020, the US stock market kept climbing to all time highs, seeming soaring ever the higher the worse the heath news got.

As I wrote this the morning of Christmas Eve, 2020, the S&P 500 is at about 3700, just a few points shy of the record high it made in the last few weeks. Lest you forget, 2020 has been strewn with a string of record highs, even as the virus news grew ever more grim. Today's *New York Times* reports[1] "at least 3,411 new coronavirus deaths and 227,522 new cases were reported in the United States on December 23. Over the past week, there has been an average of 213,472 cases per day, an increase of 2 percent from the average two weeks earlier...case numbers remain about as high as they have ever been...deaths continue to increase." On the economy, the *Times* reports[2] "personal income fell in November for the second straight month, the Commerce Department said Wednesday, and consumer spending

© The Author(s), under exclusive license to Springer Nature
Switzerland AG 2021
J. Camarda et al., *The Financial Storm Warning for Investors*,
https://doi.org/10.1007/978-3-030-77271-0_9

declined for the first time since April, as waning government aid and a worsening pandemic continued to take a toll on the US economy. Separate data from the Labor Department showed that applications for unemployment benefits remained high last week and have risen since early November. Taken together, the reports are the latest evidence that the once-promising economic recovery is sputtering. 'We know that things are going to get worse,' said Daniel Zhao, senior economist with the career site Glassdoor. The question is how much worse.'".

As I finalize the manuscript near the end of Q1 2021, the market continues to soar to record levels. Is the economy improving as vaccination rolls out? Sure. Will it be fixed like pre-COVID this year or next? No way.

So tell me, what's wrong with this picture? By fundamental measures—simple accounting math that asserts a dollar's worth four quarters and no more, and anyone who'd give you eight quarters for a dollar is nuts (but take them!)—the US stock market was way overvalued in 2019, when the economy was strong and the future bright.

Since then, stock valuations have gone bonkers, even as the COVID reaper's steered the economy off the cliff. By bonkers, I mean stock prices have gone from crazy to hopelessly hallucinatory and pathological.

Here's what I said in Forbes as the bubble was gathering. I don't care if you're in index funds, the S&P 500, or even individual stocks, you can't help but have noticed that stock prices seem to have become unhinged from the black pit the global economy has been dancing on the edge of.

Some may ask themselves why the S&P 500 is not a good predictor of the US economy. This is a valid and very important question. The implication is that stocks are high—at or near records on the Dow Jones Industrial Average, the NASDAQ, and the S&P 500—because economic good times are on the verge of coming roaring back.

Are they? Even with the cavalry of the miracle med-tech vaccine, I think that is very doubtful.

The stock market is a leading indicator, it is true. It tends to go down before the economy gets slammed and go up before the unemployment rate and other economic measures show improvement.

But Mr. Market is also a very fickle customer. There's an old saying on Wall Street that "the market can stay irrational longer than you can stay solvent." This usually is applied to short sellers, who bet that a market with no logical reason to be high must come down. Often, they get outvoted by irrational investors paying crazy prices for overvalued stocks.

Investment in the stock market always carries some risk. Stock trading is not a perfect game. Mutual funds can gyrate wildly. Knowing when to buy and sell in the financial markets is in the best of times mysterious.

Right now, things may be good on the New York Stock Exchange, but are they good in the real world where people make and spend money and fuel the profits of the companies in the S&P 500? No!

Is your chief investment your stock portfolio? Are you running it like a professional chief investment officer?

There are two massive and opposing forces acting to shape investors' views on stock prices now.

The first is the unprecedented, devastating chill COVID has placed on global commerce. For most companies—I mean the overwhelming majority, 'round the world—the lifeblood of sales revenues is way, way down. Bankruptcies were hitting the wall left and right. Businesses small and large were barely clinging to life. The economic fuel of consumer spending was decimated by layoffs and fears of layoffs. And, regardless of what the politicians or wishful thinking may say, we are really just in round one. The worst impact is yet to come and probably won't be known until 2022 or later.

This is a chilling thought but an inescapable conclusion.

It's still bad.

So why is the market partying like it's 1999? (whoops! there I go again!).

Well, the Fed has never ridden to the rescue quite like this before. Not during the Great Depression, or even during the 2008 Great Recession, has the Federal Reserve been so loose with printing-press cash, or so eager to intervene in the markets by buying to prop up demand and prices. Pretty much ditto for central banks around the world.

This is Kool-Aid of a very high order. It is literally juicing an economy on intensive care life support. And it is serving up a crack-pipe high to too many stock investors, all out of proportion to the life-support med drip to an economy barely crawling away from death's door.

Why do I say that? Ain't low rates and lots of easy, easy money good for business, and good for stocks?

Of course it is. You can bet your bottom bippy on that.

But when it comes to stock investors' expectations, what looks like all the money in the world may really be like trying to fill a mineshaft with a teaspoon. And even the open-checkbook Fed continues to be making future-is-murky-and-dangerous noises, which is of course the reason for the open checkbook.

Let's do some fact checking. Stocks are now trading well past their peaks back in 2019. Two things about 2019.

1. The worldwide economy was singing. Companies were making money hand over fist. Things are a little different now, but you couldn't tell that from stock market prices!
2. Even then, when the good times were undeniably rolling, no less pundits that the likes of Nobel Laureate Robert Shiller were warning stock prices were in a bubble and bound to come tumbling down.

Again, things are now a little different. Legions of companies' financial statements were crushed and unpredictable. The future remained so uncertain that many stopped issuing guidance of expected revenues and earnings.

So how to value stocks? It has been said that in the long term, the market is like a weighing machine, but in the short term it's like a voting machine.

In more sober times, one looks at the future earnings capacity of a company and ties that back to a fair value. Kinda like pricing a house based on how much rent you can clear. This is called fundamental analysis. It's the weighing machine part.

In the lingering COVID haze, there is no clear way to weigh. For many companies, future revenues are just unknowable. Estimating profits and assigning prices is just shooting in the dark. Even as the haze clears, much uncertainty abounds.

So that leaves the voting machine. The popularity contest. This method— prone to wishful thinking and always trumped before by the weighing machine in the end—tends to produce some whacky results, on both the under-value and over-value side.

Right now, things look to be wildly overvalued. If Shiller was warning bubble in 2019 while the economy was rocking, what does that say about now?

There is a term, *irrational exuberance*, popularized by past Fed Chairman Alan Greenspan, referring to inflated stock prices, trotted out as the 1990's dot com bubble was starting to puff in earnest. It's been described as "unfounded market optimism that lacks a real foundation of fundamental valuation, but instead rests on psychological factors…irrational exuberance has become synonymous with the creation of inflated asset prices associated with bubbles, which ultimately pop and can lead to market panic."[3]

Nobel Prize winner and Yale professor Robert J. Shiller was reportedly Greenspan's inspiration for the term. Shiller wrote a book in 2000 titled *Irrational Exuberance,* in which he says it's "the psychological basis of a speculative bubble. I define a speculative bubble as a situation in which news of price increases spurs investor enthusiasm, which spreads by psychological contagion from person to person, in the process amplifying stories that might justify the price increases, and bringing in a larger and larger class of investors who, despite doubts about the real value of an investment, are drawn to it partly by envy of others' successes and partly through a gamblers' excitement."[4] He also put it like this "a social epidemic that involves extravagant expectations for the future...social mental illness – excessive self-perpetuating feedback fed by greed, envy, enthusiasm, media amplification, regret on missing out and fear of not catching up...".

Financial texts refer to this as the greater fool theory. Per Investopedia: "an investor will purchase questionably priced securities without any regard to their quality. If the theory holds, the investor will still be able to quickly sell them off to another 'greater fool,' who could also be hoping to flip them quickly. Unfortunately, speculative bubbles burst eventually, leading to a rapid depreciation in share prices."[5]

P.T. Barnum put it much more succinctly: "there's a sucker born every minute." Gamestop, anyone?

2000, by the way, was an auspicious year. You may recall it is the year the tech-laden NASDAQ stock market index peaked, only to fall some 80% from the high. It would not break even again for sixteen years, just a few years ago.

By the way, before we get too deep into this, know that just because stock prices are bonkers high, that doesn't mean they will come crashing down any time soon. The bubble can continue to inflate on the hot air of irrationality, and big money can still be made in the markets while it does. You just have to be careful, and we'll give you some sharp tools for this in the solutions part of the book, so stay tuned for Part II.

All this blather, by the way, is way out of jibe with all you probably "know" about investing, including asset allocation and Modern Portfolio Theory. These key concepts are widely accepted as holy writ by financial professionals, advisors, and investors alike, but you may be surprised at how shaky the foundations on which these "Nobel Prize-winning" methods rest. It's important that you fit this into your thinking, so here is a quick primer.

There are two seminal concepts I want to review.

The first is the efficient market hypothesis, which in its various forms holds that stock (and other asset) prices reflect all known information and accurately reflect fair value. In other words, the market acts as an efficient "weighing machine" most of the time, so if a stock is trading at $10, the share as a faction of the underlying company's value is drop-dead worth darn near $10. The efficient market hypothesis is an extension of economic rational expectations theory which purports 1) people make money decisions rationally, with logic and without emotion; 2) they apply this logic to wisely integrate all the available information at hand, as well as their past experiences and historical outcomes; 3) because they think like Vulcans and take the time to collect and actually process all available information, their decisions come out right most of the time.

Sound like anyone you know?

Me, either (well, maybe me, but not often). This ivory tower scripture makes for fascinating academic debate, but does not describe the world very well.

From the *NY Times*, December 26th, 2020: "Market Edges Toward Euphoria, Despite Pandemic's Toll: … levels of froth reminiscent of the dot-com boom… notable for its mostly unstoppable rise …despite a pandemic that has killed more than 300,000 people, put millions out of work and shuttered businesses around the country…market is now tipping into outright euphoria…' market…foaming at the mouth'… levels last seen in 2000, the year the dot-com bubble began to burst. Initial public offerings…are having their busiest year in two decades — even if many of the new companies are unprofitable…we are seeing the kind of craziness…(not) been in existence…since the internet bubble…"[6]

How rational is that, Mr. Spock?

The second foundational concept is Modern Portfolio Theory, godfather of the asset allocation mantra invoked by advisors and investors alike. The basic points are these: Different types of investments, or asset classes, move in different cycles, such that it is unlikely that all will go up or down together. To the extent they move to different drummers, they are said to be negatively correlated. By spreading your money around, you decrease the odds of getting sacked with losers and increase your chances of at least getting some winners. If you get the mixture right, you will get the theoretically maximum possible return for a given level of risk.

Anyone who watched all of their asset classes meltdown at the same time in 2008 may wonder if this was really Nobel Prize material.

And anyone reading this on CNBC might wonder the same thing: "The S&P 500 price return year-to-date through Dec. 11 was 13.4%. Tesla's price return YTD through the same date: 634.5%."[7]

One of the big problems with theories like rational expectations is too many—academics and consumers alike—equate it with "real" science like chemistry or physics which have known and unchanging constants. An electron-volt is always the same value. It does not depend on weather or mood. A hydrogen atom can never have more than one proton. Molecular spectra will always emit precisely the same frequencies of electromagnetic radiation. By contrast, a stock's "beta"—the amount it changes relative to the market—is a hot mess of constant flux. The market index and its relative weight relative to it is constantly changing, as is the stock itself and investor attitudes toward it based on changes in the underlying company's competitiveness, the ever-changing economy, and a gazillion other things.

And let's not forget the human factor. "Rationality" is bounded and clearly varies tremendously across the human spectrum, based on intelligence, degree of interest, access to information, and prioritization of the very limited time for thinking and the action of regular unexpected events to disrupt and decay such prioritization. The notion that the collective brainpower of humanity can unwaveringly predict systemic economic outcomes is rather preposterous, and belied by its frequent and colossal miscalculations, as in the stock market was properly priced in 2007–2008, then suddenly not, even though all ex-ante factors "should" have been completely baked into pricing.

Is another meltdown like that right around the COVID corner?

Indeed, rational expectations itself do not seem to be a rational theory, given the human economic record, and findings from other social sciences regarding how human beings seem to operate. They call economics the dismal science, but it's more like the Great Dismal Swamp.

Given this, it is perhaps difficult to understand how the theory was able to sweep so much of the academic and business world into the fold, and indoctrinate so many so soundly. Yet it did, and I am prime example. Speaking from personal experience, it took me years of contrary market evidence and real-world feedback to shake dogmatic market efficiency out of my head. Sadly, I fear many advisors, and the investors who rely on them, never have.

It's not that people don't care about money. Of course they do, but some clearly much more than others. They may even think about it all the time, but not in the coolly analytic way implied by rational expectations. Are we Adam Smith-ian wealth seeking missiles? Clearly not, and Brian Tracy's "income thermostat"—where people tend to ignore wealth accumulation unless knocked out of their comfort zones—is probably closer to the mark. People are not omnipresent computers, but neither are they base animals, slavishly chasing low-level needs and pleasures to the exclusion of more noble pursuits.

Probably, the most stunning implication of the efficient markets hypotheses is not that all information is correctly known and incorporated to govern current pricing and its trajectory, but that the prices themselves are reliable oracles of the future. Anyone who remembers the Beanie Babies fad knows better.

Elaborate models to determine "proper" pricing were and can be built, but even if they are properly loaded to include complete information and accurate relationships between variables, the uncertainty of future events renders their predictive power variable, sometimes highly so. Yet the fully predetermined nature of the rational expectations hypothesis and its offspring—ignoring the certainly of unpredictable change—became as accepted and as natural and utterly mechanical as Newtonian physics, despite being an entirely different thing given the human element. Rational expectations' shortcomings—spectacularly visible in the 2008 panic—can in some ways be attributed to market practitioners' myopic extrapolations of existing conditions and "knowledge" blithely into a future assumed to be devoid of the constant and upheaving change that defines our reality. It does not square to what many of us perhaps intuitively "know"—that much of future economic phenomena are simply unpredictable and unknowable; they lie beyond the observable horizon of rational expectations' methods.

Sorry about the PhD-blather! Academic hat off and locked away. Stamped and crushed, even. And given the Junior Soprano treatment. The reality of stock prices is, I think, more faddish, unpredictable, more emotional and human, and sometimes just plain stupid.

Nothing, I think, does more to drive this point than the fact that the 2002 Nobel Prize in economics was won by a…psychologist! Daniel Kahneman explained a wide range of cognitive biases that help explain why humans are inclined to make such poor economic decisions, like, maybe, bidding stocks into the stratosphere while one of the greatest health and economic crises rages around the globe. His popular book—*Thinking, Fast and Slow*—is a gem if you care to learn more.

The short of it is that the gods of fear and greed rule stock market prices, and these often irrationally drive prices too far in each direction. When people fear stocks they sell them, even if they are cheap and good buys. When people are greedy, they way overpay and can't seem to get enough. And people, for the most part, don't know when it's smart to be fearful, or stupid to be greedy.

And when the bubblemania strikes, oh how de love to roll dem bones.

So where are we on this fear/greed spectrum in the mid-COVID megarecession world?

To help you decide this for yourself, it's helpful to learn a little about asset bubbles.

The most familiar of these is probably the great Dutch Tulip bubble which you may remember from school. Prices got so out of whack that some tulip bulbs reached a value up to $750,000 according to Investopedia.[8] That's for one flower. One seed, really. Only a flower if the bulb germinates.

While you're probably thinking that's an historical fluke, the fact is that bubbles are quite common throughout history, extending to modern times. Ron Insana put it like this, for stocks: "...price of the asset becomes divorced from the underlying economic realities of reasonable anticipated profits. Bubbles amount to massive delusion: too often, people fail to remember that trends don't go on forever, and don't learn from past. Because bubbles seem to appear in different forms, many times for many investors 'this' time really does seem to be 'different' – hence learning from the past is difficult."

From Investopedia, again: "a bubble is created by a surge in asset prices that is driven by exuberant market behavior. During a bubble, assets typically trade at a price, or within a price range, that greatly exceeds the asset's intrinsic value (the price does not align with the fundamentals of the asset)...characterized by the rapid escalation of market value, particularly in the price of assets. This fast inflation is followed by a quick decrease in value, or a contraction, that is sometimes referred to as a 'crash' or a 'bubble burst'... **bubbles are usually only identified and studied in retrospect, after a massive drop in prices occurs.**"[9]

I bolded that last bit for emphasis, and therein lies the rub. To most folks, things don't really feel bubbly, until they're not, and the money's gone.

Throughout history, bubbles have been associated with specific characteristics. One is high levels of debt. Before COVID, the US national debt was already flirting at record levels and poised to reach low earth orbit in just a few more years, as we have explored deeply in the government debt crisis chapter. This, by the way, is a global problem, which will catalyze and worsen the meltdown when it comes. For instance, the European Central Bank has been borrowing like mad to keep its economies on the warm side of life support. Italy's government debt (with the US just behind!) clocked in at around 160% of GDP for 2020. The European situation is tracking to form another "doom loop" where banks are increasingly invested in ever-shakier government debt, leading to a new financial crisis.[10] And China has more problems than you may think, not the least of which is its own "Social Security" crisis brewing because of a rapidly-aging population stemming from its long-term "one child" population control policy; its Social Security is estimated to blow up in the 2030s[11]—if you can believe the Chinese stats (it's probably way worse!). Also note that companies and individuals are feasting on cheap debt given COVID-era low interest rates....but the principal still must ultimately be repaid...or defaulted.

Another hallmark of bubbles is periods of transformative technologies. The information age is kicking into high gear now, and the world transforms daily!

A third is prevailing low interest rates and central bank easy money policies. A fourth is deregulation. Another is that credit is often very cheap and easy to get. A sixth is assets like real estate are heavily borrowed against. An obvious seventh is stock market euphoria, and a "can't lose" "risk on" mentality.

Sound familiar?

Here's a headline from a recent *Wall Street Journal*: Investors Double Down on Stocks, Pushing Margin Debt to Record.[12] Here are some brief excerpts from that article: "… Americans who are doubling, or even tripling, down on this year's highflying stock market…exposed themselves to potentially devastating losses—through riskier plays, such as concentrated positions, trading options and leveraged exchange-traded funds. Others are borrowing against their investment portfolios, pushing margin balances to the first record in more than two years, to buy even more stock…the stock market is euphoric right now…a lot of people are extrapolating from the recent past and going, 'Wow, the market's gone up a lot and I think it'll go up more.' We've seen this play out before, and it doesn't end well."

I personally called the COVID market a bubble during the summer of 2020. The Wall Street Journal and Barron's called it a tech-driven bubble in September of that year. As I wrote this in the final days of 2020, there are more mentions of frothy conditions in the press, but investors don't seem to notice, or pay it much mind. This froth continues in early 2021.

Here's a great yardstick to consider valuation. Apple—a great company!—was making about as much in profit in mid-2020 as it was two years prior. But its stock doubled in price. Does that make any sense to you? That's what price corrections are all about. Correcting out of whack prices by crashing them down.

We are in the midst of the tail end of the worst economy since the Great Depression. Consumer and company bankruptcies hit record levels and may get worse before they get better. Even with the wonder of the new vaccines, it will take years of pain to get back to 2019 good times. Stocks were arguably overvalued then, before COIVD when the economy was firing on all cylinders. Lots of bad has happened, but stocks have gone far higher. This alone is troubling, but on top of all the other risk factors explored in this book, it is downright bone chilling.

How has this happened? A theory[13] posed in *the New York Times* in early 2021 makes some sense. The economy got whacked, but national personal income did not fall very much, mostly because low income folks were disproportionately affected, and because government payouts and subsidies helped more than is widely believed. At the same time, spending dropped, since there was so much less to do in lockdown. This increased net savings, much of it in the stock market, where demand relative to supply boosted prices (in my view into space). The *Times* piece suggests that when thing normalize post-mass vaccination, spending will pickup bigtime, and savings—and stock—will be cashed in to pay for it. This alone could precipitate a big stock slide from these crazy valuation levels.

Is the mother of all stock crashes coming? I think so. Is it right around the corner? Hard to say. There's an old saying among technical analysts that the trend is the trend, until it's not. Things can keep shooting up from here, at least for a while. But there is great risk that when this bubble finally bursts, investment returns could be very lean for a very long time, right when you can least afford it.

So I will leave you to remember the great NASDAQ crash of 2000, a bubble also led up by technology stocks, as has been the COVID bubble. At that time, tech stocks plunged 80% from the high and took 16 years to break even from the peak.

If that happened again, could you ride that out, and maintain your lifestyle, with all the other financial challenges you will face in the next quarter of the twenty-first century?

Let me leave you with this from the *Wall Street Journal*, written in the final days of 2020 as the market keeps reaching for the sky. "The only way to argue that stocks aren't wildly expensive is to say that something fundamental has changed about the market environment. The S&P 500 trades at 22 times analysts' expected earnings—its most expensive level since the dot-com bubble. It also trades at its richest multiple to its inflation-adjusted earnings over the past decade...in nearly 20 years... In the early 1970s, investors believed that the 'Nifty Fifty' group of big companies that had registered years of steady growth would be able to keep growing for years to come—and got burned for it. The dot-com era rested on even more improbable expectations..."[14]

Note that as I proof this book in the now-late summer of 2021, the market has soared yet higher. Economic growth has resumed, though may industries still struggle, and COVID mutations like Delta are killing thousands and driving the hordes back into the caves. So is the mother of all bear markets coming? This is difficult to say for sure, but the confluence of the crazy run up in stock prices, coupled with the many dangers explored in this book, certainly suggest a long period of declining values going forward or at best unsatisfactory returns on stocks. Before we leave this theme, let's factor in some of the other threats highlighted in the book. Rising taxes are as bad for companies as for families, sapping wealth than could drive profits and shareholder value, and converting it into dead expense. The Biden tax plan as it stood in late 2020 looked particularly toxic to the stock market's tech-related leaders, particularly since they derive so much income from non-US sales. The plan not only bumps corporate tax rates by a whopping 33%, but in some cases doubles taxes on export income. All told, market leaders' profits could plunge by double digits from tax hikes alone, while corporate earnings in general would drop by close to 10%. If interest rates, driven by inflationary money-printing and other stimulus, rise even a little from today's zero-rate range, the price of growth stocks could drop very disproportionately. Besides raising corporate borrowing costs, it also hammers the value of growth stocks whose prices are very much influenced by the present value of distant future earnings. If the discount rate goes up, future earnings are less valuable and the stock price drops. Finally, big tech has become very monopolistic, and government pressure to regulate, strangle, and even break up tech companies is rising fast. Regardless of the social value, none of this is good for corporate profits.

When we get to the solution section of the book, we'll share tips on navigating this seemingly most dangerous of markets and explaining ways to profit from it. We will also explore potentially more profitable investment areas to consider if the stock market really does crap out, and stay down for a very long count. If you—you masochist you!—want more info on this topic, there's a class or two on it at www.fweibook.org.

Notes

1. Casselman, Ben. "New Signs of Economic Distress Emerge as Trump Imperils Aid Deal." *The New York Times*, December 23, 2020. https://www.nytimes.com/2020/12/23/business/economy/economy-trump-income-spending-unemployment.html.
2. Ibid.
3. Hayes, Adam. "Irrational Exuberance." Investopedia, January 26, 2021. https://www.investopedia.com/terms/i/irrationalexuberance.asp#:~:text=Irrational%20exuberance%20is%20unfounded%20market.bubble%20in%20the%20stock%20market.
4. Shiller, Robert J. (2015) [2000]. *Irrational Exuberance* (3rd ed.). Princeton, NJ: Princeton University Press. p. 2. ISBN 978–0,691,173,122.; Shiller, Robert J. (2017, October 19). "Three Questions: Prof. Robert Shiller on Bitcoin". Yale Insights. Yale School of Management. Archived from the original on 2017–11-29. Retrieved June 7, 2018.
5. Chen, James. "Greater Fool Theory." Investopedia, September 11, 2019. https://www.investopedia.com/terms/g/greaterfooltheory.asp.

6. Phillips, Matt. "Market Edges Toward Euphoria, Despite Pandemic's Toll." *The New York Times*, December 26, 2020. https://www.nytimes.com/2020/12/26/business/investors-bull-market-pandemic.html.

7. Rosenbaum, Eric. "Here's How Much 5% Invested in Tesla Could Have Made for S&P 500 Index Fund Investor." *CNBC*, December 15, 2020. https://www.cnbc.com/2020/12/15/how-much-5percent-invested-in-tesla-would-have-added-for-index-fund-investor.html.

8. Hayes, Adam. "Dutch Tulip Bulb Market Bubble Definition." Investopedia, January 29, 2021. https://www.investopedia.com/terms/d/dutch_tulip_bulb_market_bubble.asp.

9. Kenton, Will. "Bubble." Investopedia, October 10, 2020. https://www.investopedia.com/terms/b/bubble.asp.

10. Kowsmann, Patricia. "Banks Pile Into Government Debt, Setting Up 'Doom Loop' Sequel in Europe. *The Wall Street Journal,* December 30, 2020. https://www.wsj.com/articles/banks-pile-into-government-debt-setting-up-doom-loop-sequel-in-europe-11609324201.

11. Tang, Frank. "China's State Pension Fund to Run Dry by 2035 as Workforce Shrinks due to Effects of One-Child Policy, Says Study." *South China Morning Post*, April 12, 2019. https://www.scmp.com/economy/china-economy/article/3005759/chinas-state-pension-fund-run-dry-2035-workforce-shrinks-due.

12. Wursthorn, Michael. "Investors Double Down on Stocks, Pushing Margin Debt to Record." *The Wall Street Journal*, December 27, 2020. https://www.wsj.com/articles/investors-double-down-on-stocks-pushing-margin-debt-to-record-11609077600.

13. Irwin, Neil, and Weiyi Cai. "Why Markets Boomed in a Year of Human Misery." *The New York Times,* January 1, 2021. https://www.nytimes.com/2021/01/01/upshot/why-markets-boomed-2020.html.

14. Lahart, Justin. "Has the Fed Rewritten the Laws of Investing?" *The Wall Street Journal,* December 23, 2020. https://www.wsj.com/articles/has-the-fed-rewritten-the-laws-of-investing-11608747325.

Putting All Together—Your Total Risk Profile

Well! That was an extraordinarily frightening tour, and no mistake. As you now see, this is an exceptionally challenging time for investors and wealth holders of every sort.

Rather than reiterating the abundant dangers, this very short wrap-up chapter has one laser-focused purpose: to distill these dangers into the practical risks that face you and your family, to instill a shivering, shaking, motivational fear to spur you into action, and then help you strategize and assemble your game plan as you cruise through the Part II solutions section of the book.

For most readers, there are four primary threats, and a fifth that overlays the other four:

1. Increasing taxes that bleed family wealth.
2. Resurgent inflation that erodes wealth.
3. The risk of a deep market crash and extended bear market.
4. Inaccurate retirement planning leading risking an impoverished lifestyle and even running out of money.
5. Bad, incompetent, or abusive advice that magnifies and worsens the first four primary threats.

The first two factors act as shrouded negative return forces, sharply reducing the value of family resources. The third, of course, more obviously drags down values and hastens the day when the pot is dry. The fourth

J. Camarda et al., *The Financial Storm Warning for Investors*,
https://doi.org/10.1007/978-3-030-77271-0_10

supercharges this effect: If you need to withdraw more and more from your retirement and other accounts to keep up with the inflating, increasing cost of living after the government takes bigger and bigger pieces of your pie, while at the same time the value of what you are withdrawing from is itself dropping, you can see what a bad fix you may find yourself in. This last bit is referred to by snooty scholars as "sequence of return risk," which just means that if you start taking fixed withdrawals—like for retirement income—out of an account that is declining in value already due to market conditions, you go through the money lots faster: If the shares are going down in value, you need to cash more and more in to get a fixed dollar payout, until the shares are all gone!

So in Part II, we will explore the many taxes you pay, and the many techniques you can harness to control and avoid them. Make no mistake, taxes are acid poured on the gold of your wealth, turning it to green slime and smoke. This is true in the best of times, and taxes in recent decades have been actually low by historical standards. With the political wind now howling through Washington, they are poised to go up with a vengeance.

Once again, lest I offend some of you, I must reiterate that I don't have a political horn to blow here. I see virtue in arguments across the political spectrum. I feel for the poor and disadvantaged, and believe government must help them. There are some pressing needs the free market simply cannot serve. On the other hand, I fear government as being inherently wasteful and confiscatory. But my political leanings don't matter. Your moral compass is your own to set, and far be it from me to try to shove a lump of iron in its path. My job here is *only* to better help you protect, build, and preserve your wealth so you can use it as you will, even to give it all away as seems best to you. And from that perspective—protecting wealth loss from tax—there is no denying the political wind is now bent on enlarging the holes in the pockets of the wealthy.

I call tax the master wealth skill because it's the biggest club in the bag. Most folks—even really rich ones—swim through the ocean of taxes, oblivious to the water. They remind me of Dory in *Finding Nemo*…"just keep swimming…" To get you to hold your nose, let's take a deep dive for just a moment.

I warn you in advance that it may look like a minefield. Soon we'll give you a map and point out where to find the treasure, but first you need to know about the kinds of booby-traps that are waiting for you. A virtual zoo of financially ravenous animals awaits. You'll get the map and a bazooka later; for now, just listen to these fellows lick their chops. First, of course, is the income tax on earned income, the tax on the money you are paid for your work if you are an employee of someone else's business. Interest and much other unearned income is taxed at the same rate. Capital gains—the profit on sales of investments and other property—is also taxed, though sometimes at more favorable rates, which look to be changing in the political wind. Social security is also taxed if you have any measure of other income or hit the wrong checkpoints.

Pensions, IRA distributions, and other sorts of retirement income are taxed, and sometimes tax penalties are piled on top of the tax. If you make too much money on the sale of your home you must pay tax, though of course if you lose money you don't get any tax break. Virtually any income—with a few minor exceptions—from any source is exposed. If you have the misfortune to live in a state (or state and city, like NY City) which exacts its own income tax, you will pay this on top of the Federal income tax. You very likely pay sales taxes on most purchases. If your state imposes a personal property tax, you get to pay a "sales tax" over and over, as the value of personal property (which is any property other than real estate)—sometimes even money in the bank!—is taxed each year, as long as you own it. Sometimes they call this an intangibles tax. Sometimes they call a personal property tax a tangible property tax.

Adding a state income tax and personal property tax on top of the Federal tax on bank money can yield a real rate of return so negative you'll want to move to North Korea! You pay in a similar way, over and over, on the value of any real estate that you own, in addition to the extra taxes you probably paid when you bought it, like document and other taxes. A big chunk of the price of things like gasoline, cigarettes (you heathen, you!), and alcohol represents Federal (and sometimes state) excise taxes, often in addition to sales taxes. Tax on a gallon of gas in California? About $0.70 for state and Federal, plus some others I probably can't find. That's just the *tax*, not the gas. Register your car? Buy some insurance? There are license fees and premium taxes. Want to give some money to Grandma? There are Federal and sometimes state gift taxes. Want to leave some to grandson when you die? There are estate, inheritance, and generation-skipping-transfer taxes. Invest too well in your IRA? There are excessive retirement accumulation taxes. These are a whopping 50%, so better take those required minimum (taxable!) annual distributions! In many cases there are taxes on taxes, plus high interest and high penalties if you don't pay the piper right when he first strikes the tune. It is almost endless, like being thrust into a pit of hungry weasels. Remember Frank Zappa's *Weasles Ripped My Flesh*? Time for another listen. Plus all of your valuable time that gets consumed, without compensation or tax break, just to sort out the mess and try and get it right, or try to find a sharp tax advisor, and good luck with that.

Many taxes are almost impossible to avoid, but we will give you excellent strategies to control the major ones that can really bleed you. Try to learn and use them: All must walk this minefield, and most perish. And control them you must, or consign yourself to the quicksand. Taxes and inflation will drive you under. Deep under.

Pay attention in Part II! Freedom and untold riches await.

That's all more than a bit dark, and I'm sorry if I upset you. But you must recognize the problem, feel in your gut how important the problem is. There are many relatively easy and simple things that you can do to keep the beasts at bay, and they wait for you in the pages ahead.

We will also get into detail on how to properly do retirement planning. You can't do it with a naive calculator on the Internet—it's way more complicated than that. Most of the retirement plans and calculators you see on the net and from advisors are sales tools, not comprehensive plans. They are designed to lure you in and transfer assets. But this is your future we are talking about. We will show you how to carefully plan to take the critical multitude of factors into consideration, and way up the odds of living comfortably, not running out of money, and still being able to leave what you want to the kids.

Money has never been as loose. The Fed has been printing like mad, and over one-fifth of all dollars in existence were created in 2020 alone.[1] You better read that sentence again.

As the Biden administration consolidates power, with both houses of Congress behind it to offer agreeable laws, look for Federal spending (as well as taxes!) to go way up. The conditions for high inflation have never perhaps been more favorable, and we will give you sage advice on investment planning to protect you, and even benefit from shrinking dollars.

Also, we'll give you candid tips on finding smart advisors you can trust. You probably don't know this, but the financial advisory business is a mess. Most advisors have little training—it takes more study in most states to become a barber than a financial advisor—and most don't have to put you first; it is perfectly legal for them to goose their compensation at your expense. Many if not most work for "broker/dealers" and when you hear dealer you should think car dealer—same kind of relationship. Worse, more have criminal histories than you may think—which is no bar to licensing! We'll show you how to separate the wheat from the chafe and lots more in Part II.

And, finally, we'll give you solid guidance on what to do should we be on the verge of a major bear market. As we discussed at length in the stock bubble chapter, market values are at crazy levels. The worst health crisis in a hundred years? Market record! The worst economy since the Great Depression! Higher stocks! The political fabric of America in taters, with rioters actually invading the Capital Building sending Congress into hiding? The market hits another record! This makes no sense, and a severe day of reckoning is probably coming down the pike. We could be looking at a market crash and a long period of market declines that could devastate your wealth and retirement. We will show you how to navigate it. Look for lots of detail in Part II and lots of how-to classes at www.fweibook.org.

Note

1. Cage, Matthew. "$9 Trillion Story: 22% of the Circulating USD Printed in 2020." *Somag News*, December 19, 2020. https://www.somagnews.com/9-trillion-story-22-of-us-dollars-printed-in-2020/.

Your Countermeasures & Solutions

Charting Your Path to Financial Salvation: A Big Picture Game Plan to Survive the Storm

Thank goodness Part I's over! I've been seeing much of this coming for quite some time, now, but still managed to frighten myself as I recounted it.

Fortunately, we will no longer dwell on the horror that appears to be unfolding. Part II of the book is the good news. The gospel according to Jeffrey, if you will.

There are hundreds of things you can do to not only protect yourself and your family, but actually manage to profit and prosper through the dark times ahead. Knowledge is power. As Michael Douglas said playing Gordon Gekko in *Wall Street* (the first one), "The most valuable commodity I know of is information."

Part II is all about sharing the information that can give you a real edge to take advantage of the opportunities springing from the profound changes shaking our world.

We'll begin by giving you a thorough grounding in estate planning. This is a drop-dead critical area which is frequently fumbled, even when addressed at all. I can't tell you how often I see hit-the-mountain nightmares in practice, even for really rich people who should know better and who have spent tens of thousands on completely inappropriate estate planning that guarantees otherwise avoidable probate, drops pants, and shakes bloomers for financial predators and will contests, and does nothing to control estate taxes. Got right, you will not only avoid probate, the heartbreak of guardianship, and keep your matters completely private, but protect and secure your children for generations while avoiding estate taxes forever no matter what the tax law

© The Author(s), under exclusive license to Springer Nature
Switzerland AG 2021
J. Camarda et al., *The Financial Storm Warning for Investors*,
https://doi.org/10.1007/978-3-030-77271-0_11

changes may be. With simple language and entertaining stories, the chapter will arm you with the advanced expertise and real-world tools that escape all but the very top, six-sigma, needle-in-a-haystack planners. Just make sure you learn and jump fast, because the cheese is moving soon and once it's gone, like those old Cadbury Eggs, it's gone!

Next we'll get into asset protection planning, kissin' cousin to estate planning in the pantheon of family wealth guardians. I'm not talking about protecting your assets from confiscatory taxation and hell hounds like the IRS—that gets its very own long chapter. I'm talking about financial predators of the two-legged variety, egged on by plaintiffs' attorneys. We'll explore the nuances of first-line defenses like liability insurance and get practical detail on how to set up asset hardening structures in case the insurance isn't enough—or in case the insurance company stiffs you. This is another critically important but almost-always overlooked area and can mean the difference between being compelled by a judge to write a check for a million or more, and being able to tell your wealth-attacker to go pound sand, with a smile on your face. With the right structure, you'll be smiling aplenty, and even find would-be predators give up before ever starting.

From there we move on to one of my favorite topics, converting avoidable taxes to family wealth. As we beat to death in Part I, taxes are both the biggest threat and opportunity facing your net worth. Do you already feel like your wealth's being taxed to death? Are you making plenty of money but not keeping enough? High taxes is already one of the biggest obstacles preventing you from building wealth faster. Sadly, you ain't seen nothing yet. With taxes, it's not who you know but what you know (and there's a lot to know!). There are many tax advisors, but most barely scratch the surface, or even think it's their civic duty to make sure you pay your "fair share," whatever that is. As we will see when we get to the advisors chapters, quality tax advice can be remarkably elusive. That's no surprise given the mind-numbing complexity of the gargantuan and constantly changing tax code. Many sharp people feel that their tax advisor is not proactive or knowledgeable or strategic enough. They appreciate that truly sophisticated tax advice can mean the difference between treading water and getting really, really rich, but don't know how to go about getting truly sage tax advice. Stay tuned, because what you'll learn about tax in the chapters to come is worth its weight it bitcoin. Tax control is truly the master wealth skill. It's not what you make, but what you keep that counts, and for too many people, taxes are a hissing, sucking siphon draining wealth year after year. They prevent your kitty from really ever filling up. From the dawn of civilization, those that have access to best tax practices build wealth amazingly faster than those that don't. You are about to join their ranks, so please pay attention! The concepts you're about to learn will help you get richer faster, retire years earlier, have more to spend in retirement, and really accelerate your wealth objectives. Most importantly, they will protect you and your family wealth engine in the dark days and years ahead. We'll show you solid, mainstream ways to reduce income tax, and the related payroll taxes we lamented in Part I, and put you on solid footing to convert avoidable taxes into more wealth, better lifestyle, and richer retirement. You'll learn uncommon tips to reduce or completely avoid estate and gift taxes, not just at your death but for hundreds of years of generations if you care to plan out that far. And you'll even share the astonishing secret of how to cut your real estate taxes, year after year. That's a rare trick you won't want to miss.

We spent a lot of time in Part I discussing why the specter of inflation is now posing an increasing danger. In Part II, we explore how to protect yourself, and what actions, strategies, and investment sectors give you strong advantages to not only survive inflation, but prosper from it. You'll need this information when we move into the investments chapter, and look at the challenges and opportunities facing investments as the mid-twenty-first century unfolds.

Growing, protecting, and preserving wealth, for most of us, is not an end in itself but a means to our goals. Money is a tool. It is the fuel for freedom of lifestyle. It enables the things we want—toys, time freedom, travel, nice things and fine educations for our family, and so on.

Central to goals for most of us is retirement. While online and other retirement calculators abound, replete with happy noises and colorful, inspiring graphics, the reality is most of these are far too simplistic to rely on. Aside from the many monkey wrenches flying through the jungle of Part 1 to duck duck goose around—and traditional retirement planning systems are blithely ignorant of them—the reality is that retirement planning is a horrendously sticky wicket. It is a hugely complex problem. My PhD is in retirement planning, and I have just scratched the surface with my own study. To get it right—or as right as it may be got in our ever-changing reality—takes a very sophisticated perspective.

As mentioned, the plethora of retirement planning tools and engines are overly simplistic. They are not robust tools. Instead they are mostly sales systems designed to lure your assets into whatever fee-collecting or commission-crushing cave the retirement app is alluringly wiggling in front of. Advisors and other vendors use these to make sales, not conduct diligent planning. We will show you how to do it right, to target not only a carefree, luxuriously hedonistic retirement, but still leave plenty to pass on to the kids if that's your goal.

Speaking of advisors, there's a reason financial advisors inspire such low levels of trust. Required education is incredibly low. Those guilty of misconduct are generally permitted to continue practice. Even criminal backgrounds do not prevent licensure. And if you think those with the CFP®/Certified Financial Planner badge are a cut above, better check again before risking being cut yourself.

And this risk is by no means limited to financial advisors like investment reps and others of their ilk like insurance agents.

By contrast, CPAs and other tax professionals enjoy high levels of public regard. Sadly, in many if not most cases, this trust is misplaced, or at least the expectation of expertise is misguided. For instance, only about 15% of CPA testing is on tax—they are really-studied accountants, not tax experts. But all the world bows to their tax wisdom. Levels of finely-honed tax expertise among such professionals appear to be generally low, with the result that far, far too many families way overpay avoidable taxes. Tax is extremely complex, and most tax practitioners are just not up to it, in our humble experience.

Most taxpayers have no idea. Some suspect something is wrong, but don't know what to do. When we get to the advisor section, you will finally know what you can do to climb out of this pit. Good advice—financial and tax—can be priceless but is amazingly hard to find. If you choose to use advisors instead of climbing the Everest learning curve of the financial planning and tax disciplines, you will want tools to find the best, smartest, most honest advisors. Remember our old friend the bell curve. Most professionals are average, mediocre, by definition. That's the biggest chunk of the population represented by the bulge in the middle of the bell. Some way out on the left tail are so horrible they ought to be banned. And some way out on the right tail are so good you ought to adopt them. If you can find them, which you probably can't on your own. Most to all smile nice and look good in a suit. Heard of Six Sigma? That just means way, way out on the right tail—six σ or six standard deviations away from the mean. It's a hallmark of excellence. If you want advisors, you want a six-sigma type advisor, and I'll show you how to identify the good ones.

Regardless of if you use advisors or try to slog it alone, you must commit with what Steven Covey, in his great book *The Seven Habits of Highly Effective People*, called "sharpening the saw." By that I mean committing to ongoing financial education. This is critically important if you decide to captain your own wealth ship, and just as important if you use advisors. Why? You need to know if they're blowing smoke at you, at least until you reach the point where deep trust is earned. And still keep an eye out after that! Given the extent of ignorance, duplicity, and outright chicanery in the advisory space, you are less than wise if you close your eyes, cross your fingers, and just hope for the best. Stay frosty! Watch my classes at fweibook.org to keep sharp.

Remember, the time is nigh to take charge, to protect yourself and prosper. As we go through the golden techniques in Part II, do not forget the lessons and warnings of Part I! The pincers are tightening against wealth holders from multiple quarters.

As Keith Richards asked on his first solo album: "how you gonna keep your wealth/can't even defend yourself...."

Don't cry for Mick.

And don't wind up crying for your family.

I will teach you how to mount and execute a superlative defense.

You will become a wealth conservation god. Just make sure you muster the motivation to mount it!

Estate Planning for Protection and Control

Ah, now we waltz into the gentle exercise of planning for your death, or perhaps worse, a dive into the cognitive abyss.

Are you ready, gentle reader?

Go not softly into that black hole. Linger a bit with me, instead.

As Dylan said (the real one—whoever *he* was, to channel Paul Simon—not that Nobel-prize-winning poser from Minnesota [for whom my first son is named]): "do not go gentle into that good night, old age should burn and rave at close of day; Rage, rage against the dying of the light. …".

And Rage I will, but not this day.

This day is writ for you, and for your own good night.

This chapter—and the closely related one that follows on asset protection planning—primarily deals with educating you on the fundamentals of estate planning, critical concepts, with some advanced stuff thrown in. While we touch on tax, I save the heavy duty tax planning for the tax chapter. Tax is a critical planning objective of the book, but to properly harness it you must understand the underlying mechanisms. I try hard to make it light, easy, and fun. When you are done, you will understand more than nearly all the rich folks I've ever met, and, sadly, many if not most of the CPAs and attorneys I've met in my decades of practice.

Ready to catch some pearls? Here we go!

Dive, dive, dive!

© The Author(s), under exclusive license to Springer Nature
Switzerland AG 2021
J. Camarda et al., *The Financial Storm Warning for Investors*,
https://doi.org/10.1007/978-3-030-77271-0_12

I am going to start with a very brief overview of a typical optimal estate plan with asset protection features. For those that want more guidance—or more explanation of the underlying concepts—please continue with the rest of the longish chapter. Others may choose to skip ahead to the asset protection chapter, but note there is a very clear explanation of the what and whys of trusts later in this chapter for those that want a primer.

Before I begin, I wish to thank my longtime friend and super-lawyer John Crawford for reviewing my clumsy prose, and not letting me step overmuch into do-do.

Trusts are the centerpiece of prudent estate planning.

You want living trusts, the kind that operate while you are alive.

Testamentary trusts—the ones created at death by thick wills—often aren't worth the paper printed on. They typically don't cost any less, but they forfeit many of the advantages of living trusts, like privacy, tax savings, asset protection, and more, including avoiding expensive legal fees for probate. I suspect banking on the latter is the reason so many attorneys write them. To be clear, they *guarantee* probate, a messy, expensive, and public process.

Trust me, you want living trusts, and you want to make sure your assets are either titled directly to the trusts, or beneficiaried to them. The trusts need be written to control taxes and to control disposition of the assets the way you want, like reasonable lifetime income to your second wife, but significant assets passing intact to your kids and grandkids from previous marriages. You probably want to build features for continuing trusts down the generations, so the money stays in trust for asset protection and tax and disposition control. Using dynasty features for this can ensure tax avoidance further out than you can think, if you do it right, until the world is ruled by machines, or dammed dirty apes. And you will want layers of protection, like having investment and bank accounts held in asset protection holding companies, themselves titled to the trusts. Lots of detail on that in the next chapter. You want to make sure you have what I call the "three powers"—powers of attorney, healthcare surrogate, and living will—done with your estate planning. The healthcare surrogate is another way to say healthcare power of attorney, letting another make medical decisions if you cannot. All should be reviewed regularly with your planner and attorney and adjusted/freshened as needed.

I should emphasis that estate planning and asset protection planning (as well as income tax control, business planning, and all the other trappings of wealth management, while we are at it) are best addressed together. While we touch on smart estate planning and the other elements of wealth management in other chapters, deep details on estate planning techniques are appropriate here.

An often-overlooked feature even in expensive estate plans is trust protectors, which is an inexplicable shame. Think of protectors as guardians of the trust, the sheriffs if you will. These are something that seem to make perfect sense to most parents when asked, but we rarely find in new clients' existing estate planning. Protectors basically protect the kids (or other trust beneficiaries or trustees) from being forced to write a check against their interests, such as to satisfy a judgment, or divide assets in a divorce. In many cases, the child's inheritance is given to a trust of which the child is trustee, but a protector—their brother, maybe—takes over if a threat appears. Giving the child their inheritance in their own special trust helps to prevent it from becoming marital property and hence at divorce risk, as in "of course I love you honey and would love to put your name on the account, but Daddy set it up in a trust fund and that's how he wants it…" without restricting their access to the funds since they are the trustee (unless a threat appears, and they automatically lose trustee powers to the protector until the threat passes). Similar measures can be used to protect kids' inheritance, say if you or your spouse dies and the other remarries, from the clutches of a future stepparent. Protectors can also be used to watch over and fire trustees, like if a bank or trust company becomes unresponsive or abusive, as is often the case. And they have particular utility in making advanced tax control techniques work, to help get you your tax cake and lifestyle eating too.

Asset protection trusts (APTs, domestic or offshore) are irrevocable and transfer control to outside parties as trustees, with protectors as control. These are often overkill but useful when applicable. I've never seen the need for one, so won't get into them here.

F-BOTS (Family Bank Ongoing Trusts) have more limited asset protection power, but this can and should be shored up using personal holding companies and the other techniques discussed in the asset protection chapter. I think I coined the F-BOT term and use it to describe a bundle of features build into an advanced form of SLAT or Spousal Lifetime Access Trust, a more generic term. For single folks, we modify the F-BOT to an F-BIT or Family Bank Individual Trust. Works pretty much the same, but we need a non-spousal trustee—such as a trusted and trustworthy child.

F-BOTS, the way we do them, are the major artillery piece of estate tax control, and we will delve in detail in the tax chapter. They allow the couple complete control and access to income, while still getting the property out of the taxable estate—and eliminating estate and gift tax entirely if done right in the right fact pattern—and done before too late with stiff tax hikes on the political wind.

So-called dynasty trust can eliminate all gift and estate taxes for the family for many generations, or forever, if this is desired, while still availing the family and descendants of the full benefit of the family assets, which can compound mightily over time in the absence of transfer taxes. You can bolt these onto F-BOTS. They work by granting rights in trust assets to the family which *approach*, but technically don't *equal*, actual ownership (which would trigger estate, gift and generation skipping transfer tax for families with sufficient wealth). This is a far more elegant and effective approach than the ubiquitous "skip trust" method (which aims to game the Generation Skipping Transfer Tax regimen) since it avoids taxes for hundreds of years or longer, instead of for just one generation. Skip trusts are cumbersome and mind-numbingly complex. They also nip intergenerational wealth building in the bud. Dynasty-fueled F-BOT methods really sing and can make for incredible long-term wealth building potential.

On to more basic stuff. To begin, think hard about what you want. Often a skillful planner can help reveal really important aspect that may otherwise escape you, to your wealth's peril. It is, after all, your property. Before plotting out tax schemes, spend some time thinking about just who and how you want your property to pass. Do you want your spouse to get everything—or at least the use of it—for the balance of their life? If not, you should know that it is virtually impossible to disinherit your spouse from wealth built during the marriage without some sort of pre-/post-nuptial agreement. In most states, the spouse is entitled to at least a 1/3 of the marital property—that which is built up by the couple during the marriage (excluding inheritances), and can mount a successful challenge to your will if you try and leave them less than that. Tread carefully if your spouse is not the object of most of your wealth.

But most of us do want to provide for our partner for the balance of her lifetime, even if we wish for children from a previous marriage to ultimately get the assets. Who else, and how else, do you want the money to flow? All to kids? Your assets to your kids, and his assets to his kids, when you are both finally dead? Beloved nieces and nephews? Parents? Siblings? Charity? First set down these dispositive goals, then look for tax-effective ways to achieve them. Also consider if you are willing to live a bit less well in order to maximize your estate, or if you prefer to leave them what's left (if anything) after you have thoroughly enjoyed your retirement.

Estate planning, like all financial planning, is a fluid thing. What is important and appropriate now will become less so if you live another decade or two. At least look at it, even if you don't do (or need) a complete update, every five years or so.

Probate is basically the legal process of figuring out who should get your stuff when you die. It is a legal process, with a judge, and a public record of the proceedings which includes a list of your stuff and a copy of your will, hanging in the courthouse-wind for all who care to see. If you have a will, it is basically an instruction sheet to the judge, describing your intentions for your assets. In it you name your executor (if a woman, executrix), which in some states is called your personal representative. This is the person charged with carrying out the provisions of your will. You should name successors in case you outlive the first choice, and you should know that the job involves a lot of work and liability, so specific arrangements to pay them in the will would be nice and avoid squabbles among the children. If the will is a legal one—prepared in accordance with the requirements of your state—the judge will distribute according to it unless someone can successfully invalidate it, which is rare. If you try to trash your spouse, for instance, she may "take against the will" and thereby receive her legally mandated one-third (or so, depending on the state), with the balance pretty much flowing as you instructed. Since our intentions change with time, the term "last will" simply means the most recent one. If you die without a will—they call it "intestate," your property does not automatically go to the state! Rather, it follows a "next of kin" hierarchy, usually with spouse and kids first, then parents, then siblings, and finally the state only if a long string of relatives can't be found.

But the state's formula may not be what you want—you may prefer that nothing go to your child who stole your diamonds and defected to Cuba—and you should have at least a simple will regardless. If you want to specifically disinherit somebody, by the way, you should so state in your will: "to my son Fidel Littlebucks, nothing." If you just leave his name out, it may be ruled an oversight on your part (and you won't be in probate court to argue otherwise), and he may be cut in.

So-called probate assets are those which you own at death, and which do not pass outside of probate because of the way they are titled. Examples of non-probate assets—those which automatically bypass probate, and will not be affected by any will of yours—are things which are titled with someone else having a survivorship right (titled joint tenants with right of survivorship "JTWROS" or tenants by the entirety "T by E"), and assets which carry beneficiary designations, like life insurance, annuities, and qualified plans and IRAs. The first type pass "by operation of law," and the second "by contract," and either way they do not pass by will (or lack thereof). It is important to remember that what you say in your will won't affect these assets: the title or beneficiary designation controls.

Everything else you own comprises your probate estate—the part the judge gets to figure out. Do not confuse the probate estate with the estate for tax purposes: everything may be in the pot when we look at estate taxes, even if you have no probate assets. The distinction applies only to the mechanism by which title passes. Having a will—or at least some measure of probate assets—guarantees probate. This is a major (but far from only) reason to use a trust as a will substitute.

Even if you decide to use trusts—which for most of you I heartily recommend!—and own nothing which will wind up in probate, it is a good idea to at least have what is called a pourover will, which says that if you forget to put any property in your trust's name during your life (at least cars and such), that you want to "pour" these assets into your trust at death. This way everything will be divided according to the trust's provisions, with the trust acting as a will substitute. The attorney will probably also suggest the preparation of some other documents at this time, such as a living will (which states your desire for life-sustaining medical assistance—to "pull the plug" or not—if you are unable to speak for yourself), a healthcare power—giving someone else the right to make your healthcare decisions if you cannot (the surgery or the chemo…), and a durable power of attorney (POA, which gives someone else, whom you trust absolutely, the power to sign your name, spend your money, and attend to you affairs in case you become legally unable to do so). Be careful about this last one, because you give to another complete power over your checkbook, and because banks and others can be reluctant to accept them unless they are quite recent. But if you don't have a usable POA or use a trust as we will see in just a moment, you run the risk of being exposed to guardianship proceedings if you get to the point where you can't manage your financial affairs. Without a mechanism in place, you face the humiliation of a court proceeding the purpose of which is to prove you lack the mental capacity to take care of yourself, and that a guardianship must be set up to administer to your needs and interests. This is demeaning for all (including your loved ones who may call for it to help you), quite expensive, and is a great argument for using a living trust, especially if you are near the age where the possibility of forgetting to pay your bills is a real one.

Why use a will, or trust, at all, you say, if you can title property with a survivorship feature so that it bypasses probate entirely? Look at this unlikely but all too common scenario. Mom and Dad hold everything important (home, bank accounts, retirement plans) either in both names, or with the other as beneficiary. Their simple "I love you" will leave everything to the other, or to the kids if both die. Dad dies, Mom gets everything, and after a few years remarries. This new couple follows a similar pattern, with joint property, each other as beneficiaries, and so on. Mom dies, and everything goes to "new" Dad. The kids from the first marriage—who have lost both parents—have legal claim to not one cent. New Dad may be generous, but has absolutely no legal obligation to do so: the kids have been completely though unintentionally disinherited by their parents.

Unlikely, yes, but the possibility is important enough that you should consider planning against it. And trusts are the best solution, especially since we don't want the kid to get his hands on the checkbook at age 18. Even if your kids are grown up, and you are remarried (or think it may happen) have a good look when we talk about planning for multiple marriage situations. However you do it, the objective is to get the assets configured so that the surviving spouse can use them, but does not have so much control that she can (on purpose or otherwise) give or bequeath them to anyone but your children. And the pressures, in any marriage, to title assets jointly can be strong—unless it has been made impossible to do so.

Let's explore trust basics as background for your estate planning. The very word trust, as it rolls of the tongue, conjures images of sterling silver, old wealth, and lives of (perhaps) undeserved ease. This aura is unfortunate, since trusts are actually, at their heart, extremely simple planning tools that you need very much to know about. They are enormously easy to set up and administer, yet so flexible as let do nearly anything you want, and become as complicated as you and your attorney see fit.

A trust is simply a bucket of money, with rules that you lay down in advance for what happens to the money. There are three types of parties to any trust. The grantor, who puts the money in the bucket and gets to write the rules. The rules are written by your attorney in a paper called the trust document. The trustee, who is chosen by the grantor and is trusted to make sure the money is handled according to the rules. And then, ah, there is the trust's beneficiary, the party who gets to enjoy the money paid out of the trust by the trustee, according to the rules of the trust, or trust provisions. At the core, that's really all there is to it: the grantor puts assets in for the benefit of the beneficiary, and the assets are managed by the trustee. These parties can be anyone you, the grantor, pick: you can be the grantor, trustee, and beneficiary of the trust, use the property for you own benefit, and name successor trustees and beneficiaries to manage and enjoy the property, if any is left, after you die. In fact, this living trust arrangement is often used as a will substitute to avoid probate. It will not get you any asset protection of itself this way, since you still control and essentially own the property, and can usually be compelled by a judge to write a check to pay for your lawsuits.

Here's another important distinction: between living (or "inter vivos," which means "while alive") trusts and testamentary trusts, which get set up after you die. Living trusts are those you set up and fund (put property in the trust's name) now, while you live. Testamentary trusts are those whose terms are written in your will, and spring into life with the assets you leave them in your will after you die. You know why I hate those!

That brings up the next distinction, between revocable and irrevocable trusts. Revocable trusts can be revoked: you can change your mind, dissolve the trust, and take the property back into your name. You keep complete control, usually naming yourself as trustee, and can write yourself a check on the trust account any time you want to. It's just like still owning the property, though you have to be sure and title all assets in the trust's name (and we do forget...) if you want the trust to work for the purpose for which you set it up, like avoiding probate. Irrevocable trusts are *ostensibly* forever: Once you put the money in, you for all time give up at least some control over it, even if you are the trustee (which is usually not wise) and even if you derive some benefit from the trust property, like the income from the assets. Once in, it is no longer totally yours, and will be governed by the trust provisions, which you cannot change absent a slick attorney and an understanding judge. Of course, such trusts often are lost to fire, with their terms and obligations reduced to ash and smudge. It is a risky world. Not that I am suggesting you do this if you become tired of an irrevocable trust! And such trusts can be amended by other means, either by "decanting"—pouring—into a replacement trust you like better, or by getting an agreeable judge to change or dissolve it. Our legal team actually gets this done fairly frequently. And putting decanting provisions into an otherwise irrevocable trust can provide a convenient back door.

Why would anyone do such a final thing as make a trust irrevocable? Mostly, aside from controlling access by irresponsible or untrustworthy beneficiaries, or protecting your kids from your subsequent spouses, because it can offer enormous tax leverage. The F-BOTs we will recommend in the tax chapter, for instance, must be irrevocable to work their tax magic.

A living trust, and as mentioned, is merely one set up while you are still alive. In its simplest form, it acts as a will substitute to avoid probate and removes the need for a durable power of attorney with respect to property placed in the trust. Most are revocable, meaning you can change your mind and yank the assets if ever you decide to. You are the grantor, trustee, and primary beneficiary, getting to spend or invest income and principal as you see fit. But in most cases, you are not the only beneficiary: you decide in advance what happens to the corpus—the assets in the trust—if something happens to you. You can have the trust terminate at your death, with the money going freely to spouse, children, or cats. Or the trust can continue, with income (even principal if she needs it) going to spouse for life, with the balance either held in trust for the kids, or just paid out to them at some certain age. You name a successor trustee (and even a second successor, if only a bank to make sure at least someone's still around...but remember to add a protector to fire a bad bank!) to run the trust if you die or become incompetent according to the test you write down in the trust. If it turns out that you need someone to run your affairs, this avoids both court and the dilemma of giving someone the awesome power of a durable power of attorney (which in most if not all states can be used by your "attorney-in-fact," the holder of the power, even before you lose your faculties to spend all your assets if you choose the wrong person. Some states permit a springing power of attorney, which springs into existence if and only if you become incompetent—somewhat less risk from dastardly children stealing assets with these). If you die, there is no need to probate the trust property since title is already held in the name of the successor trustee. Works like a charm, where your primary objective is probate avoidance, and the planning for your own legal incapacity (has a nice ring, what?). And of course, like all trusts, it can do far more, depending on your goals and just how many provisions you want to build into the thing. A typical pattern might be for you to name yourself as trustee and beneficiary, with your spouse as successor trustee in the event of your incapacity or death. Or you can be co-trustees. You might name a bank or child as a contingent successor trustee to take over when the same happens to your spouse. Your spouse would be the income beneficiary at your death, with the right to withdraw principal if she really needs it. If she is the successor trustee, she would make this determination for herself; pick someone else to succeed you as trustee if she is not good with money. Your children would be the remainder beneficiaries, getting the corpus at mother's death, either outright or in trust, whatever you want. Set up this way, you get probate avoidance, a built-in trusted manager to take over when needed, and a vehicle to prevent the kids from being disinherited if your surviving spouse remarries. While most of this can be done with testamentary trusts—again those set up by your will after you die—you do not avoid probate this way, and would need to rely on a power of attorney, or face guardianship proceedings, with respect to management while you live if you become incapacitated. Use living trusts instead!

So, you see, trusts offer almost infinite flexibility to plan your affairs. By the way, "she" is the successor in these examples because women tend to live longer, not from any bias.

To make living trusts work properly you MUST title the appropriate assets to the trust's name! For you, Mr. Bigbucks, for each account, each deed, each corporate share or LLC membership interest, the title must read "J. Bigbucks, trustee for the J. Bigbucks Living Trust." Only property and accounts owned in the trust's name will be handled according to its provisions. For stuff not appropriate to be titled to the trust—typically IRAs and 401ks (because you would have to make taxable distributions to get funds out and into a trust) sometimes life insurance and homestead real estate—use beneficiary designations or pay on death features or ladybird deeds/transfer on death deeds to get it into the applicable trust at death. Also, make sure to keep the trust up with changes in the law. If you use trusts for IRA-type beneficiaries, be sure to put special tax control provisions into the trust. The SECURE Act of late 2019, for instance, produced a sea change in how required minimum distributions (RMDs) are treated for non-spousal beneficiaries. Kids can no longer stretch for their lifetimes, being limited to ten years. But they get to pick the years. If you did not change the old "IRA conduit" provision for tax control (assuming you ever had it!), this could blow up in your tax face by forcing taxable distributions at inopportune times.

The balance will pass by beneficiary designation, title, or be thrown into your probate estate, according to its nature. So use a pourover will, because you are bound to forget something. Often a will is found as the primary estate planning document, and even if the will has a trust "in" it, the advantage of avoiding the hassle (and significant expense!) of probate, as well as greatly reducing guardianship, criminal and credit risk, is lost. Setting up a living trust and putting your assets in its name while you're alive is a big opportunity often missed even by those with expensive and "sophisticated" estate plans.

Beware using joint titling as an estate "plan." Joint accounts are quick and easy, but offer little planning finesse (if you die all goes to your spouse, but if they remarry and jointly title and then they die, your kids get nothing), tax leverage, or protection from attack. If you are married by the way, and insist on joint titling, make sure you title as "tenants by the entirety" and not as "joint tenants with right of survivorship" (a common error often seen at large banks and brokerage houses) if your state permits this.

Multiple marriages can be a real pickle. You want to provide for your current spouse, but want to make sure that your own kids from the previous marriage(s) ultimately get your assets. Joint titling and simple "I love you" wills won't do, since your spouse's family will get the goods after she is gone if you die first. Ditto for her assets if she goes first. These situations are very common and can result in disaster if no planning is done. What to do? In most cases, what you want is for your spouse to have the use of the assets during her lifetime if you go first, with your property breaking out at her death and going to your kids. The same for her. The survivor among you gets to use all of the money for life, with whatever controls you deem appropriate, but at the last death her stuff goes to her kids, your stuff goes to your kids, and if you had "new" kids together, some goes to them. Or whatever else you two decide. Smart trusts can work well here, since the surviving spouse gets the use of the property—with as much control as you wish—but cannot give away or leave the property to anyone but your own darling children.

But what if you find yourself in a "trophy wife" (or trophy husband, for that matter) situation, and are now married to someone much younger than yourself, perhaps as young (or younger) than some of your older children? Odds are good that new mamma/daddy-o may live long enough to consume the assets, with nothing left for your kids when he/she goes. New spouse may even outlive them! The solution is to leave some of your assets directly to your kids when you go, or give them current income rights like you do for trophy spouse. Not only is the latter more palatable from new spouse's standpoint, but your kids won't have to wait until their own old age to see their inheritance…if any's even left!

Of course, the grand objective of this book is for your family to have plenty left, and (as the Three Stooges used to say) *how.* Tight and deeply considered estate planning is the linchpin, the chassis, the foundation of your grand family wealth structure. The launching pad, if you will of your Great Family rocket. But mind all the other chapters in Part II, cause we still need to build and fuel that rocket, and mission-control it without fail to target!

I know this has been a thick and redundant chapter. At best, the concepts are probably still pretty foggy. Sorry! It took me years to pound this stuff into my head, and I wanted to do my best to try to educate you on the critical basics. For those that want more detail or alternate explanations on this heady stuff, check out fweibook.org where there are a bunch of classes ranging from basic to quite advanced. Live long and prosper!

Advanced Asset Protection for Successful Families

We live in a litigious world. This is likely to worsen in the decades ahead, as the wealth schism—the gulf between haves and have nots, the income delta, the increasing concentration of wealth in the hands of a very few, like those reading this book—grows and expands. Most of these reasons were explored ad freakoutnitum in Part I of the book. Add to this poorer folks, desperate and lacking alternatives, becoming more inclined to sue. Then add the gasoline vapor of the socialism/redistribution political wind becoming more inclined to judicial remedy and defendants' rights.

Never before has the threat of losing wealth to lawsuits, creditors, or other financial predators been greater. And make no mistake, if you are attacked, you can't hide your real wealth, unless it's gold bars in cement underneath Jimmy Hoffa.

You get sued, you gotta turn over your records. It's called discovery. Watch *My Cousin Vinny*, for gosh sakes. Try to hide it or lie about it or transfer it to your sister, and not only will the judge probably find out about it, but she's (the judge, but your sister too!) likely to get very pissed, and undo the transfer as a fraudulent conveyance.

Never before has it been as easy for predators and their attorneys to gauge your net worth, and discover what hole(s) conceal your treasure. Services like Wealth-X (wealthx.com; based in Singapore) have for *years* used Internet scraping to compile "dossiers" on fat cats like you, and sell the information to all comers, no questions asked. I ran one as a test for a client—crazy scary the accuracy and detail of the report. The advent of AI will just hockey-stick

© The Author(s), under exclusive license to Springer Nature Switzerland AG 2021
J. Camarda et al., *The Financial Storm Warning for Investors*,
https://doi.org/10.1007/978-3-030-77271-0_13

this trend. Never before has our wealth been so easy to find and see, and so easy to attack. With the dizzying proliferation of information technology, this problem will only become more acute as time passes.

So burn this into your brain: Asset protection is the art of fortifying our wealth so that it becomes extremely difficult or impossible to extract. It is the art of controlling everything and completely "owning" nothing.

There are two basic levels of asset protection planning.

The first and most basic is making sure there are adequate levels and types of liability insurance. It is important to make sure there are no gaps, and that all exposures—businesses, real estate, and personal (including vehicles, boats, planes, etc.)—are covered for all exposed individuals and assets. Miss this, and you have a soft spot in you armor leading right to your honey pot.

Usually, umbrellas (both personal and business) are used to extend the liability limits of underlying policies and should be maintained at levels keyed to a family's net worth. It is important to be sure that underlying policies and umbrellas are properly structured so that there are no gaps, and this should be regularly reviewed with an agent or financial planner expert in these areas. But this is just the first fence. The insurance company could walk away from the claim, leaving you naked (unlikely but possible), or the judge could award more than the insurance will pay.

Here in lil' ole' Jacksonville, I like to use the example of getting in a wreck with a Jacksonville Jaguar. Hit a key player making tens of millions, and the ambulance chasers are gonna come a-callin. No matter the Jags play like the Saints of old and I want to put a bag over my head (the shame of it all, you know). Got a $5 M umbrella! Great. Pay him $10 M. What if you fail? You go to jail! Not really, but that's what you get for making whoopee. Sorry, I wandered off. Anyway, no discounts for helping to put a hopeless team out of its misery! If the judgment exceeds the insurance limit—or the insurance company is successful in wriggling out of the claim (as they are wont to do) your assets are on the hook. Pay up!

The second level of planning is structural and involves how assets are titled and in what types of entities. A very basic tactic for married people in states like Florida is using tenancy by the entirety (TbyE) instead of the far more common joint tenants with right of survivorship—with TbyE at least both spouses would have to be successfully sued to lose the wealth, instead of just one. This is strong if only one spouse gets sued, but worthless otherwise—like if he is driving your car, both of you are libel—your property, idiot husband's fool driving. By the way, we find most brokers and banks are clueless—or just don't care!—about giving you this little bit of free asset protection. Demand it! Beware the ubiquitous JTWROS!

But a little bit of work will pay off in far more effective planning. For instance, assets in qualified retirement plans, or in IRAs, can enjoy far greater attack protection than those in individual or joint accounts. Using LLCs (Limited Liability Companies) with the *right* ownership structure and the *right* operating agreement provisions in the *right* states (these three are ALL critically important and often gotten wrong) can offer tremendous protection for passive assets like bank and brokerage accounts, for operating businesses, and for real estate holdings (just be careful not to mix the asset types! Putting the right eggs in the right baskets is of supreme importance! That $2M brokerage account in the same LLC as the rental house that burns? Tenants sue, everything in that LLC silo is exposed. It's all gone...).

The tremendous asset protecting power of *proper* LLCs over corporations is something we frequently see business owners—and their lawyers!—missing, to their peril. Just these simple, basic steps—and they really are quite simple for clients to implement, so long as they have expert guidance—can solve most folks' asset protection needs. For the more complicated, advanced techniques like equity splitting (where we separate various parts of a business into different companies, to make the whole harder to grab), trust layers, and using "foreign" (out of state) and "alien" (non-US) trust and companies layering can make it so hard and expensive to chase your assets that even the most implacable adversary will give up, or settle for pennies. But most of the time, that's way overkill. Using the right LLCs is typically plenty. Did I mention getting it right is hard to find?

Getting this right is dicey. Like for tax and estate planning, it is worth paying for six-sigma advisor quality. All the stars need line up—right secret sauce in the operating agreement, right assets and right silos, right ownership structure, and so on. For instance, Florida has a very strong LLC law for asset protection. Georgia's is nearly worthless. And no, Virginia, you don't need to be a Florida resident to make it work. But you do need someone who knows precisely how to write the sonnet, and tether it to Florida, and few do. But well-written, and they're nearly bazooka-proof. Advisors—investment, tax, legal—are legion. All have opinions. Many if not most are inexpert to downright wrong. And mostly impossible for consumers to tell the difference!

So the de rigor of asset protecting planning is a two-pronged strategy. Prong one is using cheap (compared to your wealth) insurance to encourage attackers' lawyers to take the quick and easy money (and legal fees), settle any claims against you, and leave you alone. The second prong (by far the sharper one) is using entirely legal structures to make it so difficult, expensive, and time consuming to pursue claims against your assets, that they just don't. In a nutshell, you map out a path of least resistance *before* any trouble arises, and, if it does, the predators slide down the path that leads away from your treasure.

Let's look at some specifics.

Let's reiterate that by noting that asset protection (like estate planning and so much other legal strategy) varies by state. This material is written from my practice perspective of Florida, and while there are important similarities between states, it is best to make sure a proposed plan will be effective in your state. In many cases, non-Floridians using Florida structures get enhanced protection, so long as it's done right. We do quite a bit of this work across the country, but always partner with lawyers we screen in respective states to make sure all lines up properly with applicable law.

At its core, asset protection is the art of making it harder to chase your assets than they're worth. The objective is to structure matters so that it costs so much time and money to get and collect a judgment that an adversary will give up, or settle for a pittance. We do this by setting up hoops, splits, levels, and layers—instead of a pile of cash on the table, it's positioned in different places, and secured by safes within safes within safes, figuratively speaking. The million-dollar-bill is cut in many pieces, and the pieces are hidden separately. For most people, effective planning can be very simple, but still have this effect. It is important to note that this planning is usually fairly inexpensive to create, but extremely expensive to defeat.

That's great leverage.

A few thousand can protect tens or hundreds of millions.

But hark! And beware!

One final, extremely important point: to work well, such planning needs to be done before you think anyone's got a reason to come after you. Do it then, and it's sound planning. Try to it after you know about a threat, and you will probably find your pantlegs tied tightly around your ankles. While there are techniques for those already entangled, they are more complicated and uncertain. Be smart, do your planning before any threat appears. Since most techniques go hand in hand with estate planning, it is usually much more effective to combine asset protection planning with an estate planning review.

Liability insurance—the kind that pays if you become responsible for damage to someone else—is the essential foundation for asset protection. Unless you engage in high-risk activities, the coverage is usually pretty cheap. It is important to have adequate insurance levels (liability limits) and make sure that all potential exposures are covered (real estate, vehicles, boats, planes, and rocket ships). You will want at least several hundred thousand in coverage for each risk (a half million is even better) with a high limit payable per individual, not only per incident. "100/300," for instance, means the policy will pay a maximum of $100K per individual and $300K per incident, meaning the most any person could collect would be $100K—not nearly enough to keep them from coming after your assets if they have a good case. "300/300" means a single person could collect up to $300K (so long as no one else was hurt in the incident). Also, bear in mind that if ten people are damaged by you—in a car wreck, say, or because there was a fire at a rental property—that $300K would be spread awfully thin, and risk to your assets goes way up. Again, you will want at least several hundred thousand in coverage for each risk, but should note that multimillion dollar awards are fairly routine, so you should consider your limits accordingly. Usually, the maximum available on your home and auto policies is $500,000 (sometimes less).

The same rationale is true for business: make sure each liability exposure is covered, and the limits are adequate. A good property and casualty agent can be indispensable in this process, but select carefully as there is wide variation in quality, as with any profession, and a careless agent can leave you thinking you're well protected when you are not. Make sure you understand what you need, and *get assurance you have what you need in writing.*

A big concern with this type of insurance is avoiding gaps in coverage, such as where you think your liability coverages are overarching, but some exposures are not covered, leaving a direct and clear path to your assets. Again, a skilled agent can point out concerns like this should they be present.

Umbrellas are policies that sit on top of your basic policies, and extend liability coverage to 1, 3, 10 million, or more. Different umbrellas are required for personal versus business interests. The proper underlying coverage needs to be in place for the umbrellas to actually work, if needed. Umbrellas are usually dirt cheap ($300/year per million is typical) and indicated for virtually everyone with exposed assets.

Finally, as in all markets, different companies pursue different markets and have products more approximate for them. Companies like Chubb, Fireman's Fund, Chartis, Zurich, ACE, PURE, and others cater to the high net worth market.

IRAs, 401ks, and other types of retirement plans offer excellent asset protection, in most states. Remember, like life insurance and other types of assets, these accounts pass by beneficiary, and the asset protection status becomes somewhat murky once a payment is made at death. Also, like most other asset protection shelters, one should assume the protection only applies so long as value remains in the shelter—once removed for consumption, investment, or other purpose, the risk of it being seized goes up considerably. While IRA and pension accounts usually offer much more flexibility in investment choices than life insurance and annuities, and typically many more low cost options are available than for insurance products, investment options are still much more limited, in most cases, than is generally true for taxable investments, unless you find enlightened advisors who know how to expand your choices. Finally, most of these plans are tax-qualified, meaning that any withdrawals trigger income tax, and maybe penalties, in addition to possibly exposing the value to creditor attack.

LLCs (Limited Liability Companies) are probably still among the most misunderstood vehicles around. I myself did not get a very good grasp until the early years of the twenty-first century, when I became interested in learning about asset protection, despite pretty much continuously studying financial planning and wealth management since I began with the CFP® way back in 1990. Most folks have at least a rudimentary understanding of corporations, partnerships, and even limited partnerships, but LLCs remain a mystery to many.

So let's spend a little more time talking about what these are. LLC, again, stands for Limited Liability Company. Two key words: limited liability, which is precisely what we are after in asset protection. We want to limit our liability to little or nothing. This is the major advantage of this company form. The LLC is basically a partnership that has the limited liability of a corporation. Owners are called "members," unlike partners for a partnership or shareholders for a corporation. Because of the partnership element, the entity enjoys *charging order* protection if you pick the right state for jurisdiction. This basically means that if you own the right kind of LLC (more in a moment) and an adversary succeeds in getting a judgment against you, they might get the bank accounts titled just in your name or as JTWROS, or even TbyE if your wife hits someone in a car titled to you, but can't force assets out of an LLC to pay it. Moreover, unlike a corporation (business owners take note!), if you are sued, it is very difficult to take your membership interest away. To clarify, if you own shares in Tesla or in your own business, these can easily be lost in a lawsuit. LLC membership interests, again owing to the partnership roots, are very difficult to take in satisfaction of a lawsuit. So, we are protected from the "outside"—losing the asset protection structure. As important, the "contents" of the LLC—the bank and brokerage accounts you have transferred to it, perhaps, or the tractors you use in your business—are protected from being ripped out in satisfaction of a charging order to pay a judgment. So long as the asset stays in the LLC, it is very well sheltered. Take a distribution from the LLC, of course, and the money's in your pocket and on the table. However, a little commonsense creativity can be utilized to work around this.

It is important to stress that the LLC can be utterly your creature—you own, can put assets in or take them out without restriction, and is pretty much invisible when it comes to taxes. It is a very easy creature to live with. My expensive collector car and big boat are very happy in theirs, with equity stripping to other entities to keep you litigious dastardly readers at bay.

For asset protection, in many states it is absolutely essential that you have "multiple members"—more than one owner. This is so due to the partnership aspect of the entity (much as you may wish, you can't be a partner just with yourself!). Someone else (a spouse, child, or sibling perhaps) needs to own at least a very small interest in the LLC to get the protection. And the rights of this minority member can be virtually nil, but we need multiple members to keep the wealth safe. And also note, unless the state LLC law is asset protection favorable, even a perfect structure won't help. My lawyer pals tell me Florida's LLC law is fearsome, Georgia's worthless.

It is also vital to have the right "operating agreement." This is like a corporation's bylaws or a partnership agreement, and basically defines how the LLC is structured and what the members' rights and duties are. I cannot stress enough that this needs be drawn by an attorney quite familiar with asset protection if it is going to work! In my humble, non-lawyerly, experience most are not! And often the client and the lawyers don't know it! Please, no online forms, or Office Depot kits. Most CPAs and attorneys in my considerable experience miss the mark on this. Any idiot can set up an LLC and pay the state fee. But getting it right is absolutely critical if your asset protection plan is going to work if and when a threat darkens your financial door.

LLCs, of course, have broad applications as business structures, and while a treatment of business applications is well beyond the scope of this already too-long chapter, we will touch on a few of the more important business aspects below.

Virtually all readers, business owners and not, should consider using LLCs as personal holding companies for liquid assets like bank, brokerage, and mutual fund accounts. Follow the points regarding ownership, operating agreement, optimal state, and so on above. And do NOT mix these assets in the same LLC with those (like operating businesses or real estate) that might incur liabilities that could be satisfied with your liquid accounts. Got a million in the same LLC as the balloon company? The million may crash with the passengers in the hot air balloon. Keep them separate, and safe! Put your riskier assets in their own LLCs; typically each business should be encapsulated in its own LLC. Some real estate investors put each property in its own LLC, others group bunches of properties in separate LLCs—commercial in one, residential in another, and so on, and deal with the property risk primarily with liability insurance. Having a lot of LLCs can become a chore to keep up with, so this becomes a balancing act between protection and practicality. Smart practitioners can minimize the needed number of tax returns, which is really smart. We basically use one master LLC and one tax return in a variation of the Delaware Serial LLC concept. And note that if properties are mortgaged, any attachment in judgment is subject to any mortgage, making (perhaps depending on equity) these assets less attractive to satisfy a judgment. The mortgage acts as a poison pill. Properties with minimal equity need minimal asset protection, but keep an eye out as you pay them down. Also, getting them into LLCs can be a pain, needing lender approval and probably new expensive doc stamp taxes. Sometimes recording a mortgage to yourself (and putting the note in another LLC) can solve this—to take the deed they have to pay you off first, which should scotch them good. This latter is one type of equity splitting.

As mentioned above, it is much harder for a plaintiff to take membership interests in the right LLCs than for a stock in an S or C corporation. This is a major advantage that is not used by far too many business owners! If you are one, please take note. To summarize, both LLCs and corporations protect your personal assets from attacks on the business. I call this a bottom up attack. If your employee shoves a customer in a pizza oven, they can sue the pizza shop corp but not get to your personal bank accounts—unless you helped push!

But only proper LLCs protect the loss of your business from attacks on you: top down attacks. If you are liable in an auto accident for which an award exceeds your insurance, assets held in your name (including your incorporated business) could be lost to satisfy it. *Proper* LLCs—and most are laughably improper!—are much, much harder to crack, and this is the reason you have seen so many of them in the past few decades. Now you know why. Did I mention only the right LLCs work for this and most we've seen are worthless as asset protection?

From a tax perspective, LLCs are pretty invisible, and you can choose—by checking a box on the IRS form—to be taxed as a partnership, S-corp, or C-corp. Just don't choose sole proprietorship, because that would mean a single member LLC and the asset protection would be lost in many states. Depending on the state, it also raises needless IRS red flags as I hope I remember to address in the tax chapters. For those business owners who consider converting corporations or partnerships to LLCs (and all should consider this), make sure you run it by a sharp tax advisor to make sure this would not trigger capital gains recognition, which might be bad. Even where this is the case, you may have other options to improve asset protection, such as perhaps having the corporation be acquired by a new LLC you set up.

Remember, the essence of asset protection is diversion. Smoke and mirrors. Keep those pea shells moving. More hoops to jump through discourage potential attackers. For those with a lot of liability (or a lot to protect), a bit more complexity can take fortification to the next level. One idea is the Delaware-style serial LLC (which is basically a holding company with subsidiaries (one each to hold a rental property, for instance), whose intent is to minimize filing fees and red tape hassle, but I like the simplified Florida version my team came up with better. Another way to apply this concept is equity splitting, where one splits a company into pieces to protect value. In this scenario, a school bus company would be split into a holding company which itself owned 1) an LLC which owns the buses, 2) an operating company which employs the drivers, and 3) a management company that collects the money from the school district and contracts for service from the bus and driver divisions; if a driver goes whacko, the buses and the contracts with school districts are insulated. You can even have another company that finances the buses and holds notes and liens against them. Get a bus or ten in a judgment? No keys until you pay off those loans, bubba!

Added protection can be afforded by using a holding company in an asset-protection-progressive jurisdiction, such as Nevada. This is also a great way to get anonymity, if important. And it never hurts! A casual adversary may try to check things out in Tallahassee, but is unlikely to go digging in Carson City. You can even have holding companies owned by other holding companies. The more hoops, the better protected. Even the robots will scratch their heads.

Another technique is using mortgages and promissory notes, as discussed above and reiterated below. In the previous example, if the buses are encumbered by debt that you own in another entity, even if a judgment attaches to the bus subsidiary, for a creditor to get the buses, they would first have to pay off the debt—which means giving cash to you! A final technique is using an LLC variation of the old family limited partnership, or "FLIP" technique, which used to be very useful for estate freezing to avoid estate taxes before the F-BOT came to town. In my view, FLIPs are pretty obsolete. And, by the way, just in case I didn't mention it, the best time to do asset protection planning is at the same time as estate planning—results tend to be cheaper, better coordinated with other wealth goals, and more effective. Note that "limited partnership"—"LP"—configured LLC units can be real poison pills in asset protection planning. If a creditor accepts such a unit in satisfaction of a judgment or settlement, they get no real assets, and no income, but may have to pay tax on undistributed income! As you can imagine, this can be very effective at keeping the bad guys at bay. Or screwing them over if they're less well advised than you. Limited liability limited partnerships—"LLLP"s—properly built are real bunkers, by the way. For you itching to jump ahead to estate planning, ain't no reason in the world you can't put LPs or LLLPs into your F-BOTs, shugah!

If you find a reason to use this borrowing equity splitting technique, it is important to follow the form to actually have a legitimate and defensible note. While I'm no lawyer (despite being admitted to grad work at Georgetown Law, so please don't construe any of this book as legal advice!), I strongly suggest you to follow the UCC (Uniform Commercial Code) format in terms of setting up the notes. It is important to execute, and properly record, such notes, if you want the judge to respect the structures, they need to be legitimate, not obvious shams. Note for instance Florida imposes a tax on note documentaion. Commerce being what it is, a cottage industry has sprung up to service such needs as these in south Georgia, and many who need to do this find themselves slipping north of the boarder to execute their notes, in places like Kingsland/St. Mary's, GA (conveniently located off I-95, a mile or so into the Peach State), or on their way to a cultural event in Savannah or Atlanta to get notes officially executed. Frugal is as frugal does, Forrest!

This technique works because debt is a higher obligation than equity. If you own the bus, but owe against it, a predator can't take the bus unless they pay the note off first. Ditto for real estate, just make sure such debt is evidenced by a recorded mortgage (hard to beat the recording tax on this one). So the basic technique is to lend money from one, low risk entity (a personal holding company, say) to another entity which pledges assets (real estate, buses, cranes, whatever of value) as security for the loan. Make sure to follow the form of legitimate debt, including reasonable interest (this is tax neutral in most cases since you are just taking money from one pocket to another). If the crane crashes into a bridge, the company that owns it can be sued, but the crane itself can't be taken unless the note is paid off first. Again, too much trouble, not enough to get, the attackers are encouraged to settle for pennies or go away entirely. Eureka!

We have covered a lot of ground in this chapter. While some of the concepts may seem complicated—and asset protection, as an aspect of the broader discipline of wealth management should be meticulous to work properly—a good plan is actually quite simple for clients to set up and live with, provided they get good advice (sadly this is frequently not the case, and a good reason to get a second opinion). The important thing is to take the time to get your plan in order, or reviewed if you have one. For the great majority of families, this is simple, quick, cheap, and easy—if action is taken before a problem appears. If not, and fortune's winds blow the wrong way, the result could be complicated, unending, extremely expensive, and hard—not to mention painful, and devastatingly expensive!

Before leaving this seminal area, here are common errors we see nearly every week, and some simple thoughts on how to correct them.

1. **Using the spouse** as the asset protection "plan." We see this a lot, particularly with doctors concerned about malpractice exposure. While this does offer scant protection, it ignores the risk of losing the assets if the "safe" spouse dies first or is themselves sued for some reason—like getting in a car wreck. The "technique" also introduces both perceived and real asset control issues that may prove unpalatable—like if loving spouse refuses to write a check out of the "protected" account, or argues in divorce proceedings that the assets transferred were a bona fide gift, and hence no longer marital property. Shite!

2. **Inadequate divorce protection** not properly segregating non-marital assets—inheritances, wealth acquired before marriage, etc.—can put into play assets that would have been impervious to the divorce axe. This applies as much to your kids as to you, and not using the right kinds of trusts, with protectors, can lay your treasure bare to the attacks of your children's soon-to-be-ex spouses, who you always knew to be soulless barbarians anyway. The right trusts can often also function as very elegant pre- and post-nup devices, without souring the romance the way traditional pre-nups can.

3. **Titling errors** risk assets—cars, boats, planes, non-homestead real estate, etc., should be titled to an encapsulating entity like an LLC, or at least in the name of the principal operator: his car in his name, and so on. Joint titling or other mistakes can engender needless and expensive liability.

4. **P&C gaps** in any asset protection plan, liability insurance is the very first line of defense. Not having adequate insurance for vehicles, toys, business and real estate exposures, as well as proper levels of business and personal umbrellas is a problem we see all the time. While this area is complicated and exposing gaps takes some work, the insurance is usually cheap and well worth exploring. It's the first line because marauding plaintiffs' attorneys can be often placated (get a nice percentage fee without much work) instead of going after your real assets... and in today's hyper-Google world, it won't take them long to find out where your treasures buried.

5. **Underutilized qualified plan opportunities** business owners particularly leave a lot on the table here. Not only do they often fail to maximize the tax shelter offered by the right kind of tax-deductible plan, but fail to appreciate the extremely strong asset protection properties for them in such plans. Worse the business owner is usually the plan trustee, giving them radioactive liability for stuff like employee investment losses, which they probably think their advisor is liable for but almost never is.

6. **Personally-held business stock** if you own an incorporated business, know that the stock (your business) is on the table if you are successfully sued. You may need to hand it over in a judgment. Having it just in your name (or with a piece to you and a piece to your spouse) is needlessly risky; TbyE (see #2) is better, but a multi-member LLC is, by far, superior.

7. **Not using an LLC (or LLP, or LLLP).** Limited Liability Companies (and their cousins, the Limited Liability Partnership, and the Limited Liability Limited Partnership). These have been around for a long while, but are still poorly understood. Let's face it, you want limited liability, don't you? You wouldn't be reading this otherwise. What an LLC does is protect your personal assets from claims against your business or real estate (yes, I know a corporation does that, too) AND protects you from losing your business if claims are successfully pressed against you (which a corp can never do— get a judgment, hand over the stock). An LLC seals both ends—and that's a very big deal.

8. **Single member LLC.** For the LLC technique discussed in #8 to work, in many states there needs to be more than one owner (LLC owners are called "members"). So make sure your wife or daughter or girlfriend or grandson has a small stake (that has no control or rights to compel income). And remember, this separate interest must be in their name alone, not joint with you.

9. **Waiting until you're fired upon**. Too many people with lots to lose don't get serious about asset protection planning until they smell a lawsuit, or have already been filed on. All of this stuff works really great if you take the time to plan your defenses in the happy sunshine, before the hordes gather for a dawn attack. Once potential liability appears, all the planning in the world may be deemed a "fraudulent conveyance" sham, and much less effective, or entirely so. "Not so fast!" Says the judge! "You only put it in your daughter's name cause you got sued! Get it back or to the hoosegow you go!" So be smart—build that brick house, while the wolf is still at the other pigs' places.

Let you that have ears, hear. Be smart. Get your fortress built now, while the sun is shining. Get started today, while it is fresh on your mind, and before some financial predator starts to huff, and puff. With all the other dangers and threats that are circling round your head right now, not spending nominal time and expense on making your fortune bulletproof makes no sense. Integrate it with your estate and tax control planning, get 'er done, and sleep easy! And again, those that want more can pick up free asset protection classes at fweibook.org.

Converting Avoidable taxes to Family Net Worth

As a teenager, one of my favorite authors was Robert A. Heinlein. I love his quote that "One man's 'magic' is another man's engineering." (And also "Beware of strong drink. It can cause you to shoot at tax collectors—and miss." But that's the stuff of a different chapter...) Another SF writer of the era, I forget who, maybe Clark or Asimov, said something like "the technology of a sufficiently advanced civilization is indistinguishable from magic."

So as I start to weave my spells of tax magic, I want you to bear those thoughts in mind. You may find the efficacy of some of these techniques hard to believe. You may encounter naysayers—typically other tax preparers and advisors—who pooh-pooh the kind of techniques you're about to learn. They may tell you it's poppycock. They may say you'll go to jail. They may merely shake their majestic heads in faux-sage bewilderment.

I call such folks "poo-poo heads," because they generally speak from crass, and sometimes even pompous, ignorance. It's like the CPA who tells me "you haven't been allowed to write off boats for 30 years..." when I see clients writing off their expensive boats and boat trips each and every year, even after being audited where the boat deductions stuck.

I remember one IRS agent saying "I'd like to take my boat to the Caribbean and write it off..." We showed him the law, then said "so go ahead!" Not one nickel of deduction was lost.

As "Rich Dad Advisor" Tom Wheelwright said in *Tax Free Wealth*, "there are millions of people who legally pay little or no tax...(because) they simply

J. Camarda et al., *The Financial Storm Warning for Investors*, https://doi.org/10.1007/978-3-030-77271-0_14

understand how the tax law works." As he warns, you must "beware of tax advisors who really work for the government…many are afraid of tax law so they won't learn how to take advantage of the law for you" or are "more interested in protecting themselves than reducing your taxes." You got an amen to that, Tom!

Not this guy. I am supremely passionate about helping you drive family wealth by saving taxes. As we get into this, there's a couple of caveats I want to warn you about.

The first is helping you understand that the tax code is not set in stone. It is not a black or white thing. It is one of the most complex, convoluted, and internally contradictory documents ever created—and it keeps changing almost by the week. And that's just the law, which itself is endlessly draped in rulings regulations, memos, advisories, and other interpretations which run the gambit from having the force of law to IRS blue-sky wishful thinking.

It is also important to realize that tax laws are written by human beings who are not perfect. They forget stuff and can't cover every conceivable base. Unintended consequences of imperfect legislation breed endless loopholes smart planners can throw big bags of clients' gold through. Loopholes are almost always not intended—but the law is the law and all you need to abide by.

Many efforts are made to try to counter the tax reduction strategies that the most proactive taxpayers (and their advisors) keep coming up with to legally keep wealth in their families' pockets. But for IRS, it can be a game of catch up, with the best advisors finding new—and legal!—opportunities faster than IRS can lobby Congress or Treasury to close old ones. Great complexity can breed great opportunity. Tax avoidance is perfectly legal, and often remarkably easy, if you know where to look. Too many taxpayers (and their tax advisors) believe in "death and taxes" inevitably, that you "gotta pay what you gotta pay." The truth is, it is perfectly legitimate to use the portions of the tax code that support the reasonable position that results in the least tax—or no tax at all! This is a key concept; tax liability is a function of code interpretation, and astute advisors mine the complexity of the code to build the most favorable positions for taxpayer clients.

Have I mentioned finding astute advisors in this and other finance can be hard? Use what you learn in this book to sharpen your judgment and pick better ones!

The second is opening your eyes to tax arbitrage opportunities. Arbitrage just means taking advantage of different prices for the same thing in different markets. If you can buy gold for $1500/oz in London and sell it for $1700 in Dubai, you can make a riskless $200/oz—that's arbitrage. Gold is a pretty efficient market—prices are consistant worldwide—but it makes a good example. For instance, tax arbitrage—using the differences between tax rates applicable to different kinds of entities (C vs. S corporations, for instance) or different individuals (you and your children, for instance)— can save some people a real bundle. Another way to apply this concept is doing IRA ROTH conversions (paying the tax on the IRA in exchange for the remainder to grow tax free) in years when you are in a low tax bracket because you may have business losses, lost a job, or high deductions from medical expenses, for instance. A great example of arbitrage is the so-called corporate inversion, a super "loophole" that basically lets corporations swap high US tax rates for near-zero ones in places like Ireland; this for years generally remained perfectly legally though somewhat dicey in application. It looks to be rapidly dying in 2021, though many opportunities spring anew.

The third is remembering the most basic, go-to platforms to enable super-charged income tax savings: owning at least one business and/or investing in real estate. The Trump-era Tax Cuts and Jobs Act expanded tax opportunities for business owners, while at the same time further choking deductions for employees. These two platforms will be your main guns in the income tax battles to come, even if TCJA gets gutted.

It has been said that taxes are a science, but they are really a dark art. The various government laws and codes which promulgate taxes—crowned by the bloated Internal Revenue Code ("IRC")—are so vast and internally conflicted that there is often no clear answer to the question "what do I owe?".

Most of us want to pay the "right" amount, what the law says we fairly owe. But the more one studies the tax laws, the clearer their lack of clarity becomes. Instead of a right/wrong, yes/no answer, in many cases we find endless shades of gray, especially for business owners or professionals whose tax returns are more complicated and nuanced than the typical W2 employees. If you are reading this book, there's a fair chance you own or manage a business, invest in capital assets like stock or real estate, and it is quite likely that you are overpaying your taxes and can benefit enormously from this material.

Most taxpayers—and far too many of their tax advisors—tend to be overly conservative, and far, far too much needless tax is paid every year as a result of ignorance, laziness, or unreasonable fear.

What most people assume is a precise, just system is, in reality, a seat-of-the-pants flight through interpretation, with the best pilot usually winning. And not just the hot-doggers. Lots of ultraconservative positions that even the IRS would advise you to take are routinely missed. The venturesome have even more opportunity. I do not mean to give the impression that there are no rules; rather, there are such a dizzying number of conflicting laws morphed into legitimate interpretations of what the laws mean and how to enforce them, spun by the case law of tax court decisions, that a HUGE amount of wiggle room and latitude is hopelessly baked into the system. You would probably be astonished to learn the amount of horse-trading and deal-cutting that goes on in most audits and the forget-the-rules-let's-get-it-done attitude that revenue agents can take in order to "do business." Many folks think that IRS auditors come in guns blazing, prepared to work past midnight checking every receipt. The reality is many would rather just cut a deal and go to lunch.

If you are not a simple W2 taxpayer, "do the right thing" becomes "find a strong position." By that I mean you should find and take tax positions that are reasonable and can be defended by citing applicable sections of tax law. I'm talking about well-considered arguments that are likely to be accepted by the taxing authorities (such as the IRS) if your return is ever questioned, not wild arguments or fringe ideas.

The reality is that the person with the best advice and strategy usually pays the least, and those with poor advice or no strategy pay through the nose! The cruel irony is that such overpayment offers little protection against audits and harassment from the IRS or other taxing authorities. Actual tax paid and audit flags are two totally different realms, really.

My objective in this book is to point out a number of mainstream techniques that are commonly used by enlightened tax advisors and their clients. But remember, these are just the tip of the iceberg. In most cases, there are many more powerful methods to save you even more tax but they require knowledge of an individual taxpayer's fact pattern to discover the particular opportunities.

But learn this well! You have no idea how much family wealth is wasted to bad tax advice. No idea how much of your money could be just burning away for no good reason.

Forbes says a whopping 93% of business owners overpay their taxes.[1] David Ramsey says "Every year, more than 2 million taxpayers overpay their income taxes—and we're not talking about pocket change."[2] Even the Federal government admits business owners overpay their taxes by $50 billion each year![3] How much of that huge number is yours?

A nice lady recently gave me an antique sculpture. It's a clown pushing a cart full of money to IRS. She gave me that sculpture after I showed her how to save a ton on taxes. She's quite savvy, a single mom who built an impressive fortune alone, from scratch. With more tax smarts, she's getting even richer. Much faster. She gave me that clown to remind me to keep reaching out to help folks like you. To teach the powerful tips you'll see later in the book. Tips that can put a rocket booster on your wealth and help you and your family keep more of what you make, faster and easier, with less hassle and stress. Don't you be that clown!

Smart tax strategy is without question the most powerful, effortless way to increase your income, and supercharge your wealth—faster than you now believe possible. And with the tax storm that's coming, it may be the only thing between your wealth and the clutching hand of a starving government. This is important stuff, and maybe the difference in being able to continue with the things you really care about. Like nice things and trips for your family. Education for kids and grandkids at good schools. The power to retire sooner and better. And the wealth to create a fine legacy your kids and descendants will cherish and remember you for generations.

So that's why I call tax strategy the master wealth skill. More than anything else, it can make the difference between just getting by, and getting really rich. Smart tax tends to be the least appreciated wealth skill, and many consumers seem to downplay the value of searching for and paying for this expertise. Don't make the mistake of making the chore of getting taxes done more like dry-cleaning than the incredibly complicated master-art it really is when practiced well. Don't just drop your taxes off and get them "done" cheap! With so much cash at stake, it constantly amazes me how many people value cheap over good tax advice. Would you do that for medical care? Don't sell your wealth care short! More than ever, you must seek out the rare true masters, and not be resistant to paying for quality advice. This advice is usually not cheap, but is often one of the very best investments you can make, with tax savings typically many, many times the cost of the advice. I've said it before, and I'll say it again.

Getting good tax advice can cost you a small fortune.

Not getting will cost you a large fortune!

More than in any other profession I've seen—law, medicine, engineering, academia, whatever—I have found that true experts are extremely rare, and so outnumbered by the legions of barely-competent, "you gotta pay your tax" software-junkie button pushers as to be nigh-impossible to find. Like financial advisors, it is very difficult for even very smart consumers to tell the difference between truly excellent tax practitioners and those who merely smile winningly and look good in a suit, or golf shirt. Savvy consumers may smell something amiss, but are clueless as to specifics and remedies. This sad state, coupled with the dry-cleaning mentality of most consumers, means that vast sums of family wealth are typically lost to legitimately avoidable taxation. While we have enjoyed some modest tax reduction in the late twenty-teens, I am utterly convinced this is a brief holiday only, and that taxes will rise with a vengeance for the rest of your lives, and those of your children's, too.

I mean a hockey-stick meteoric rise, with that stick squarely swung at fat cats like you!

Remember Mike Meyer's *The Cat in the Hat* as pinnata? Go not easy into that Sunday morning!

If you don't watch out, taxes will choke your family's wealth. Don't let them!

Enough soapboxing! Time to sharpen the axe. Turn the page, and let's put it, and your nose, to the tax cutting grindstone. And if you want to get really good, plenty more tax ed at fweibook.org.

Notes

1. Gunderson, Garrett B. "Entrepreneurs: Stop Overpaying On Taxes." *Forbes*, June 9, 2015. https://www.forbes.com/sites/groupthink/2015/06/09/entrepreneurs-stop-overpaying-on-taxes/?sh=6cad03cc3f70.
2. "How to Get Your Cash Back If You've Overpaid the IRS." November 26, 2019. https://www.daveramsey.com/blog/how-to-get-your-cash-back-overpaid-irs.
3. Gardner, Diane. "Stop Overpaying Your Taxes." https://www.taxcoach4you.com/books/stop-over-paying-your-taxes/.

Converting Income Tax to Family Wealth

Let's start where most wealth starts, with the production of new wealth we call income.

No more chest-thumping on why keeping more and paying less in tax matters. No more reiterations or accusations of hyperbole. By now, you know how I feel.

When I say income tax, I lump other income-related taxes in, like FICA payroll taxes, capital gains, the gnatty NIIT (Net Investment Income Tax), and others of its ilk into the stew.

Also, I will not bore you with the basic stuff you read in the papers toward the end of each year, like maximizing expense recognition in one or the other year based on expected brackets, doing tax loss harvesting on investments, measured ROTH conversions in low income years, and not pulling the trigger on Social Security while you still have high employment income (unless you don't expect to live long).

You don't need me for that stuff. Google away if you want a primer. Or read the *Daily News*.

I bring you the heavy guns. The *Iron Man 2* Cohibas. The killer power of Justin Hammer's "ex wife." Or what he said it was, anyway.

Before we trot them out, know this. There never was much dancing room—by infernal design—for W2 employees. Trump-era tax reform squeezed them even more, sharply limiting time-honored deductions like state income tax, employee business expenses, and the venerable exemption, wellspring of the more-dependents tax dodge (at least for higher income folk).

J. Camarda et al., *The Financial Storm Warning for Investors*, https://doi.org/10.1007/978-3-030-77271-0_15

Wage earners' (and I include the unjustifiably-high-salaried among them—ye swarthy tax-challenged pirates!) hands are really tied. Does that mean you should curse, spit at my image on the Internet, and demand a refund for the book?

Arrrrdly. But it does mean you need to find a way to open the business deduction treasure box, as a business owner or real estate investor. More on these boons soon.

A few more points before leaving W2 land. The first is if you have any influence whatsoever on your employment status, try hard to get reclassified as an independent contractor. This way you get paid on a 1099 instead of a W2. Not only is this way better for you, it is also much cheaper for your employer. Why? Because they save a bunch of FICA taxes and other costs, and you get a ton of write-off opportunities that are denied you as an employee. It basically converts your status to independent business person and opens the entirety of the toolbox discussed below. IRS hates this for obvious reasons, but provided you are able to meet the test—basically a control one where you self-direct your work instead of being tightly supervised—they can hate it all they want. Satisfy the law, and the law is on your side.

Also, if you get stock bonus options, restricted stock units, or other incentive comp of this sort, pay careful attention to how you recognize income on them. This can be a wickedly complex area and is beyond the scope of this already-sprawling book, but hark! Those of you in this space often have many choices to make that govern eventual taxation, primarily the difference between ordinary income and capital gains rates. As you remember from Part I, under current law the former can be about twice the long-term latter, meaning if you get stuck paying ordinary income taxes your bonus can shrink considerably. To navigate these stickiest of wickets, read your bonus explanations or plan documents carefully, and if you feel the very slightest shred of uncertainty, get with a tax pro who can figure it out with you. Since the good ones can be very hard to identify, read the chapter on finding good advisors twice and get solid advice instead of seriously shellacked. It's not hard—if you know where to look and bone up—but sadly it seems few do.

On to the big guns of real estate and your own business. The first gem is you want to set these up as separate companies, and not put the tax accounting on your personal return. Lots of taxpayers do this—put business accounting on the Schedule C and/or real estate on the Schedule E of their 1040 personal return—but this is a big mistake. There are several reasons for this. Using Schedule C generally induces avoidable self-employment tax (calculated on Schedule SE of the 1040). The second reason is for asset protection as discussed in that chapter. But the third big reason is audit control. Welcome to the gentle art of tax return cosmetics! Where the law gives you multiple ways to present your information, the wise choose those which look best and waive nary a "IRS look at me!" red flag. Revealing your business accounting on your personal return is dropping your bloomers needlessly. You are offering red-flag trip wire info that you are not required to that may prompt an audit. Whether or not anything is untoward, you may invite avoidable scrutiny. This really goes to the venerable school of tax return cosmetology, which holds that the better you look, the easier life is. Tax law gives you many options on how to present your numbers, and you are wise to try to avoid needless attention.

So if you are smart, set up the right kind of LLC, or, gosh help you, a simple corporation if you must. Avoid general partnerships which engender unlimited liability. This way, instead of dropping your drawers and gushing all your numbers across your personal return, just one number links the returns. Since most readers—even sophisticated ones—probably are not familiar with this, here's a simple example. If you have an S-corp (or a way smarter S-elected LLC), the accounting goes on the corporate return, the 1120S. If you have a partnership like makes sense for an asset protection family holding company, the return is called a 1065, but the process is the same. The company files the return (1120S or 1065) with all the revenue, expense, and what-not numbers. The company issues you a form called a K-1, which really (mystery solved!) is just like a 1099. The K-1 summarizes company accounting data but really just basically shows how much your interest in the company made or lost, and that one number goes on the Schedule E, then flows on to other applicable schedules of your 1040 personal return. Get it? Just the one number. No home office, unreasonable meals, or excessive auto to flag attention. No yacht trips to the Caribbean. Just one debit or credit, to get summed with all your other simple numbers, like dividends and capital gains and your (I hope you're choking now) W2 income. So instead of having one roadmap return (with the map pointing to an unlubricated pain in your butt), you now have two—or twenty—blackbox returns with very little connect-the-dots traction. Better yet, the way IRS is currently configured, odds may be that different divisions review your personal versus business returns. Talk about one hand not washing the other. You have to pay a little to file multiple returns to get to this happy place, but believe me, it's worth it.

Before we stray too far from this enchanting note, we should comment on the veracity of the deductions that you, gentle and moral reader, may seek to claim on your stealth-mode returns. So, once again, know this: There is no black and white! There is a spectrum of positions, from "you freakin' fraud you're going to jail get in the trunk I'll drive you myself" (and I am a very tolerant man!) to "I'll pay double the taxes I owe I don't care what deductions I can take just so they leave me alone!".

I suspect you are in neither camp, though your advisors may be sequestering you in the latter, whether you smell it or nay.

The spectrum starts at tax fraud (don't do that!) and ends at overcompliance. Most taxpayers lean, unintentionally, to the expensive right, here. In between, there are varying degrees of reasonable positions supported by some bit of tax law or regulation, or other. The AICPA (American Institute of CPAs) has published a number of guiding documents[1] on this, which mostly say something like this "A member should not recommend a tax return position or prepare or sign a tax return taking a position unless the member has a good-faith belief that the position has at least a realistic possibility of being sustained administratively or judicially on its merits if challenged." There are many others in the CPA canon which put a much finer point on it, but the clear point (I hope) is this: There is a very wide range of reasonable positions. If you take one and it does not hold, you are not going to jail. Odds are you will even get penalties and maybe interest abated. Odds are decent you will prevail on exam (audit), because you have a smart advisor and the examiner wants to go to lunch. In the end, you must decide how much IRS risk is acceptable. But my counsel is this: Far too many taxpayers cringe in fear of a less-than draconian IRS. Ditto for tax preparers, who sadly may care less for your own wasted tax dollars than their own. Take a reasonable position, that saves you serious tax. Better to give it up later—and that day may never come!—than to lay down and never take it at all. Go gently not into that tax-sucking good night! What's a "reasonable" position in the eyes of the IRS? Only a bloody third of chance of being deemed right! A one-in-three chance! That's how low the bar is to avoid penalties and other nasty stuff. Not that I advise you to go that low in your tax research. But I bet you believed—and your CPA made you believe—you had better be 99% right to avoid trouble. Just ain't so, mate!

The major benefit of running a company is the ability to take deductions. While it should be obvious, let's review the basic tax equation. You pay tax on taxable income. This number is derived from a series of plusses and minuses. For employees, you get one big plus with the W2 and very limited minuses these days besides the standard or itemized deductions, 401(k) contributions, and the like, none of which move the needle very much. But if you— or your spouse—have a deductible business, that unlocks a whole tier of potential minuses, which are the expenses of the business, a bonanza of ideas we present herewith below. Often such items include legitimate business deductions for things you consider personal, like auto or maybe home expenses. This includes depreciation, a non-cash but tax-deductible expense. The rules for depreciation got much more liberal in recent years creating mucho opportunity for business owners. Real estate is great for this, to the point where deductible depreciation and interest can drive tax losses to offset other income, even if the real estate is cash flow positive! To harvest such losses against other income, you may need to meet the so-called real estate professional test. This does not mean you need a license, it is a tax code test that requires, according to TheTaxAdvisor.com, that "(1) more than one-half of the personal services the taxpayer performs in trades or businesses during the tax year are in real property trades or businesses in which the taxpayer materially participates, and (2) hours spent providing personal services in real property trades or businesses in which the taxpayer materially participates total more than 750 during the tax year."[2] This is a pretty easy test for you or a nonworking/part-time spouse to meet. To activate it, you need to check a box on the back of the Schedule E. We see this missed all the time—even where it drop-dead, no-question applies, like for folks whose only income comes from apartment buildings. It is astonishing how much bad tax advice chokes taxpayers like this.

By now it should be obvious that owning a business seriously purposed toward earning a profit (to avoid the "hobby rules" trap) offers incredible leverage to deduct legitimate expenses that are utterly lost to W2 employees who work for others. Appropriate business write-offs can be profound, if you spend a bit of effort to learn the rules, or find someone who knows them well and eschews an "you gotta pay your taxes, mate!" attitude.

The rest of this chapter is devoted to sharing the tips and tricks that can drive big deductions to minimize your taxable income and convert wasted tax dollars to family wealth.

The first is not overpaying yourself as an *employee* of your own business. Most tax advisors will tell you should take a salary from the business you work in, and that's correct. You should. But most advisors seem happy to see you overpay yourself, which is bad because you have to pay FICA and other payroll taxes on your W2 salary. You don't need to overpay yourself and FICA taxes. You only need to satisfy the reasonable compensation test. There is tons of wiggle room on this. $20K is too low in most cases, but $50–$70K is reasonable in many situations. What does this mean? You need to pay FICA on the part of business income that represents you working as an employee in it. You don't on the part that represents profits on your ownership of the business apart from your personal employee efforts. That's why you don't pay

FICA on your dividends from your IBM stock. Get it? Seek to reasonably minimize your W2 to save FICA!

As mentioned above, don't put your business reporting as a "disregarded entity" on your personal Schedule C or E. Use a real entity instead. Save self-employment tax, and fly under the avoidable radar.

If your business has few or no non-family employees, think outside the 401k box when it comes to pretax/tax deductible retirement plans. There are many, many more flavors to these than the employee contribution variant of profit-sharing plan authorized by Section 401(k) of the IRC or Internal Revenue Code. One big gun is the old defined benefit plan, also called a pension and sometimes a cash balance plan. I call them a "super 401k" because it communications the concept, but is a misnomer. But better you understand than be confused by jargon, right? Without getting into too much detail, these plans define the benefit—like the lifetime annual pension—and not the contribution like 401k plans. That means the contribution required to fund the benefit can be way higher in the right fact patterns, like for older folks closer to pension age with less time to build up the kitty. The maximum "standard" allowable *benefit* for 2020 is $230K,[3] and depending on how you slice the dry actuarial math, it can go even higher. That's a big gun! You don't need to be a rocket scientist to see that you need to shovel a whole lot of tax-deductible coin in to fund an annual pension of over $200K that could last decades. We often find the deduction ceiling so high that folks don't have the cash flow to max it out. Annual deductible contributions of $150K per owner are common. $150K deducted in the 40% tax bracket is an easy $60K in tax savings = heavy coin in your pocket now. Note this does not work so well if you have full-time employees, because the required kicking in for them can get expensive. If you have more than a few employees, move on to other ideas. But where it works this is a really big deal, totally plain vanilla, around forever—but breaking news to many CPAs and tax "pros" whom I regularly educate on this all the time, more's the pity!

I can't make this point loudly enough. Business owners can often use tax deductible retirement plans much more to their advantage than is typically the case, if the objective (as it nearly always is) is to pile up tax deductions while putting way more dollars in owners' accounts than for employees. Sadly, this is really business tax planning 101, straight down the fairway, but I am continuously amazed at how often it is missed by even high-dollar tax advisors. I recall a case where a Manhattan CPA advised a fellow to use a SEP, with deductions in the $20K range. Not even these were maxed out! This was like under half of the allowable defined contribution limit. Mind you this client lives near NY city and pays NY state and municipal income taxes on top of the Federal burden, meaning he really got whacked. We showed him how, in his fact pattern, using a 401(k) would more than double his CPA-suggested deduction, but that what he really needed (and eventually did) was a defined benefit plan, boosting deductions to about $150K a year. The guy saved pushing $100K a year in taxes, like waving a wand. Note you may have to goose your W2 income a bit, and pay more FICA, to drive higher contribution deductions, so be prepared to do some exploratory math to optimize this. You trade off some lower rate FICA for real big higher rate income tax savings. It's actually much better than that because the ratio of W2 increase/deduction increase is often much lower than one. So, gee willikers, this is HUGE where it fits. I just checked the file on the above guy, and here are his 2020 deduction choices, straight from the actuary "the minimum required contribution is $154,273; the recommended contribution is $310,000: and the maximum deductible is $542,077." That's powerful tax medicine.

Back in the 401(k) box, but with a little-known twist, is the ROTH 401(k) This very-little-known tool has emerged as one of the most powerful tax-control techniques around. Most know that ROTH accounts grow tax free, which is as good as it gets. Many don't know that wisely structured ROTH 401(k)s (not ROTH IRAs so much) have enormous flexibility as wealth building machines. My team counseled one sophisticated real estate developer who'd on his own figured out how to do lucrative projects inside his ROTH 401(k) such that all the appreciation and rent flowed tax free. This itself is a leap well beyond most tax advisors' strategic acumen. He had that rarest of treasures—a very tax-sharp CPA. The problem for my team was not to control the income tax—he already had that knocked—but to figure a way to get the residual multi-millions of projected ROTH value out of his already-taxable estate, which we did, yielding a real cake-and-eat-it-too tax magical situation. Another very cool feature is the ability for the ROTH to borrow to invest in real estate. This magnifies the tax-free potential far beyond what would be possible on actual contributions to the plan alone. Let's say that again: You can only put limited dollars into a ROTH—but you can pretty much borrow unlimited dollars with the right plan set up which can balloon the tax-free asset engine enormously. Unlike the defined benefit plan—protests of the unlearned hordes aside—*this* strategy is quite sophisticated, and every i must be dotted lest you fall deeply into the malodorous abyss. These must be very carefully structured, deeply researched, and well-documented to demonstrate congruence with tax law. Don't try it at home! And don't ask your tax guy/gal, who will likely tell you it can't be done (just like you can't write off a boat). But man, these can really sing, especially combined with estate tax shields like the Family Bank Ongoing Trusts (F-BOTs) you learn about in the estate tax chapter. Done deftly, you can even get a large, fully-depreciated real estate portfolio, out of the taxable environment, into a tax-free one, and beat the estate tax in the bargain. This is tax alchemy of the highest order.

Let's talk partnership tax law for just a bit. Really too deep to more than wet a toe here, the complexity of partnership (as opposed to corporate) tax law offers vast opportunity for deft dancers to optimize their positions and mint significant additional wealth from tax savings. A great example of this is how hedge funds' so-called carried interest facilitates the transmutation of high-bracket ordinary income to much lower bracket capital gains treatment. Even better, the alchemy promotes tax deferral until such capital gains are recognized. Deft dancers, with the right profile, may even be able to use tax-free borrowing out of the partnership to free up needed cash without triggering capital gains recognition. Done right, you can tweak such a structure to where most high-bracket ordinary income is transmuted to capital gains, and you can defer capital gains recognition until the cows come home and your tax profile pleases you, but still access the cash flow via tax-neutral borrowing. Talk about a home run! Theoretically you can do this for generations, so even if the proposed 40%+ capital gains rate sticks, it won't matter.

In considering the partnership structure, it is important to balance against opportunities spawned by current C-corp rates, and the new qualified business income (QBI) rules. If you split a business into C-corp and non-C-corp parts, you can income split and funnel some profit to take advantage of the lower C-corp brackets, and dump the rest elsewhere (like into an S-corp) to avoid hitting potentially higher C-corp rates. QBI basically makes 20% of a qualifying business's income tax free.[4] It's not hard to qualify for many small business—so if you are just setting up a new one, structure it to make sure yours does. For many business owners, the big prize in the 2017 changes may be the QBI rules. These apply to partnerships, S-corps, and Schedule C sole proprietorships (as well as their LLC analogs). They also apply to shareholders in REITs (Real Estate Investment Trusts) and owners of publicly traded partnerships like MLPs (Master Limited Partnerships). The big "news" is the "deduction" of 20% of (generally) operating profits. In other words, only 80% (generally) of profits is now taxable, with the other 20% essentially tax free, on top of reduced tax bracket rates. Before leaving QBI, business owners, know this: This sweet plum is *still* amazingly missed by too many tax preparers. We see returns all the time that overpay because of this. Make sure it's checked by someone who knows what they're doing!

When it comes to expenses, we find most business owners understate them, so both old hands and new entrepreneurs please pay attention! You should look at this from the perspective of every bloody cent you spend has a legitimate business purpose unless proven otherwise. Go to dinner with your partner spouse and talk business? Who doesn't? Write it off!

The Good Code sayeth, at Sect. 162, that "There shall be allowed as a deduction all the ordinary and necessary expenses paid or incurred during the taxable year in carrying on any trade or business..." Key words are ordinary and necessary—clearly open to wide interpretation. So ponder deep! Use that vehicle for some business-related stuff—like picking up envelopes or inspecting your rentals? Driving to the bank? Business purpose!

Also note for vehicles: actual expenses—fuel, tires, repairs, washes, insurance, tags, etc.—tend to way outweigh the standard mileage, so think hard and use that, even if you have to estimate. Don't forget legal, accounting, and other professional advice. We find a great exercise with clients is to go through their credit card bills item by item, and flag reasonable business-related expenses. You may be surprised by what a pile you come up with—and how much tax you save! This is really one of my pet peeves. Far too many business people—largely on the advice of their too-conservative, or ill-informed tax advisors—simply do not write off perfectly legitimate expenses, and wind up essentially doubling their costs for these overlooked business items. I am firmly convinced that many tax preparers would rather see clients pay excess tax than face the bother of additional tax research. Don't be afraid—or let your tax advisor convince you to be afraid—to take legitimate deductions. You would be amazed at even some of the extremely aggressive positions that have passed muster during an IRS audit!

Worth its own paragraph is the home office expense. With the advent of COVID, it is MUCH easier to meet the test of regular and exclusive use of a part of your home, and that it be a principal place of business.[5] Even writing off just a portion of your home—and the pro rata taxes, interest, landscaping, utilities, cleaning, Internet, depreciation, and on and on—can yield a huge number to offset other income. What sayeth the blessed Code about this here? Kindly turn your hymnals to IRC Sec 280A, where it is writ: "exclusively used on a regular basis...(A) as the principal place of business for any trade or business of the taxpayer, (B) as a place of business which is used by patients, clients, or customers in meeting or dealing with the taxpayer in the normal course of his trade or business, or ..." Note the very ambiguous lack of an "and" or "or" between subsections (A) and (B). (Do I sound like Bill Clinton's "It depends on what the meaning of is 'is'"?) These days, a Zoom is a "meeting." Following the letter of the law is key to success.

Another big opportunity is called income splitting, such as with C-corps above, or with family members. Here's how it works. This is a great boon to families, a way to give meaningful "gifts" to your kids or grandkids on a tax deductible basis. Find a way to employ your children in a way you can document their work such as making copies, cleaning, running errands, and entering data. You can shift your high-bracket income to your kids low/no bracket rates. Let me say that again—you can shift your high bracket income to much lower rates and still keep the money in the family. This is one way, for instance, to get a tax write-off to fund college costs. This can save the family thousands or tens of thousands or more. Your kids have the right to file their own returns and their earned income as opposed to the radioactive "Kiddie Tax" investment income. Earned income is taxed at very low rates for low income earners and can generate valuable deductions as well. This is Tax Planning 101 but is too often a missed opportunity. Works for older kids, too, and parents. In the latter case, a way to get write-offs for home health or other care. The whole key is bracket arbitrage—shifting taxable income to those in lower brackets. You need to do some proforma math, but the payoff can be huge.

A similar angle comes from playing the entity tax brackets. There are many creative ways to split a business into separate entities. For real estate investors, one co can do management, another repairs, for instance. For 2020, the first $50,000 of C-corp income is only taxed at 15%, likely lower than your other brackets. So make one low-profit piece of your operations a C-corp. Playing with this, available QBI, and the right qualified plan can whip up a lovely low-cal tax brew.

The depreciation rules for non-real estate assets have greatly eased up, allowing high percentage and sometimes complete deprecation of assets in a signal year. We frequently see this missed as well, but combining available "bonus" depreciation, the old Section 179—now good for $1 M + in 2021!—and other flavors can make for huge write-offs. For real estate investors, cost segmentation depreciation—which greatly accelerates write-offs on wear items like rugs and doorknobs instead of waiting the glacial 39 years for commercial real estate for instance—can shift lots more money from IRS to your family.

Another oft-overlooked area is the research and development credit. Credits are way better than deductions. If you are in the 40% bracket, a $1 deduction saves $0.40 in tax; a $1 credit saves $1 in tax—it's one for one. Credits are gold. If you engage in developing or designing new products, prototypes, software or processes, or work on improving these, this is definitely worth looking into. Again, just make sure you read and understand the applicable Code section—or find some who does!

Here are some other common business tax mistakes we often see. Don't let it happen to you!

If you or your business own real estate used in the business, and you pay yourself rent, the rent is maybe subject to sales tax, depending on the state. This can amount to a lot of money that could otherwise wind up in your pocket or be reinvested in your business. There is, however, no requirement that you pay rent to yourself (or your entity that owns the real estate), so avoiding this one is easy…just stop paying rent! There is no income tax effect from this, you just save the sales tax. Why? if your company pays rent to you, the company writes it off, you declare the income, it's a wash. By the way, it is usually unwise to have your business own the real estate, for two big reasons. First, entwining assets like this can make things difficult to unwind later. If you want to sell just the business or just the real estate having them part of the same entity adds a level of complexity and confusion. Second, from an asset protection standpoint, the liabilities of one asset can expose the other— if you are sued over one asset, the other can (often needlessly) be lost if the legal winds blow the wrong way.

As touched on above, many businesses have the wrong type of qualified retirement plan. This is a common mistake and offers potentially huge tax savings. "Qualified" plans are the kind that let you put money away pre-tax, which means that the contributions are tax deductible. They "qualify" for the tax deduction. Most people think of these as 401(k)s, though 401(k)s are only one very specialized type of plan; there are many different types to choose from, with some much better than others, depending on the situation. This is a very powerful tax savings tool because in the top income brackets, you can wind up investing almost twice as much into a plan like this than otherwise. Using $100,000 for example, you can shelter a full $100,000 pretax compared to merely investing $55,000 after taxes in a 45% combined bracket. That is, put $100,000 of income in a qualified plan and control it all to grow your wealth; if you take it as income instead, you'll lose nearly half of it to taxes. Significantly, what works for $100,000 can also work for $1,000,000 or more, depending on your situation. Most employers use "cookie cutter" plans that tend to treat all employees the same, instead of enabling owners to choose to concentrate the benefits where they see fit, such as on themselves and their key people. Where applicable, making this change is a no-brainer in most cases since business owners would prefer to do more for their own and their family's benefit and as a reward/retention tool for key employees. This can be difficult to accomplish without sound advice—always hard to find!—but employers have considerably more flexibility than most realize. The reasons are twofold:

1. Qualified plan advice is such an arcane and rare discipline that many employers never even encounter an advisor (including their accountant and 401(k) salesperson) who really knows the material and can expertly guide the owner to tax savings.

2. The industry is dominated by insurance companies, whose primary product is the "prototype" 401(k) plan. This kind of plan is dominant probably not because it is best for the companies who buy them, but because they are easy to manufacture, deliver, and sell. Uniform manufacturing and dumbed-down sales distribution makes proper customization nearly impossible to deliver, even though most plans could be vastly improved with customization. Typically, large commissions are paid to 401(k) salespeople to push cookie cutter programs. Since most business owners and their accountants don't have the information to really know about more beneficial alternatives, the sale is easy.

The fact is that in many cases, business owners can vastly improve their situation, increase deductible contributions for themselves, cut substantial taxes, and often lower plan costs. And then there is the f-word. Fiduciary. (I always want to say that with a Curly Stooge lilt—fa-DOUCHE-i-ary!). These plans put a huge amount of liability on the business owner, who typically does not know how to offload it. This is killer important, but the stuff of another book. If the shoe fits, getting a second and expert opinion on this from someone who knows what they're doing can be a huge deal for you. This is because most owners underestimate the tremendous liability they have as plan trustees—for selection of vendor investment options and performance, employee education, plan costs, and more. ERISA (Employee Retirement Income Security Act of 1974) trustees—that's what you are if you are the 401 k trustee, dear business-owning bubba—carry the absolute highest, radioactive liability of all types of trustees—something to consider if your employees' spouses listen to some you-been-wronged class-action lawyer in the next market crash and decide to gather the pitchforks and come for you. I know you believe the "advisor" is on the hook for this. That's what they want you to think! If you want the lowdown on how exposed you are, email me for my whitepaper on this.

Many business owners with partners don't have smart transition agreements in place. In some cases, "stock redemption" style buy/sell plans (as opposed to "cross purchase" types) can result in needless taxation when one partner dies and the survivor(s) buy them out. Here's why: With a cross purchase, the (income) tax-free <u>life insurance proceeds</u> are paid to a partner, who then takes them and buys the deceased partner's stock. This purchase increases the surviving partner's tax basis, so when he eventually sells his share, capital gains are smaller and more of the sale proceeds are a tax-free return of basis. In contrast, with the stock redemption style, the insurance money goes directly to the company, wasting the tax-free benefit of the insurance and keeping the survivor's tax basis the same. If you have a buy/sell agreement, getting an expert opinion and updated review could save you a bundle.

If you have a business to sell, note this. When you negotiate to sell, you and the buyer are at cross-purposes when it comes to tax treatment. You want as much value allocated to goodwill, personal goodwill, and going concern value since this shifts more taxable value to lower-rate capital gains treatment, and less to highest rate ordinary income/earned income treatment. This is especially important to avoid since the proceeds from the business sale itself will probably push you into the highest bracket, if you are not already there. Under current law, this rate is pushing 40% and very likely going up, versus 20% for capital gains at the current rate, plus applicable NIIT (Net Investment Income Tax, an Obamacare extra capitial gains tax). On a $2,000,000 sale that is a savings of over $400,000! The buyer will attempt to shunt value to "earn-out" things like a personal consulting contract for you, fast depreciation period assets, and so on, to accelerate write-offs and manage their own tax position. Saves them, costs you. Beware!

The important thing to remember is that you must have strong and expert tax counsel during the negotiation process and not just after the sale. Like the buyer, you want to protect your own tax position and, once a deal is cut, it is much harder to finesse the tax angles. Higher taxes mean a much lower net on the business sale and the net is what you should be concerned with. Don't get infatuated with deal heat, only to find yourself with a tax nightmare later.

One final warning, really too important not to include. If you keep sloppy books—or don't keep books at all—invariably errors will creep in, expenses will be missed, and needless taxes will wallop you. To say nothing of being unprepared or even unpreparable should IRS come a callin'. We have seen instances where non-taxable loan proceeds (a couple hundred grand in one case) were carelessly added to the income statement instead of the balance sheet, overstating taxable profit by a huge amount. If we had not been called in to clean up the books and tax position on this case, they would have paid something like $100,000 in extra taxes, and no one—neither he nor his previous well-paid CPA—might ever have known. Unless the person doing your books really knows what they are doing and is very careful, you can really be getting soaked. Remember that tax accounting and "regular" financial accounting can have very different rules, and it can be better to run a set of tax books along with the regular books you use to steer the business the whole year rather than trying to "pull them together" months after the fact. Doing it right the first time usually costs less time, money, and taxes than letting things pile up to the fermentation point. Not Boss Hogg duplicitous books, two sets of legit books using different applicable rules. One provides management steering data, the other tax results.

This was a long and heady chapter, and I apologize! Much as I like to keep it clear and funny, taxes can be dry as dust. To keep it moving I've also not gone very deep on some of the strategies, but there should be enough for you to flag opportunities in your personal situation, to try and put a team together to study and smoke out big savings. As should be disgustingly clear by now, finding the right, competent team can be so difficult as to seem impossible, but is absolutely critical to your success! Be careful! Study the guidance in the finding advisors chapter, ask hard questions, and use your nose! And again, loads more on tax at the free fweibook.org site.

Notes

1. American Institute of Certified Public Accountants. "Statements on Standards for Tax Services No. 1, *Tax Return Positions*." Accounting Topics of Interest – Resources for Your Expertise. Accessed January 27, 2021. https://www.aicpa.org/interestareas/tax/resources/standardsethics/statementsonstandardsfortaxservices/downloadabledocuments/ssts-no.1-tax-return-positions.pdf.
2. Nitti, Tony. "Navigating the Real Estate Professional Rules." The Tax Adviser, March 1, 2017. https://www.thetaxadviser.com/issues/2017/mar/navigating-real-estate-professional-rules.html.
3. Internal Revenue Service. "Retirement Topics – Defined Benefit Plan Benefit Limits." Topics. Accessed January 27, 2021. https://www.irs.gov/retirement-plans/plan-participant-employee/retirement-topics-defined-benefit-plan-benefit-limits.
4. Internal Revenue Service. "Qualified Business Income Deduction." Tax Reform. Accessed January 27, 2021. https://www.irs.gov/newsroom/qualified-business-income-deduction.
5. Internal Revenue Service. "Home Office Deduction." Small Business and Self Employed. Accessed January 27, 2021. https://www.irs.gov/businesses/small-businesses-self-employed/home-office-deduction.

Converting Estate Tax to Family Wealth

Welcome back, children. We continue in the land of happy tax, the happy part being where we tell you how to use smart strategy to keep your family wealth. So back we bounce again to the outstretched hand of the Federal government, this time glistening with the convoluted sparkle of the Unified Transfer Tax. This, as you recall, is the part of the Code that tries to snatch a piece of every asset you try to give to another, either during life or after death. For the most part, the estate tax and gift tax parts work in parallel fashion, though they diverge occasionally. Let's drill down a bit on that concept, at the risk of being a trifle redundant. The basic premise is this: You can't beat the estate tax by giving your wealth to your kids before you die. If you try, you are subject to gift tax. While there are significant differences between estate and gift tax, they are collectively integrated in the Unified Transfer Tax which aims to take a piece of wealth you want to transfer to others, like your kids.

You can't win.

Well, actually, you can, if you figure out the maze and find the secret doorways leading to tax avoidance.

The primary concept for this is called the estate freeze. My seventeen year old loves Arnold Schwarzenegger as Mr. Freeze in the campy movie *Batman & Robin*. Use him as your emoji to stay ice, I mean crystal, clear on the concept.

Under current law, and for as far back as creaky professional memory stretches, there has been a threshold estate value level under which no Federal

J. Camarda et al., *The Financial Storm Warning for Investors*, https://doi.org/10.1007/978-3-030-77271-0_16

tax is imposed. (States often impose their own death taxes, but these variations are very situation-specific and beyond the scope of this brief, humble tome. But know that for many states—like NY—the estate tax can kick in at *much* lower wealth levels.) They call this the exemption amount, for the amount exempt from tax. Back in the day it was $600,000 per spouse, so if you worked the wickets right (not as simple as one might hope!) taxes were not imposed until a couple's estate value exceeded $1.2M.

Don't confuse this with the annual gift tax exclusions, which for 2021 is $15K, indexed for inflation going forward we may hope. That's the amount you can give—so long as the gift is structured and accounted for right—away each year without fear of gift tax or using any exemption up. That's $15K per donee (the person to whom a donor gives a gift) by the way, and if you're married it can double to $30K. Two kids and two spouse can gift $60K a year. Two kids and four grandkids boost it to $180K a year. Get the picture? It can really add up, but you have to absolutely give the money away with no personal interest strings to use it. It needs to be a present interest gift, the arcane definition of which I won't bore you with in *this* book.

Back to the exemption, which is the big gun. For 2021 until and unless the law changes (count on it!) the exemption is $11.7M per individual, a decent sum. Under existing law (don't count on this lasting very long!) the exemption reverts to $5M in 2026, plus some change for inflation. Not to put too fine a point on it, but current priorities of the Party in Power are to drop the exemption to $3M, plus for the first time I am aware of, impose a capital gains tax at death on top of the estate tax for especially fat cats. Other voices—and mounting fiscal pressures—argue for even lower threshold exemptions. But we covered all that scary stuff in Part I. Back to happy tax.

So the freeze reference refers to icing the exemption. In other words, freezing the estate value below the taxable amount. Remember the transfer tax is unified? So the exemption applies to gifts as well as estates. With a hypothetical exemption of $1M for an easy number, you could give away $500K during life, and leave $500K at death, and owe no tax. Get it? You add up the gifts and estate to calculate the unified taxable amount.

Time to trot out grandfather. Time-honored tax doctrine holds that actions taken under existing law are typically honored after the law changes. Of course, this is called grandfathering. New tax law is overwhelming prospective, applying only to future transactions after an effective date. Congress can do whatever it wants and the government has the guns (most of them anyway), but the imposition of tax hikes retroactively is awfully bad form, and in my view extremely unlikely. In other words, count on planning based on existing law to be grandfathered, and effective going forward, provided it is done right and timely. Did I mention I think we're running out of time? Note as of proof time (August 2021) Federal legislation is pending for a *retroactive* capital gains hike, as you no doubt know. Ain't law yet, and ain't no pending estate tax increase—yet. But the retroactive bit smells and sets a bad precedent. Estate tax savers, gather ye rosebuds, if you wait to finalize (not begin!) a plan until after some unknowable future back date gets inked, you are screwed. It is later than you think!

So let's pull this ice age together. If you give your wealth to wisely structured family trust and dot all the i's, you effectively freeze the estate. If you get $1M out with a $1M exemption, it is out of the estate tax arena forever, even though it may grow to $100M. Shazam. Under existing law as I write this, a couple can get $23.4M (2 x $11.7M) out this way. Actually, you can get quite a bit more out using slick discounting techniques, such as structuring the trusts and transactions to diffuse control and restrict marketability, the rationale being if Dad gives me something I can't sell or vote on, it ain't worth nearly as much as if I could cash it all in and split for Vegas. Drat, Daddy! Properly structured, valuation discounts on the order of 30% are not unusual, giving an effectively freezable budget of some $33M (2 x $11.4/0.7) per couple. Gohhhhhh-ley!

"That's great Jeff," you mumble as you spit on the floor, "but did you say I have to *give it away?*"

You caught that, huh?

Perhaps you were planning on using that wealth for a comfy retirement, and screw the kids if it means living in poverty? You selfish so-and-so, you.

This minor sticking point has long be the bane of (what I consider) bush-league estate planning. The ubiquitous GRATs (grantor retained annuity trusts) used for this purpose have a major flaw—you really give the property away, and can't eat it—except for a token annuity income payment (which is another way to get a valuation discount, but clearly one I don't like). Also popular in the minors (in my humble view, dear colleagues who take another view!) are so-called skip trusts (generation skipping transfer trusts) that typically enable parents to disinherit their children (wealthy or otherwise) and pass the dough directly to the grandkids, thus skipping the tax at the kids' (but not the parents' or grandkids') generational level. Skip trusts' genesis comes from the generation skipping transfer tax, an additional estate tax intended to be imposed where parents give so much to their kids that it makes sense to skip a generation with the surplus wealth. Want to skip the kids on some wealth to avoid estate tax at the kids' level? Not so fast! IRS sayeth: pay extra generation skipping transfer tax! This is what skip trusts are intended to manage, and there are legitimate applications of these for really wealth folks

($35M + +) for whom my F-BOT and other techniques below are powerful but insufficient, but such readers will be rare enough that we won't trudge through that particular swamp here. Check out the classes at fweibook.org if you want more info. This applies when there's so much wealth—or planning was delayed so long—that there's no hope of getting it all out under the exemption, and some tax must be paid. Still, in my view dynasty planning—discussed below—is way superior to skip techniques for most wealthy families. If you think you're in the skip category, drop me a line and I'll get you some specific material. And don't you DARE buy life insurance as an "estate tax plan." Back when I was a commission slug, a lawyer working for a life company teaching "advanced planning" joked "the definition of estate planning? the orderly conversion of estate assets into commission dollars!" Beware! But the real icing on the estate freeze cake comes from having it and eating it too. Skips don't do that well. I know you love your kids, and want to save them as much tax as you can. But's it's your money, by golly, and you want to enjoy it. I feel the same way! I like my comfort. So the real magic of estate tax planning is figuring a way to beat the tax, but still enjoy and control the property.

If you feel the same way, you're going to love the tricks I'm about to share.

Before doing so, I want to spend a little time on family limited partnerships (FLPs), or "flips" in the planners' vernacular. These have been largely supplanted by stuff like the F-BOT, but we still see quite a few of them, and new ones do still have application in the right fact patterns. But these are rare, and I suspect most FLPs are created by practitioners that have not kept up with modern planning, out of moribund inertia. The kind of traditionalists who still put Social Security numbers in wills (which eventually become public documents!) If you must have a FLP, these days, you'll want to use a partnership-elected LLC to avoid the pants-down liability of being unlimited general partners, like old or clumsily crafted ones often make ma and pa. And we still see quite a few of these obsolete and needlessly risky ones created on fresh paper.

FLPs can be really nifty devices to both insulate assets from creditors as well as save hefty amounts of estate tax. They work best for illiquid things like closely held businesses ("C" but not "S" corps), farms, and real estate, but you can mix in other assets like marketable securities as well. If you use real estate, you eventually give up any tax shelter from losses, but by this point your properties are probably fully depreciated, and you are making money hand over fist, anyway. Here's the nuts and bolts. You form a FLP and transfer the desired assets into it. This is not a taxable event since you effectively still own—and pay income taxes on—the assets and the earnings. Within the

FLP, you allocate value to "units"—which are kind of like corporate stock shares—with most of the value going to limited partnership units, and just a touch—but at least 1% and better more—going to general partnership units. Initially you, and your spouse, own all the units. The general partnership units carry all control of the property, including the right to distribute income in any fashion that you as general partner see fit. The general partner gets to run the business or manage the assets, to distribute income or not, and to pay herself reasonable compensation for doing so. As a practical matter, the general partner can pay virtually all income to himself, if he chooses. The limited partners, on the other hand, have no control, and no right to income unless the general partner says so. Note that the limited partners may have to pay income tax on their "share" of the partnership income, even though none may be paid out to them. Making distributions to them in the amount of the tax owed can alleviate this, if desired. It's good for the kids, so hush their mouths.

Initially, you and your spouse own all units, both general and limited. The default plan is often to gift out enough limited partnership units each year to maximize your annual gift tax exclusion, which in this case will amount to more than $15,000 per year per donee. You'll actually get more because of discounting. Why? Limited partnership units can look so unattractive as an investment: you get discounts for lack of control, and lack of marketability and illiquidity—can't sell 'em—who would be crazy enough to buy?—and can't cash 'em in. So effectively, you transfer far more in underlying value than the $15,000 per donee per year that you claim. How much more? It varies from case to case, but discounts increasing the tax-free gifts by as much as 50% are not unheard of (though pretty aggressive), though 25–35% might be more reasonable. Of course, gifting big chunks by using up your unified transfer tax exemption is faster and makes more sense in the current environment, since that number is expected to shrink big time. At the end of the typical FLP rainbow, when done, you've gifted out tax free up to 99% of the partnership value on a deeply discounted basis, and hung onto the 1% that entitles you to all income and iron-fisted control. Plus with the help of Mr. Freeze, you've gotten all growth out of the estate, into the tax-hands of your children.

At death, if the partnership agreement is so drawn, the partnership can dissolve, producing clear, unencumbered title of assets to your kids. Or you can pass control to a designated child to serve as a de facto "trustee" by acting as general partner, managing the assets for himself and his siblings. You have nearly as much flexibility as with a trust. All partnership assets, and all growth on them, will have escaped gift and estate tax, if the estate is not too awfully large, and you have begun early enough. The only downside is that the capital gains torch has been passed to your kids, because your basis—on gifted units only, not any that pass at death—carries over to them. For this and other similar gifting techniques, you'll miss avoiding capital gains tax since the tax basis won't be stepped up to the value at death. In many cases, this is a small price to pay, and with the rumblings of eliminating the step up now shaking the halls of Congress, it may not matter anyway. In fact, this may be the only way to beat—or at least defer past the date of death—the capital gains tax. Ditto for F-BOTs. There are other ways to control income taxes like the capital gains tax, but you're in the wrong chapter. FLPs also can keep the creditors at bay, since no one wants to own a unit in another family's limited partnership, and the creditor, even if he takes the limited units, has no control and no claim on the underlying assets—but gets to pay the annual income tax. What to do with the units? Can't sell them. Can't demand income or liquidation. In fact, were the units to be accepted as part of a judgment, the creditor might find itself paying tax on cash that it would never receive, because the owners of the limited partnership units must pay tax on their share of income, whether distributed or not! How would you like to pay tax on the money that someone else is using to tour the world? The creditor protection is very poison-pill effective.

There's a whole menagerie of weird-sounding estate planning tools I won't bore you overmuch with. Buzzwords abound. Besides GRATs, there are GRITs and GRUTs, CRUTs, CRATs and more. As Captain Ron might have said, "this is the land of voodoo and hoodoo and all kinds of weird....stuff." These have limited application in limited, special situations, but I generally don't have much use for most of it and don't think it's worth your while to get into. I prefer what I feel are far more effective techniques. But before getting to my favorite tax control techniques, we need to talk life insurance. At this point in your life you may not need it, and the needless sale of high-commission, cash-value-type policies is a real pet peeve of mine, knowing the business like I do being a reformed life insurance man myself. Believe me, I can tell you some real horror stories! So beware—most life is sold for the benefit of the agent, not the insured! Still, if you have life insurance, you need to know the death benefit will be included in your taxable estate if you have any "incidents of ownership" or real control over the policy. I know the agent said it was tax free, and probably even believed it, but that's only for income tax on the death benefit, not estate tax on the death benefit or even income tax on the cash value buildup if you aim to make withdrawals. So if you have life insurance, be sure to get the death benefit out of your taxable estate. The knee-jerk method for this is the old ILIT (irrevocable life insurance trust), which properly crafted can be a real tax savings wonder. There are lots of other ways to get it out, like outright giving it to your kids or using more sophisticated trust planning. Just be sure it's on your planning radar so the death benefit is out of your estate!

Let's talk just a bit about the venerable step up. Here we manage to avoid the capital gains tax when we transfer property at death. This is because the basis—the amount we paid for the property, less any depreciation taken—is stepped-up to its value on the date of death (or to the alternative estate valuation date, if used. Forget I mentioned it). Cash, of course, has the same value before and after death. But what about that rental house you bought for a song 20 years ago, and have depreciated down to zero basis? Or the shares in Walmart you bought in 1965, which are now worth a gazillion times what you paid? You have probably kept them long long time because you were reluctant to pay the tax, but under the law existing as I write this, the capital gain vanishes at death. So even though the market value on the date of death must be included in your estate, at least the capital gains demon goes away. A good planning technique can be to leave highly appreciated property to pass at death—in the estate not frozen outside of it—and to minimize or plan for the payment of estate taxes using another method. If you sell the property while alive and hang onto the proceeds, you pay the capital gains tax plus the estate tax, not a happy outcome. If you give the appreciated property away during life, your basis also passes to the donee, and so does the capital gains specter (though at the donee's tax rate). Harken unto this next point. This basis step-up does not apply to lifetime gifts. When you make a gift, the donee (the person to whom you give the property) takes over your basis. If zero, then the donee has to pay capital gains tax on the entire sale proceeds if he gets rid of it. But the amount of the gift tax—imposed if the gift's value exceeds the annual exclusion amounts—is figured on the fair market value as of the date of the gift. So here we have the unhappy likelihood of both taxes on the same property. This can be a real issue in GRAT-land, boys and girls, so if you go there gift that GRAT before you see much appreciation in the rapidly-appreciating assets that are the best grist for GRATs and their ilk. So better, if you make gifts, to use things like non-highly appreciated property or cash, which do not transfer carrying a capital gains "tax lien." Be careful about this, especially if the potential size of your estate is in taxable territory. Even something so innocent as adding someone's name to a deed (except for spouses, since the unlimited marital deduction applies both to gifts and bequests) may ultimately impose some gift tax. Remember that lifetime gifts over the annual exclusion amounts must be tallied when your estate is figured, where they will at least burn up some of your unified credit, which is another term for the exemption (or more precisely the saved tax on the exemption amount).

You must bear this in mind as I roll out my favorite estate tax control techniques. Since they involve lifetime gifts to conjure up Mr. Freeze, you will lose any potential step up. This means your heirs need hang onto the property long long time, so as not to sell and invoke the tax, or use income tax control strategies to mitigate the income tax if you want to sell. Of these we have magnificent dozens. Remember enough offsetting deductions will wipe out capital gains tax concerns. All things considered, I think this is a very attractive tradeoff, and a no-brainer if the step up is legislated away.

So we enter the magical kingdom of F-BOT land. I am pretty sure I coined this to mean Family Bank Ongoing Trust. It's my team's enriched variation of the more generic SLAT, or spousal lifetime income trust. From this you clearly infer you need a spouse—at least for a very short time!—to make it work best, though we have designed effective F-BOTs using the F-BIT variant for non-spousal situations. Besides doubling the exemption to into the twenty-millions before discounting, we need a spouse for two other critical reasons, besides warmth and comfort. The first is to get easiest access to the money. The second is for trust the structural asymmetry required to make SLATs sing.

Here's how it works. We, after deep and careful consideration of all the angles with an erudite planner, design two irrevocable trusts that are enough structurally different in terms as to not be reciprocal. They can't have mirror image provisions, but can be similar enough this won't be a livability issue. You probably won't even notice. Then you fund the trust with different assets. Mom puts in the real estate empire. Dad contributes the family business and the stock accounts. You get the picture. You may have to do some title shuffling—converting joint accounts into either hers or his, for instance—before funding the trusts. You will also need to get bona fide third-party valuations for the file, and file gift tax returns to complete the process, so don't dawdle if you fear an imminent law change! The gift tax return—Form 709—is a critical piece. Mom gets to be trustee of the trust for Dad's benefit, and vice versa. Dad wants a new car? Mom cuts the check. Gets to be real easy to live with. The kids—and future descendants—are the beneficiaries after Mom and Dad pass.

So what have we accomplished? We freeze the estate, and get up to about $33M out of the taxable environment by using our asset-discounted unified exemption to avoid gift tax. The property ain't Mom's and Dad's anymore, but they retain a bundle of rights close enough to actual ownership that they won't care much. They can control the assets, spend as they wish, pretty much do what they want. When the first spouse goes, a friendly trustee takes over to keep the assets gushing for the surviving spouse. This trustee succession bit is very important, though beyond the scope of this girthy book. You want to write the trust carefully and with enough protections and teeth that the surviving spouse has enough soft control to not risk being unpampered. This is a really cool outcome, and far superior to the old FLPs in my view. Taxes avoided, money close at hand.

Using dynasty provisions, we can pretty much avoid estate tax further out than your blurry mind can visualize. Since the law against perpetuities ("…legal rule in the Anglo-American common law that prevents people from using legal instruments (usually a deed or a will) to exert control over the ownership of private property for a time long beyond the lives of people living at the time the instrument was written" – thank you Wikipedia!) was repealed in most states, these things can go on long past the time machines rule the earth or humanity heads to the stars. In my adopted home of Florida (left high-tax N.Y. in my 20s), we can go out 360 years, long enough to make my head spin. So to avoid tax down the mists of time, we use the same technique we did for Ma and Pa. The kids get a bundle of rights so close to ownership it hardly matters, but they don't actually own it! Since only owned assets are in estates to be taxed at death, this beats the tax as far out as you care to gaze. To be clear—kids control assets, but don't own them to the extent they are in their estates at death. In the words of a great planner, "own nothing, control everything!" Not much difference in using the wealth, really. For most families, way better than those byzantine skip trusts, FLPs, and other oft-misprescribed gobbledygook. For those a bit nervous about the stability of their marriage, note that deft planners can build in lots of post-nups safeguards, without ever using that word and pissing off your already unstable spouse!

By the way, whenever I hear "dynasty" I remember a multi-level-marketing upstart named that which was nipping at Amway's heels back in the day, which clients would occasionally ask me to research. Some of the Amway folks referred to it as "die-nasty!" Charming blokes.

For the single fat cat who won't consider an economic marriage of convenience to double their exemption, there is a somewhat less attractive alternative. I call it a Family Bank Individual Trust, or F-BIT. In this case we set up a so-called grantor or defective trust—these confusing terms just meaning the trust is taxed to the client (the grantor, or founder of the trust) instead of the trust being a distinct taxable entity. Another word on defective trusts. The trust is "defective" only in that regard—it is defective as a discrete taxable entity—which is good cause trust income tax rates are sky-high. This trust, like the F-BOT, is irrevocable, so craft carefully! One way to play it: The grantor then sells assets—on super EZ terms!—to the new trust, which pays him or her lifetime income. We get The Freeze, and income access, but less control than for F-BOTs. Mail order spouses, anyone?

There you have the keys to the kingdom! Enough tax-free dancing room to found or perpetuate your own Great Family, you Medici you! Just be sure to get it done right! Read the chapter on finding good advisors twice. With irrevocability risks and the very high tax stakes, you want to be sure this does not get screwed up—and since you probably won't be alive to tell the difference, make sure you ride that long thin good tail of the bell curve to six-sigma excellence! For more, check out the advanced estate tax control classes at fweibook.org.

Controlling Other Expensive Taxes

A while ago, I founded another firm called TaxMaster. I am so proud of the logo I designed; I want to share it with you. Looks like this:

That's Ben Franklin, of course, for whose name (and wisdom) I have a special affinity. My second middle name is Franklin (first is Michael, and no snickering!), after my maternal grandfather, Franco Traina, and my Dad's long love of American history, which he taught passionately for many decades, before wearing it out later in life, and switching to teaching European history, which he came to find more meaningful and interesting, and taught with profound gusto until retiring at the tender age of 89. Dad's given name, BTW, is Rosario, anglicized before my birth to Russell.

Anyway, old Ben was as sharp as they come. He is said[1] to have said, in 1789 in a letter to Jean-Baptiste Leroy, that "Our new Constitution is now established, and has an appearance that promises permanency; but in

© The Author(s), under exclusive license to Springer Nature
Switzerland AG 2021
J. Camarda et al., *The Financial Storm Warning for Investors*,
https://doi.org/10.1007/978-3-030-77271-0_17

this world nothing can be said to be certain, except death and taxes." Many forget the constitutional context of this quote and infer the inevitability of taxes, instead of the intended constant of change. He is also misquoted as saying "A penny saved is a penny earned" probably derived[2] from the 1737 Poor Richard's Almanack's "A penny saved is two pence clear," which basically means savings beat the pants off mindless consumption on credit—better a pence in the pants than spending a penny down and another on EZ credit.

Why, dear reader, do I wander so far afield?

When I founded TaxMaster, my muse was to meld these concepts together. TaxMaster's slogan is something Franklin never said, but I wish he had had— "taxes saved is wealth earned!" Or better, taxes saved is wealth created. Like nothing else, tax smarts can create fortune out of thin air. Nothing else comes close.

As I have propounded often in this book, I believe tax savvy to be the master wealth skill. For those who already have a significant income or net worth, nothing can blast the wealth rocket higher than smart tax advice, fleeting will-o'-the-wisp though it may be to find.

Despite the grandiose beginning, this will be a short chapter. Taxes are ubiquitous burrs in the saddles of the well-heeled, but we hit the main ones in the last couple of chapters. I can't cover them all in the book, but here are a couple more worth shooting at. Apply the same logical process, and all kinds of taxes can be whittled.

Let's start with sales tax. Nettlesome on most purchases, these can get really big on stuff like cars, boats, RVs, and other major purchases such, perhaps, as art or antiques.

Sales tax is imposed at the state level (mostly) and a go-to gusher of fugetaboutit revenue. For this, as with most tax, a careful study of the law often yields amazing strategies to avoid it.

I live in Florida, land of the mega-yacht. You see lots of these babies "flagged" in exotic lands like the Caymans, and lately Jamaica, an emerging sales tax haven. Why? To beat the Florida sales tax or the de facto reciprocal sales taxes of most other states. Flagging just means registering and titling the vessel in the sunny island of choice. While this strategy can beat the sales tax, it also makes life complicated, since the boat can't stay long in Florida without leaving US waters periodically and reapplying for a US cruise permit. Fuel and crew costs add up! And believe me, the Florida Dept of Revenue agents prowl the docks of the marinas, looking for violations with sales tax nets at the ready.

While this approach is de rigueur, it always seemed crazy to me. Here's why.

When clients have approached my team about sales tax control, we researched the Florida statutes and discovered that for vehicles purchased for leasing activities, the sales tax is due on the rental or lease amount, not the purchase price. The statute is silent on reasonableness of the rent amount—the legislators forgot to scribe a formula linking the value of the property for and the lease terms. Tax codes are replete with such unintended consequences, and smart planners drive Mack trucks through such "loopholes." So a business owner sets up a leasing company, buys a Lamborghini, with Rolls, and leases it to herself. Florida Dept of Revenue issues the tag and title in leaseco's name, and presto, no sales tax. No questions asked. Just a yawn over a routine transaction. Client pays maybe $1,000 a year for the rent and pays $70 in sales tax to drive a $300,000 car—on which the sales tax would have been $30,000. She owns the company that owns the car or boat or plane or RV bus or whatever. Titled and kept right here in the good ole US of A, with no midnight runs to the Bahamas to beat the revenuers. You just need to learn and follow the letter of the law. Now, I can't tell you how many folks have taken umbrage to this, not believing it, or morally pounding their chests that it just ain't right. But "right" is in the heart of the beholder. Legal is all that is required.

This is a real critical point in all tax work. The "bible" of practice before the IRS is called "Circular 230."[3] With regard to client tax work, the following is illuminating. Thou shalt not take a position that " (A) Lacks a reasonable basis; (B) Is an unreasonable position… not advise a client to take a position…unless the position is not frivolous.…A practitioner may not advise a client (in a way) … that demonstrates an intentional disregard of a rule or regulation unless the practitioner also advises the client to submit a document that evidences a good faith challenge to the rule or regulation…"

Sorry, and that's the Cliff Notes version. The actual document runs some forty-four fine-print pages. But did you notice something? It doth not say "you must follow the black and white letter of the law." Why? When it comes to tax, there really is none. The Internal Revenue Code (and most other tax codes) is a seething pile of hot contradictions. Skillful practitioners weave applicable bits of law into reasonable positions that save client's tax. Provided you have a reasonable basis, you are acting legitimately. Just don't be frivolous. That's not a bad as fraudulent (talking jail time for that!) but it's still just plain stupid!

Let's take property tax, like on real estate. These are the taxes Tony Soprano's consigliere lamented, "yeah, and you gotta pay *those*." As opposed to the income taxes they illegally evaded. And while you have to pay *some*, you don't necessarily have to pay the number on your annual bill. Detail courtesy of Adam Rosenfield, who on my TaxMaster team has helped save money for clients for years and with me shaves my personal real estate portfolio bill pretty much each and every dang year.

Most taxing counties or other municipalities use something called a computer mass appraisal system. This process takes a base assessment value and ratchets it up (or very rarely down) annually using a pretty dumb algorithm. Typically, no human inspects the property for fair value. The machine just spins the wheel and spits out a bill. Problems with this approach? Well, the base number—lost in the mists of time—could be just plumb crazy wrong. Increasing it by x% each year won't make it any more right. Second, the percentage annual adjustment may be completely wrong for the situs of your property. In my neck of Florida, houses at the beach appreciate a whole lot faster than those next to the interstate on in the bad part of town.

Don't squawk, don't save. I've personally gotten millions of assessed value off my holdings, and we revisit for opportunity every year. Significant reductions of taxable value are commonplace if you try properly. Most people—or clumsy practitioners—who try this start at the end. In Florida, "magistrates" on "Value Adjustment Boards" are charged with making things fair—if you complain. Most of these folks do an honest job, but it is still a very gray area and your reasonable position may differ from theirs. Some outliers are pigheaded. I've personally appeared (when I was young and tender and ignorant) before some jokers who "ruled" that "the law doesn't' require I drop the value, boy, and I won't!" I call this the bad judge syndrome. Remember Jimmy Reed's *When You're Hot, You're Hot*! ("he let my friends go free/threw the book at me!"). Avoid playing in that sandbox.

Better, as Adam puts it, to "take two bites at the apple." Smarter to start with the property appraiser, whose job it is to fairly and accurately assess property. Our team gets value reductions most often at this stage. Faster and cheaper for all—including the appraiser! With regard to date of assessment which is typically January 1st of each tax year, present reasonable condition, cap rate (return on investment, relationship of net rent to value) and comparables arguments, and often you will walk away happy, while holding the second bite of the Value Adjustment Board (or whatever it's called in your local) apple in reserve.

Obviously, there are many variations on this basic process across the fruited plain, but from the jurisdictions we've probed, it's pretty consistently done this way. Happy hunting!

The last section in this not-so-short-as-I'd-like (and potentially endless) chapter is on sate and municipal income taxes. Like those inflicted on the pal of mine paying city, state, and Federal income taxes, and whose high dollar NYC CPA had not taken (or remembered) Tax Deductible Retirement Plans 101.

For you burdened many, please re-read the income tax chapter here in Part II, for much of that wisdom will apply in droves for you.

Beyond this, you have two heavy artillery pieces to ponder.

One is changing residency to a no-tax state like Florida or Nevada. From our friends at nolo.com: "currently, six states – Nevada, Ohio, South Dakota, Texas, Washington, and Wyoming—do not have a corporate income tax. However, four of those states—Nevada, Ohio, Texas, and Washington—do have some form of gross receipts tax on corporations. Moreover, five of those states—Nevada, South Dakota, Texas, Washington, and Wyoming—as well as Alaska and Florida currently have no personal income tax. Individuals in New Hampshire and Tennessee are only taxed on interest and dividend income."[4]

Such mumbo jumbo induces much dancing room for reasonable positions to avoid state income taxes. Because of the endless permutations and need to research individual states' tax laws, we will fly above the weeds. But this can be easier than you think! Like changing residency to a no-tax state. Florida[5] has some simple steps, like getting a driver's license, registering vehicles, registering to vote, and so on, not all of which are required. The acid test (and document all for your old high tax state is bound to howl, slather, and demand proof!) is residency for the majority of the year—six months and a day. Believe it or not, there are cottage industries whose only mission is helping you prove just that, down to mailing addresses and cell phones.

For retirees this is simple. For business owners it is feasible. For those who physically work in high-tax states, we have more of a challenge, though much more opportunity in the post-COVID work-from-home (servicing Mass clients from our home office in sunny Florida?) world.

Another option for business owners to consider. Combined with estate planning techniques learnt in other chapters, consider shifting business value to a F-BOT-style trust beneficiaried to children or others in low/no tax states. This would take some deep thought, with the objective of paying tax on your reasonable W2 comp—but not on the torrent of S-Corp or whatever profits—in your high tax state. This is income splitting of the highest order, but certainly feasible if you have the right brains on your team!

Sadly, cherished reader, it is time to leave the wonderland of tax and get on to other critical countermeasures areas.

Remember! Wealth management is a tapestry! All the threads must sing to make it beautiful! And don't forget the (still!) free classes at fweibook.org.

Notes

1. Pirie, Madsen. "Death and Taxes." *Adam Smith Institute* (blog). November 13, 2009.   https://www.adamsmith.org/blog/death-and-taxes#:~:text=It%20was%20on%20November%2013th,%2C%20except%20death%20and%20taxes.%E2%80%9D.
2. "7 Things Benjamin Franklin Never Said." The Franklin Institute. https://www.fi.edu/benjamin-franklin/7-things-benjamin-franklin-never-said#:~:text=%E2%80%9CA%20penny%20saved%20is%20a,saved%20is%20two%20pence%20clear.%E2%80%9D.
3. Department of the Treasury, "Regulations Governing Practice before the Internal Revenue Service," (2014). https://www.irs.gov/pub/irs-pdf/pcir230.pdf.
4. Steingold, David M. "Nevada State Business Income Tax: What kind of tax will you owe on Nevada business income?" Nolo, June 18, 2018. https://www.nolo.com/legal-encyclopedia/nevada-state-business-income-tax.html#:~:text=As%20just%20mentioned%2C%20Nevada%20is,important%20state%20taxes%20at%20all.
5. "Florida Residency." State of Florida. https://www.stateofflorida.com/residency/.

Investment Strategies to Prosper in the Storm

Once upon a time, I was a hard scientist. I don't mean crusty (OK maybe that too!), but rather a physical scientist.

I was actually thought a rather brilliant inorganic chemist by my undergraduate professors. I still remember a poster in the Chem building that read: "If it stinks, it's chemistry. If it's green and slimly, it's biology. If it doesn't make any sense, it's physics. But if it stinks, is green and slimy, and *still* doesn't make any sense, it's psychology!" (I did take psych and sociology too, for balance). Remember psychology is a social science—you will see why!!

I was trained with scientific structure and rigor. The scientific world is ordered, predicable, and repeatable. An electron volt, by golly, is an e-volt $(1.602 \times 10^{-19}J$—thanks Google!) the multiverse around. Spectra from hydrogen atoms are fingerprint-specific here, on Pluto, or in Andromeda. One plus one is two. All this stuff adds up the same every time, and is laser-flat consistent in hard science. (Of course, even this is ever more doubtful as "real" scientists slurp ever more deeply of the nothingness of the quantum soup, but I am out of metaphoric rope.) These are unshakable laws of the universe.

Not so in the social sciences like economics (dismal for a reason!), or in my own Ph.D. areas of finance. Social scientists think and act like hard scientists, believe in rigor, and seek logic and order in their research. Many if not most believe they capture it. But they are many of them deceived, for it remains green and slimy, and quite squishy. I was among the greediest Kool-Aid guzzlers, with my hard science background and deep CFA® schooling

© The Author(s), under exclusive license to Springer Nature Switzerland AG 2021
J. Camarda et al., *The Financial Storm Warning for Investors*,
https://doi.org/10.1007/978-3-030-77271-0_18

in Warren Buffett/Columbia Business School fundamentalism and fair valuation. I did the math like a crackerjack, but don't really believe overmuch in it anymore.

Wither we wander with this, you wonder? Because I have come to believe a lot of what you read about investment best practices is misguided at best, and can really come back to bite you. Most financial and investment theories assume precision, and rationality and quantitative valuations. Social scientists apply hard science methodology and believe they discover repeatable financial principals and laws. But stocks ain't electron volts, and people are not robotically identical hydrogen atoms.

I spent a lot of time in Part I bashing Nobel Prize-grade theories like rational expectations, modern portfolio theory, and the efficient market hypotheses (yes, there are several), so I won't scorch the same earth anew. These theories—from which I had to be dragged kicking and screaming from after my hard science background and long financial training from CFP®, ChFC®, and CFA® through masters and doctorate degrees—assume hard links between financial data and investment values. P/E ratios, dividend yields, convergence to means, and valuations based on discounted cash flows and profitability analyses imply a certainty of valuation only occasionally disrupted by market manias and panics. The University of Chicago-school mantra that "there is information in prices" implies a predictive value I have come to believe is at best elusive and at worst illusory.

All this mumbo jumbo (sorry to use the term yet again, but Dr. Evil's a favorite of mine) describes what we in the trade call fundamental analysis. This approach is numerical-data based, like the above and more, using debt to book, debt coverage, and all kinds of other accounting-based metrics and perspectives.

The other school is technical analysis. This is the art of inferring market behavior based on charts. Back in the day—lasting for decades for me—I would ridicule such as being as baseless, and subjective, as using astrology to divine stock moves, or casting the chicken bones by light of silvery moon.

No more. I have truly come to appreciate that technical analysis—the so-called tactical approach—does a remarkably good job of capturing market sentiment, buy/sell trends, and the overall supply/demand condition of stock and other investment markets.

Because that's, me buckos, the real force which determines stock prices. Not the pseudo hard science of the fundamental school, but what real world, sweaty, monkey "logic", irrational, poorly informed, oft-stupid, greedy, and fearful human creatures feel decide and do.

Supply and demand have nothing to do with the Shiller CAPE ratio, beta-weights, or companies' projected profitability. This does not mean fundamentals don't matter—they are critically important and should be considered and born in mind. But they rarely drive prices in the hot/cold market near term—fear and greed do. While long-term averages that revert to the mean over long periods may track fair valuations well, the short-term chop—crazy runs up and free-fall plunges—can wipe out your accounts, eviscerate your returns, and leave you high and dry. Why?

It has only to do with "I want!" or "I don't want!" With buy/buy/buy "I don't care the price it's going UP!" or "sell before it becomes worthless!" Take wisdom from The Great Lewbowski—"sometimes you eat the bear, sometimes the bear eats you!".

These are the true forces that drive the market. If the crazy froth of the 2020 and 2021 markets—sky-high stock prices while the world teetered on the doorstep of economic doom—doesn't prove this to you, nothing will. And don't think that highbrow investment pros are any less susceptible to the fear/greed emotional feedback loop than the Robin Hood/Gamestop masses. Or that the fancy program trading algorithms written by humans are not infected with biological decision rule bias.

An important overall point is that it is possible to consistently beat the market. Just because the textbooks say it's impossible doesn't mean it can't be done. As with most things, superior results come from study, intelligence, discipline, and skill. In the treacherous markets I foresee ahead, this ability will be supremely important in making returns and preserving wealth. Another important point is a dash of cold water on index mania. I know "everybody knows" 1) you can't time the market (false!) and 2) you can't beat the market by sector or stock picking (false!), so you are better off just buying cheap index funds (maybe not!). Index funds can be cheap (and also crazy expensive for the same index depending on the brand—better check!), but they can expose you to dangerous concentration and dummy risks. The addition of Tesla to the S&P 500 in late 2020 is a great example of both. For one, adding a bemouth like Tesla—market cap of nearly two-thirds of a trillion dollars—gives you a very lopsided exposure to this stock. Since most indexes are market-cap-weighted, you have way more Tesla than of smaller stocks. The bigger the total value of traded stock in a company, the more of your S&P index dollar is invested in it relative to others—you are NOT evenly divided and diversified among 500 stocks! When Tesla was added, its market cap exceeded the next biggest nine carmakers combined![1] Index investors have a very big bet on this arguably nose-bleed overvalued stock. That's the concentration risk. On the other hand, the price of Tesla keeps soaring well beyond all reasonable valuation metrics. That's the torpedos-be-damned BUY/BUY/BUY risk.

The dummy risk is index investors can wind up owning the stock at puffed up prices after smart traders buy cheap in anticipation of mega index fund buying. From a fellow *Forbes* contributor: "this creates an opportunity for active investors to take advantage of the index-funds' lack of flexibility. Once the announcement of Tesla's forthcoming inclusion in the index is made public, the "mechanical buying" that index-tracking funds will be forced to carry out becomes in effect a fait accompli. It is a certainty that the passive funds will be forced to buy $50 Bn, $80 Bn, perhaps $100 Bn worth of Tesla (depending on the share price on the effective date). With that knowledge, active investors can start to position themselves to profit from this surge in involuntary demand. They can buy at the November price and hope to sell to the captive buyers at the December price."[2] We in fact did this at my firm…and it peaked 27% higher after the index funds loaded up; we sold half but then rode the trend-train a few more stops before unloading the rest. Note that from a fundamental rational expectations perspective, Tesla was and still is way overvalued. The stock was and is crazy-priced based on all my fundamental training. No rational investor should want it. But we made a real nice, quick hit riding the technical trend, just like the textbooks and buy and hold Kool-Aid says can't be done.

My objective in this chapter is twofold. I wanted to impress on you the basics and value of technical analysis, which, I think, is especially critical to protect you as the stock markets float up into space. I hope I have done that. At the end of the chapter, I'll share some technical analysis basics for those who want to try to learn themselves, or at least tell if a prospective advisor's blowing crack smoke. These techniques can be amazingly powerful and applicable to virtually any market, from motor oil to cryptocurrency. The candlestick system you'll see later was actually developed by Japanese rice traders in the nineteenth century and is quite sophisticated, a virtual I Ching of market divination. The technical analysis school attempts to discern overall market sentiment and direction by integrating and visualizing price movements as representative of collective market participants' thinking. If you think—and this is an admitted stretch—of the myriad human and computer market players as cells or nodes in an integrated brain or decision process directing investment price movements, then technicals are a method not only to read this mind but to profit by anticipating it.

My second chapter objective is to offer some suggestions for asset classes that seem to have good upside and inflation protection to profit in the expected storm conditions ahead. We'll get into that now.

If we assume inflation, borrowing money at today's fixed rates to leverage and invest makes good sense. Getting fixed rates are important—if inflation rages, interest rates will rise with a vengeance, and variable rate borrowers will find rising payments chewing through their net worth lunches. So why borrow fixed? If you can lock in low—like I just did at 3.4% on some commercial real estate and 2.25% on some residential—and inflation comes roaring back, you repay the debt with increasingly cheaper dollars. In other words, your debt goes down in value in real value terms. This is like monetizing your own debt, which I referred to as the banana republic solution in Part I. By definition, inflated dollars are less valuable. With fixed interest, your payment does not go up. So you get to pay off the debt with payments that actually decline over time. That 3.4%, by the way, was a rate accommodation on an existing 4.1% mortgage. All I had to do was ask. No refi, just a rate modification. For a $5K fee, I'll save some $10K a year on interest for the five years left on the note. No fuss, no muss. The bank is happy to keep the note. But you have to ask! Since I expect to be able to make far more than the tax-deductible 3.4% cost of the money, I am very happy to a borrower be. The 2.25% was a refi with another lender because the replaced bank wouldn't play ball on the old 3.85% loan. So I switched. By the way, if I'd had time I would have tried to place the debt privately by running classified ads in the WSJ like I recently did with some rental property I want to sell. Demand for rentals—and even ultra low interest rate debt—is fierce in the early 2020s.

If in inflationary times it is better to a borrower be, the flipside is you don't want to be a lender since you are the one taking the incredibly shrinking payments. That makes bonds denominated in an inflating currency bad. Remember as a bond investor, you are actually a lender. By the same logic, you don't want to be selling assets like real estate or businesses by holding paper, especially at fixed rates. Even variable rates will merely pace, but not beat inflation. Fixed rates are death to lenders.

And God help you, lest demons trash you, if you lock in shrinking lifetime payments by buying an annuity! At least when rates are low and at risk of shooting up.

Another danger area is go-go high growth stocks, as most tech is hoped to be. The reason is so much of a current growth stock's value is based, from a fundamental standpoint, on future earnings. To collapse these earnings into the current stock price, we discount them using a de facto interest rate. The higher the discount rate, the lower the value of the stock as represented by the discounted present value of the future cash flows, representing the growth stock's profits. If interest is 0%, a dollar in ten years is the same as a dollar now. At 5% that future dollar is worth $0.61 now. At 10%, $0.38. At 15%, the dollar then shrinks to a quarter now. You get the point. Higher rates driven by inflation crush the present value of growth stocks. A big reason they've flown so high is rates have been so low, al la the TINA syndrome (there Is No Alternative to stocks since you can't make a nickel on interest). With inflation, the ground shifts, and alternatives aplenty emerge. Rising rates and a herd mentality switch from greed to fear could utterly crush over-valued tech stocks and make the 2000-era NASDAQ meltdown look like a picnic.

The longer the period—before a bond matures, the period of discounted future stock profits, whatever—the worse this interest rate risk effect is. At 10%, a dollar in one year is worth 90 cents now. In ten years, 38 cents. Long is wrong!

When I say bonds are bad, by the way, this is only true for inflating currencies. Stable or deflating currencies are better bets. For instance, late in 2020, Chinese government bonds were paying 3.15%, nearly 2.5% more than comparable US Treasuries, before inflation effects which favored the Chinese bonds even more.[3] If US inflation spikes and China's doesn't, you would also see sharp price appreciation as the red bonds became ever more valuable in shirking US dollar terms. So bonds in stable or deflating curren-cies, or those inflating less relative to the United States, can offer hard shelter. The same goes for other assets like stocks or real estate denominated in more favorable currencies. You'd also make money trading non-US denominated assets back to dollars. The non-US currency would rise relative to the green-back, so you get more dollars when you cash out. Just be sure to spend them fast before they shrink!

This currency effect is a big reason things like gold do well in inflationary times. All commodities have prices keyed to the currency in which they are traded. If the dollar falls, gold goes up in dollar terms. So some commodities offer opportunity, but we need to be careful and consider the supply/demand factor as well. If oil demand dries up in a greening world, oil may rise in dollar terms relative to other currencies, but still tank big time relative to higher demand items like lithium (batteries for computers, cars, wind farms, you name it), and rare earth metals, for instance.

Real estate has been a traditionally strong inflation hedge and a great tax shield as discussed in the tax sections. But before loading up on rentals or securities that invest in them, a few caveats. First, COVID has accelerated an inevitable shift from many forms of commercial real estate. Malls and office buildings and lots of traditional retail may never fully recover. Amazon and Zoom have crushed them. So if you think real estate, think maximum utility going forward. Residential is solid—people have to live somewhere, you can't upload them to the Internet. Warehouse and logistics space to support goods delivery from e-commerce look like sound bets. Theme parks in the emptying malls, not so much. Second, the real estate market—particularly for suburban housing—has soared with the stock market and may be headed for a big 2008-style crash. I flipped my first house in 1982 and owned 100 units at one point, and I can't recall seeing this market so frothy. Full disclosure: I still have 30 rental houses left, and as I write this am seriously considering dumping them to look to get back cheap later. A very smart broker buddy of mine thinks he can get a couple hedge funds in a bidding war over the package. Go figure! That said, the mid-2021 trends for sharp increases in residential housing values and rents are very robust, driven mostly by a sharply constricted supply of existing and buildable houses.

The old real estate mantra was location, location, location! Here's a twist you probably have not considered. You want to pick your jurisdictions very carefully. Besides the (slight) risk of places like NYC never fully recovering from the COVID ghost town malady, fiscal pressures and the socialism wind will grind hard on some locales. They get ground, real estate investors get ground, in terms of higher taxes and fees. As such costs go up, they become inescapable shackles on real estate values, choking the life out of them. Think rent control on the one hand, and rising taxes on the other. Ain't much left for ma and pa landlord, and the housing value becomes a grease spot. Such are long-term trends you must learn to sniff and avoid if you tread into this space. New York's a good example of this risk. On the one hand, there is strong philosophical and political pressure to subsidize housing for non-fat cats, and control profits for fat-cat landlords. On the other hand, the state's a tax-burning furnace running out of money hand and fist to pay for social and other programs ad infinitum. Income taxes you can move away from, but you can't take your dirt with you and the value can get crushed in the death spiral of controlled revenue and escalating operation costs.

Another example is Alaska. I remember chewing on this a while ago for a very sharp entrepreneurial pal of mine with extensive housing rental holdings in the Great White North (left). I met him and his family at an anchorage (Great Sale Cay, don't ya know) on my first cruise to the Bahamas in the early 2000s. He'd even back then figured out how to run his empire off his catamaran from anywhere in the world. So consider this. Alaska's economy is 80% dependent on petroleum. Drops in demand and prices are devastating. Before the COVID bust, Alaska was one of only two US States with a contracting economy, and both the United States worst unemployment and worst population loss from people leaving the state.[4] Couple that with this ethos: "The idea of a universal basic income — a check sent out by the government to every American, no strings attached, just for being alive — is sometimes decried as un-American, as a way for people to get money they didn't work for. But America contains one of the few places the policy has been tried at scale…Alaska has figured out a way to use its oil wealth to give all its residents cash for free and wipe out extreme poverty — and it doesn't appear to be harming its economy in the process."[5] This free-money mentality has been baked pretty deeply into the state's culture, and such ways are loathe to mend. Love it or hate it, it doesn't take rocket science to blend these trends and spell "Oh s___!" for Alaska real estate. Let him who has snowshoes, walk.

Industries with social pricing control are other danger areas. Not just rent control, but utilities pricing, and maybe, soon, health care and tech services. Many of you are probably aware of the tale of two Canadas, where most doctors don't make much, and most patients have to wait forever for care—with a parallel concierge healthcare industry for those rotund fat cats who can pay really big for health care, on top of paying via high taxes for the pedestrian sort. Standard health care—and associated industries like pharma—just ain't good investments where pricing is cranked down for the good of the people. Look also with mildly jaundiced eye upon tech. Regulation and perhaps antitrust dragons are on the wind, and forget not what they did to my Bell, Ma.

I call asset classes disfavored by inflation to have negative inflation-alpha. Alpha, of course, is geek shorthand for returns in excess of the market. Bonds in the preceding discussion would have negative inflation-alpha because inflation chews up their returns. Positive alpha would come from investments for which inflation serves as a tailwind, like the Chinese bonds in the above example—provided the relative inflation rates hold. While there are clearly many moving parts to investment calculus, the impact of a declining currency can't be underrated if you, as I, fear inflation's resurgence.

There are a lot of ways to play this besides using investment assets denominated in more favorable currencies. Unlike real estate, stocks should not generally be assumed to be automatic inflation hedges. It just depends on the business dynamics (have we forgotten buying stocks represents owning tiny pieces of hopefully profitable businesses?) of the shares at hand. For instance, per the *WSJ* "from 1973 to 1979 the core consumer-price index, which excludes food and energy, rose at an average pace of 7.3%, while the S&P 500 fell 8.5% over the same period."[6] But wisely selected inflation-alpha stocks should prosper even if or while indexes flounder. Look for dominant growth companies able to grow revenue and profits at rates significantly faster than inflation. Consider those with strong demand/pricing power—leading companies in industries that can control supply and pricing where consumer demand is robust and regulatory controls benign.

And just for a flyer, think outside the box. Space, for instance, is huge (sorry for the Trumpian lapse). Not long ago no less than Goldman Sachs predicted the next and biggest-ever gold rush to soon begin…in space. "…while the psychological barrier to mining asteroids is high, the actual financial and technological barriers are far lower," Goldman Sachs analysis concluded. "Prospecting probes can likely be built for tens of millions of dollars each and Caltech has suggested an asteroid-grabbing spacecraft could cost $2.6 billion." The payoff? The "world's first trillionaire."[7]

This demand/pricing Goldilocks recipe works in all sorts of markets, products, services, commodities whatever. Of course, conjuring up these opportunities before they explode is easier imagined than banked. Recall the discussion with which we began the chapter—on the power of charts and technical analysis to infer trends and the path to profits. Of course, such divination can also be applied to currencies, crypto, or otherwise, and pretty much any market where prices are reported and reasonably transparent. Again, this chapter concludes with a primer on that mystic art, after a short bit on crypto.

Before going there, consider so-called alternative investment areas, such as direct investment in your own business or the right real estate at the right price. If you look here, be sure to learn how to crunch the numbers to clearly understand risk, cash flow, pro forma returns on investment, and tax advantages. These areas are beyond the scope of this book, as is private equity (PE), another hugely promising area increasingly open to most investors. PE of course is just owning stock in companies that are not publicly traded; the same inflation-era caveats extend here with respect to business models and prognoses.

Cryptocurrencies present a newish way to transmit value between members of society. Also referred to as *virtual currencies,* "crypto" (for short) is one of three types of currency: commodity monies (backed by physical assets like gold); fiat currencies (paper money backed by the promise of the issuing government); and virtual currencies (backed by social convention or beliefs).[8] Cryptocurrencies are typically traded over exchanges—digital marketplaces where users can convert a particular cryptocurrency into another virtual, "real," or fiat currency.[9] As of 2019, 2,140 separate cryptocurrencies are currently in circulation with a total market capitalization of over $1.7 billion.[10] Of course the size of this market has exploded since. People not only exchange cryptocurrencies but they also speculate and use them to purchase goods and services from vendors.

Cryptocurrencies are often issued and transacted using blockchain technology. A blockchain is a process of encrypting and automating digital transactions including the mining, issuing, and trading of cryptocurrency. Mining basically just means solving complex computer puzzles and being reward with a free crypto "coin" if successful. Cryptocurrencies and blockchain—while commonly paired in conversation—are distinct and mutually exclusive ideas.[11] Cryptocurrencies need not necessarily involve blockchain technology, and blockchains are used in several ways outside of cryptocurrency. Think of blockchain as a decentralized ledger; rather than a central authority tracking ownership as is the case with stocks, the information containing owner identities and transaction histories is encrypted and stored in copy on every exchange member's machine, making it nearly impossible to hack or otherwise manipulate. It is a very smart and anonymous ownership verification system.

Bitcoin, the archetype of all crypto, is mined by high-powered computers that spend time and resources solving increasingly complex algorithms. Despite a new unit being mined, say, every 10 min, the number of available Bitcoin may drop by half every four years. Thus, by the year 2140, all 21 million Bitcoin are expected to be in circulation. As an investment, Bitcoin (and other crypto) is highly volatile but is uncorrelated with the stock market and other traditional asset classes. Some finance gurus cast doubt on the prospect of Bitcoin as a suitable hedge in one's portfolio due to its high volatility.[12] Many ascribe a hot-air, zero value to crypto.[13]

When it comes to owning cryptocurrencies like Bitcoin, you mostly have three options if you want to keep your investment affairs stateside while minimizing counterparty risk. First, you can set up your own mining system complete with high-powered machines and the associated high electricity bill. Note that the next block that is mined and then added to the blockchain comes about partially by computing power and partially by chance. Thus, there is technically no guarantee you will ever be successful in mining a single Bitcoin. Instead, you can join a mining pool, adding your computing power to the group and split ownership of any mined crypto. Second, you can invest in a vehicle like the Grayscale Bitcoin Trust,[14] an open-ended private fund (structured as a trust) that began trading publicly in 2015. Its objective is to track the value of Bitcoin much like SPDR ETFs (exchange-traded funds) track the S&P 500 Index. Grayscale is only open to accredited investors, though, so be sure to have those tax returns and proofs of net worth ready! Also keep in mind that owning a share of Grayscale is *not* the same thing as owning Bitcoin. Yes, you gain exposure to the ups and downs of the virtual currency, but you will not own it directly by investing in Grayscale or any investment company.

Alternatively, you can invest in various ETFs and other investment companies, like ARK Next Generation Internet ETF, who invest a share of their assets in Grayscale from time to time. The problem here is with this "fund of funds" arrangement, the fees can pile up and erode the expected return. As the end customer, you will not only pay the ETF's fees but also Grayscale's management fee. This market is evolving rapidly and dabblers no doubt have many other options to invest now.

Third, you can start a business (the benefits of which we've covered in earlier parts of this book) and accept Bitcoin and other cryptocurrency as payment for your goods and services. If you are feeling particularly enthusiastic about crypto, you can do all three. Now, it's possible to venture beyond the US borders and gain exposure to other avenues of crypto ownership such as foreign currency and derivatives exchanges (e.g., Bitcoin futures), but doing so incurs several types of risk, you can avoid if you stay inside the United States, namely foreign political risk, counterparty risk, currency risk, and foreign interest rate risk. You can also invest in an assortment of crypto exchanges that are *not* registered with the SEC or any domestic regulator, but do so at your peril. There is little-to-no recourse here if things go sideways: No FDIC, SIPC, nothing. If the platforms or any nefarious players take your money and run, you'll be the one standing there awkwardly holding the bag.

You may ask why not, as a fourth way, just buy some coin directly? The devil is in knowing what you have and not having a guarantor like FDIC at your back. The essence of crypto is anonymity. Ethereum—another crypto variety—is aptly named. Ether is an old physics term for the immaterial nothingness of outer space. Nothing to grab. Invisible. Is it really even there, that coin you bought? What are you buying from whom? Robin Hood will let you buy it, but what's really in your account? You still may face massive counterparty risk. Do you have the money, time, will, and manpower to properly vet this stuff? Want to pay big bucks to hire tech personnel to ensure the Bitcoin is legit, inspect the servers and Bitcoin mining operations of an individual or company, etc., and verify what they tell you is really what they sell you? Individual investors are pretty much SOL. Not even your ultra-wealthy are likely to deploy that kind of capital on the front-end, and that even assumes they know what to look for. And, if you are taken, ain't nobody going to help you. The SEC would probably say something like, "This is why we don't directly regulate it and have only provided minimal guidance on crypto." There is one exception to this rule: Apex Clearing—the custodian of Sogotrade, a broker-dealer, both of whom are registered with the SEC. Keep in mind, however, that you face severe limitations if you decide to invest in crypto directly, including no retirement accounts, 1% commission on each transaction, a $50,000 daily purchase limit, and no margin ability on crypto assets.[15]

Again, things are evolving rapidly here, and if you are really interested bone up on current events. There are plenty risks (in addition to common investment dangers) associated with crypto. One is political risk. The United States as a whole—particularly the many agencies that constitute the Federal government—has not worked out how to classify or regulate cryptocurrency.[16] Depending on whom you ask, crypto may be a security, a commodity, a currency, or a digital asset. The first three are regulated by different agencies, while the fourth is caught in the middle of various Federal and state regulators.[17] While the SEC, CFTC (commodities futures trading commission), IRS, and state governments have all issued guidance on cryptocurrency, the larger, national conversation is far from over, in particular how to regulate and tax crypto while maintaining user privacy and market fairness through security and transparency. In addition to political risk is the counterparty risk regarding cooperatives or pooled investment platforms. Because there is as yet no publicly listed direct investment vehicle in Bitcoin, coupled with the anonymous nature of crypto users, unsecured trust in the system is a big issue.[18] As of this writing, none of the cryptocurrency exchanges have registered with the SEC to become a national exchange. The closest anyone has come thus far is Coinbase, the largest US-based crypto exchange, which began the filing process in 2020 to launch an initial public offering (IPO) sometime in 2021.[19] Similarly, NYDIG, a spin-off of Stone Ridge Asset Management that specializes in Bitcoin and other crypto investments, filed with the SEC to launch a Bitcoin ETF sometime in 2021.[20] While either of these would be a giant leap forward in secure, domestic crypto investment, we recommend that if you decide to place some of your hard-earned money in crypto, make sure you do the due diligence to acquire at least basic understanding. And note, you tax-treetop flyers you, that crypto investors are required to brightly wave the "look at me! look at me!" red flag to IRS. Crypto disclosure is now the very first question on the Form 1040, with failures to come clean having distinct criminal implications. Tread carefully!

Now, back to traditional assets. As mentioned, there are two basic schools of stock market analysis: fundamental analysis and technical analysis. Fundamental analysis looks at numbers and "hard data"—earnings and debt load, growth rates, currency rates, and competitive environments, and so on, while technical analysis studies charts and historical price patterns as a proxy for human market behavior and attempts to predict future behavior based on the interpretation of past patterns.

While the tools of technical analysis are timeless, the Internet age has made once-tedious work a snap. There must be hundreds if not thousands of software packages and Internet sites designed to help with this. This is also true for fundamental analysis, though charts are much more amenable to adroit interpretation than accounting numbers which demand a deep due diligence that may be absent in many online aps.

The cardinal rule of technical analysis is to invest congruently with the direction of identified trends. Investing with the trend is like swimming downstream, easy, predictable, and relatively safe. Bucking the trend is said by chartists to be like going against the current, hard, exhausting, and perilous. Trends can be said to exist for all investments, from broad market indexes to individual stocks (which may or may not be moving with the major trends). Investments whose trends match overall market trends are thought to be easier to predict and profit from.

Using a "top down" approach simply means first looking at the big indexes, like the DOW, S&P 500, and NASDAQ (the "top"), then looking at market segments, and finally at individual stocks. You want to first establish what you think the major market trend is; that is what we mean by "top" down. Trends can be up, down, or sideways.

Since things never go straight up or straight down, an uptrend is described as a series of "higher highs and higher lows," a downtrend as lower highs and lower lows, and a sideways or "trading range" trend as a pattern of level highs and lows that the stock seems to bounce between for an extended period. You will also notice that there are shorter-term trends within the intermediate (lasting several months) trends, and that nimble traders could have made money exploiting them. Often, short-term trends in the sideways intermediate market show some remarkable opportunities of their own.

After a little practice reading charts, spotting trends is quite easy. Reading history is a no-brainer once you get the hang of it. Much tougher is predicting the future…but such prediction is the basis on which profits from technical analysis depend.

For those beginning technical analysis, it is probably best to try and identify short and intermediate term trends, and then try to extrapolate and trade on them. I cannot overemphasize the importance of two critical rules:

1. Your trade strategy must match the timeframe of the trend you are predicting. An intermediate sideways trend would dictate one strategy,

and a short-term up trend following short-term down trend quite another. Timing is everything, if you will forgive the pun.

2. The markets—and their trends—can change with blinding speed. Once you decide to make a trade based on your opinion of a trend, you must be extremely attentive to changes, and be prepared to act when this happens. You must have a "Plan B" to exit your trade in case you are wrong, and to get out with a decent result whenever things change, even when you are right. You must be constantly watching, and know what you are going to do before it hits the fan. If you wait to formulate strategy on the fly, you may be doomed.

The next basic concept is learning how to make the trend you have identified really work for you. Some things go up far more in an uptrend than the underlying market in general, and such investments can really magnify your gains. In a down trend, some dogs go down far more that the indexes would indicate, and gains can be bigger if you bet against these than against the market in general.

This concept is generally referred to as beta (β) where a higher number for β suggests a stock will go up more in good markets and down more in bad ones than the market in general. $\beta = 1$, same as market. $\beta = .5$ goes up/down 1/2 as much as market. $\beta = 2$, twice as much. And remember, unlike an electron-volt, the value for metrics like beta are in a constant hot flux of change.

A good way to work this is to study how particular industries or sectors are *currently* performing verses "the market." I stress the "currently" because, as we have just said, things can change with blinding speed. You have to be vigilant to spot these shifting anomalies.

For instance, pull a sector graph of the best and worst performing sector groups, for simplicity. Sectors include many industries, so a graph by industry would include many more data bars—and many more opportunities. But the sector graph makes the point pretty clearly. The overall market trend during a given period could have been generally sideways. But those attentive investors who had been aware that a given sector—such as technology—was "on a roll" could have handsomely profited, had they made the right moves.

In most markets, some things are usually doing far better than others. Your task as a trader is to spot and exploit these discrepancies. One of the big reasons for this stems from the activities of large institutional investors like mutual funds and pensions as they collectively deploy their huge asset bases. While investors of this sort are widely perceived as poor forecasters when it comes to profitably employing their clients' money, it cannot be argued that their gargantuan capital flows move the markets, at least in the short and intermediate terms. Remember the Tesla to S&P example. Since they must, with billions of dollars to marshal, move much, much slower than smaller, nimbler investors like us or you, spotting the trends they are making, *in time to capitalize on them,* is very possible, and "riding their coattails" (to use a Warren Buffett expression) can be enormously profitable. Here is one way to attempt this.

Charts can be displayed to show relative performance, as in which industries or sectors are doing relatively better than the market, and which worse. In the end, stocks (and other markets) go up because more "people" are buying then selling, and go down because sellers outnumber buyers. With their huge capital flows, big-money investors can't help but move the markets—up or down—as they modify their investment strategies. Tracking relative performance can be a good proxy for what the "big money" is doing, and riding such a trend can really pay off. Bucking it can make for a rough road.

Such a chart, for instance, could show the relative performance of several industries in the basic materials sector, over time, so you can see trend shifts. In an example from one of my old whitepapers, the chemical manufacturing industry went from being in the bottom 16% in July to in the top 7% by September. Many technical traders would feel it flashed a buy signal (you read such charts right to left), as it went from red to yellow, to green, as the relative performance (the number often depicted in a red/yellow/green colored square) kept improving. Easy as red light, green light, one, two, three.

The first important point to make is that the market does not have to move up for you to make money. There is much profit to be had in any sort of market, if you know how to call and play it.

The simplest way is to buy higher β stocks during up trends, and short higher β stocks in down trends. In sideways trends, simply buy near the bottom of the cycle and sell near the top; more conservative traders will simply wait for the stock to head back down before buying again, and the more intrepid might short at the top of the trading range.

It is important to note that shorting stock means selling stock you do not own: You borrow from a broker and sell a stock you think is headed down at a higher price, expecting to be able to buy ("cover") later at a lower price, thus returning the stock you borrowed to sell. This can be quite risky, since if you are wrong the stock could theoretically go up infinitely high, leaving you to chase it to the moon to buy to replace the stock you borrowed (yes, they make you do that!). This is how the little guys in 2020–2021 stuck GameStock to big players who had shorted the arguably dog-doo-doo company. So-called inverse ETFs can give you short exposure without the "chase the moon" risk, but unfortunately are not nearly as profitable for a given down move as a genuine short. You can up the octane by buying leveraged inverse ETFs—lie 2x and 3x—but these are slippery devils and must be watched daily. The reason is they price-reset every day, meaning that even if you are right about a downtrend you can get slaughtered if you stay in a 2x and the market does not go straight down, as it rarely does.

Options are another way to exploit trends and offer the opportunity of leverage—the ability to earn (or lose!) a greater percentage profit on a stock than the stock itself moves. There are many ways to use options, far more than we will make words for here. The simplest are directional plays, like buying a call option on a stock you think will go up, or a put on a bearish expectation. Many people who do this lose, since even when they are right, the options can expire before the stock makes the expected move. Safer is selling calls (make sure you own the stock, so you are covered! Selling naked calls is very risky…the stock could theoretically go up an infinite amount, and you are obligated to buy it to cover or satisfy the promise you made to sell it at the call price) on stocks you expect to move sideways, or not up as much as where you sell the call. Probably my favorite (and one of the safest strategies) is the so-called short vertical spread. Despite the weird name, it really is a pretty simple play: You sell one option (call or put) with a "strike" (exercise price) close to the price the stock is trading at and buy one of the same sort with a strike farther from the stock's price. The "spread" is the difference in price between the strike prices. Since you sell closer to the stock price (closer to "the money") than you buy, you get paid more for the one you sell than you pay for the one you buy, which is why they call these "credit" spreads—you wind up with a net influx of cash…at least at the beginning. The reason these are lower risk is because your loss is sharply limited if you are wrong—that is why you buy the option farther from the money. Here's an example: a stock is trading at $50, and you are bullish—your analysis indicates it will go up. You sell a put at a strike of $45, and get, say, $3 for it; you buy a protective put with a strike of $40, and we'll say that costs $1. (The $45, $3, and $1 are per share prices; you will be dealing in real money in intervals of 100x these.) So you pay $1, get $3, and net $2. If you are right and the stock goes up, the puts expire worthless, and you get to keep the $2. This is the goal. If the stock goes down, your loss is capped at the $5 loss on the stock (the $45 put you sold makes you buy at $45, but the $40 put you bought lets you sell at $40), minus the $1 you paid for the protective put, plus the $3 you got for selling the $45 put; this adds up to a *maximum* loss of $3. If you were attentive and got out before the trade went to heck, you could have controlled your loss at far less than $3. Anyway, those are the basics of how short verticals work. You use calls if you are bearish (down trend), puts as described if bullish, and can use either in a sideways market, or even take both sides, which is called an Iron Condor. To be clear, I am trying to compress some pretty complicated stuff into overall themes here. If you want to do this, better bone up big time, or find an advisor who really knows their stuff! And learn enough to sort the psychobabble rap from the real deal.

So do not mistake the "simple" in this section title for "easy"; developing skill in technical trading requires a massive commitment to learning and discipline, even if you have the aptitude. You still need the time...and the guts...and the discipline. It is very easy to lose your shirt trying to time the market, and many if not most have, and many more will. Probably most will. Most market timers and options players lose money. As is oft-said, "the only problem with market timing is the timing..." This is not meant to discourage you, but rather to make sure you appreciate that developing such a skill—which you would use to compete with legions of other sharp, professional, and profits-hungry investors, all fighting to make sure it's your money and not theirs that gets lost—requires a strong commitment to learning and studying markets on a continuous full-time basis. As well as iron will and Vulcan logic. Like a sport, you must constantly train, or you will lose your edge and get burnt. But for those with the time and aptitude (or those who choose to seek out skilled professionals to do it for them), the rewards can be very satisfying! But to say you can't time the market consistently is just rubbish. Many, many do.

I had planned to give a short discussion of chart reading methods here, but choked-chained myself back. There's lots of material on the Internet about this, and maybe I'll coauthor an upcoming book on tech analysis with my darling wife and business partner Kim, or brother Jonathan, each of whom is just a dandy analyst and very sharp trader.

But I do want to leave this chapter with a taste of one of many more sophisticated approaches than the typical line charts with moving averages you are likely to see in casual studies. So let's look at the so-called candlestick style, a method developed by nineteenth-century Japanese rice traders as a way to visually and efficiently capture a lot of trading information. Without getting too much into the details, the color of the "candle" tells us if the day was up (white or green usually) or down (red or black) (Figs. 1 and 2). The bull patterns generally show an up day after a down day, the bears the opposite.

In addition to all the quick visual information—it takes lots of training and practice, but once mastered (and maintained!) you can see an awful lot with just a quick look—the patterns of the candles themselves and the cluster

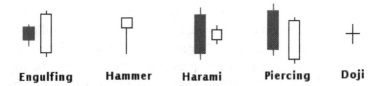

Fig. 1 Bullish Candlestick Patterns

Fig. 2 Bearish Candlestick Patterns

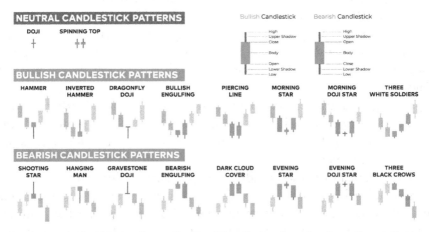

Fig. 3 Candlestick Series Patterns (*Source* "Forex Candlestick Patterns Course + Cheat Sheet." ForexElite. https://www.forexelite.com/forex-candlestick-patterns-course-cheat-sheet/)

patterns they form can be remarkably illuminating to the adept. While there are likely thousands of patterns, with many including three or more candles, here are a few of the most basic (Fig. 3):

Again, these are very basic patterns, and there are many variations of each.

In this kind of chart analysis, major turning points—the bounces to the upside—are indicated by hammers. Turns down are indicated by "the hanging man," another basic pattern which is the same as the hammer, but occurs at resistance, instead of support as for the hammer.

Try to find such patterns on a chart and think about the context in which they appeared. Remember, a trader is making decisions before the chart "happens." A good way to practice is to hold a card over the chart, and slowly move it to the right, first trying to predict what will happen next from the parts of the chart you have already revealed. Good luck!

Everything you have been reading about here can be applied to charting virtually any market, from currencies to commodities (like gold or our friends the old Japanese rice traders), numismatic coins, or the prices of muscle cars from the '60's. Not that fundamentals are not just as important to these other markets as to stocks, but they have different things to measure. Remember, financial chartism is essentially a way to try and read collective market psychology, and predict what the market will be doing based on the prevailing net mood. That's it, really. Human brains—and the various mobs and human-programed computers which *are* the markets—make money decisions pretty much the same way, whether they are buying a car, selling a house, or speculating on gold. If you can learn to read the mind of the market—and that's what technical analysis really is—it should work wherever you apply it.

Do you want to be a trader? Then ponder this. Here are two fundamental truths (and sorry for the bean counter pun):

1. You CAN learn to become a very effective trader. You can almost certainly do it, regardless of circumstance, education, or lack of genius intelligence, IF you have the will.
2. You CAN NOT do it easily! If you are to succeed, you must commit to— and follow through on—a significant amount of time dedicated to intense education. This stuff is not hard per se (like my CFA® curriculum was hard…man, that was *hard*!), but it does require diligence, concentration, tons of memorization, and lots of practice. You must also resign yourself to an ongoing commitment to working the techniques and the market. This is not a passive activity; rather, it is like running a business. You can to some extent pick the hours, but you must put in the hours or it all goes to the devil. Finally, you must accept the fact that you will lose money. Some of your trades will lose money—forever—that is part of the game. And you must learn to master your emotions and overcome your fears and gut instincts. All that matters is your indicators and rules. In the beginning, you will lose on most trades, and you have to make peace with that going

in or it will drive you nuts. Or worse, it will drive you into a death spiral of increasingly bad decisions that could leave you broke.

So! As we said at the beginning, technical trading can be an enormously profitable practice, one well worth including in your investment strategy. There are several ways to go about this. You can learn yourself, if you have the time and the passionate interest; many who start are thankful for the basic knowledge, but find they would rather pay a full-time professional to do this for them, considering the small fee a small price to pay to avoid the hard work, time commitment, and enhanced risk of "practicing" with their own money. Basic knowledge is still very valuable, especially in being able to spot true professionals who actually know what they are talking about in this regard, from among the vast sea of those who may merely say they do. Many of these ignorant sayers believe what they say, and many others will look you in the eye and lie with a smile.

So of course, Diogenes, finding that expert, honest advisors is not as simple as might be wished. Finding a skilled investment advisor can be a nightmare task in itself, but finding one who can put all the critical disciplines—tax, estate, asset protection, financial planning, and on, and on!—together would challenge Hercules. There are many quarterbacks, few Tom Bradys.

In an upcoming chapter, we'll show you how to size up the draft, and make your best play to find a winner. But first, let's work on untying the thorny knot of a secure and comfortable retirement.

Of course, we teach a bunch of classes on this technical analysis stuff, check out fweibook.org for details. Look for the one called elite investor for a good overview.

Notes

1. Wayland, Michael, and Lora Kolodny. "Tesla's market cap tops the 9 largest automakers combined – Experts disagree about if that can last." *CNBC*, December 14, 2020. https://www.cnbc.com/2020/12/14/tesla-valuation-more-than-nine-largest-carmakers-combined-why.html.
2. Calhoun, George. "Will Tesla Break the S&P 500? (Part 2) – The Mechanics of Market Turmoil." *Forbes*, January 4, 2021. https://www.forbes.com/sites/georgecalhoun/2021/01/04/will-tesla-break-the-sp-500part-2--the-mechanics-of-market-turmoil/?sh=6a82862d1843.
3. Jakab, Spencer, Aaron Back, Justin Lahart, Nathaniel Taplin, Jinjoo Lee, and Telis Demos. "How to Avoid Paying the Cruelest Tax: Inflation." *The Wall Street*

Journal, October 2, 2020. https://www.wsj.com/articles/how-to-avoid-paying-the-cruelest-tax-inflation-11601631007.

4. "Best States for Business 2019." *Forbes.* https://www.forbes.com/places/ak/?sh= 62cf0c186800.

5. Matthews, Dylan. "The amazing true socialist miracle of the Alaska Permanent Fund." *Vox*, February 13, 2018. https://www.vox.com/policy-and-politics/ 2018/2/13/16997188/alaska-basic-income-permanent-fund-oil-revenue-study.

6. Jakab, Spencer, Aaron Back, Justin Lahart, Nathaniel Taplin, Jinjoo Lee, and Telis Demos. "How to Avoid Paying the Cruelest Tax: Inflation." *The Wall Street Journal*, October 2, 2020. https://www.wsj.com/articles/how-to-avoid-paying-the-cruelest-tax-inflation-11601631007.

7. Wehner, Mike. "Asteroid mining will produce the world's first trillionaire, according to Goldman Sachs." *yahoo!finance*, April 23, 2018. https://finance. yahoo.com/news/asteroid-mining-produce-world-first-trillionaire-according-gol dman-201817072.html.

8. Kiviat, Trevor. "Beyond Bitcoin: Issues in Regulating Blockchain Transactions." *Duke Law Journal, 65*, no. 3. (December, 2015): 569–608.

9. Jackson, Olly. "PRIMER: regulating cryptocurrency exchanges." *International Financial Law Review*, (February, 2019). https://search.proquest.com/ope nview/455d327860c3e078721076e2c5c1de22/1?pq%09origsite=gscholar& cbl=36341.

10. Prewett, Kyleen, Roger W. Dorsey, and Gaurav Kumar. "A Primer on Taxation of Investment in Cryptocurrencies." *Journal of Taxation of Investments, 36*, no. 4 (summer, 2019): 3–16.

11. Fernandez-Villaverde, Jesus. "Cryptocurrencies; A Crash Course in Digital Monetary Economics Cryptocurrencies." *Australian Economic Review, 51*, no. 4 (December, 2018): 514–526.

12. Vukovic, Vuk. "Bitcoin Is Not A Hedge Against Inflation." *Seeking Alpha,* January 11, 2021. https://seekingalpha.com/article/4398232-bitcoin-is-not-hedge-against-inflation.

13. https://seekingalpha.com/article/4397513-worth-exactly-zero-crypto-and-bit coin-pure-techno-babble.

14. Best, Richard. "2 Funds that Invest in Bitcoin." *Investopedia*, January 21, 2020. https://www.investopedia.com/articles/etfs-mutual-funds/042816/2-funds-invest-bitcoin-gbtc-arkw.asp.

15. "Welcome to Apex Crypto!" Sogotrade. https://account.sogotrade.com/Help/ ApexCryptoFAQ.aspx#.

16. Howden, Ed. "The crypto-currency conundrum: regulating an uncertain future." *Emory International Law Review, 29*, no. 4 (summer, 2015): 741–798.

17. "Digital and Digitized Assets: Federal and State Jurisdictional Issues." American Bar Association, December, 2020. https://www.americanbar.org/content/dam/ aba/administrative/business_law/buslaw/committees/CL620000pub/digital_a ssets.pdf.

18. Zhang, Li, Yongping Xie, Yang Zheng, Wei Xue, Xianrong Zheng, and Xiaobo Xu. "The challenges and countermeasures of blockchain in finance and economics." *Systems Research and Behavioral Science, 37*, no. 4 (July/August, 2020): 691–698. https://doi.org/10.1002/sres.2710.
19. Ennis, Dan. "Crypto exchange Coinbase files for IPO with SEC." *Banking Dive*, December 18, 2020. https://www.bankingdive.com/news/crypto-exchange-coinbase-files-for-ipo-with-sec/592446/.
20. Reynolds, Kevin. "NYDIG Files for Bitcoin ETF, Adding to Firms Hoping 2021 Is When SEC Finally Says 'Yes'." *Coindesk*, February 16, 2021. https://www.coindesk.com/nydig-files-for-bitcoin-etf-adding-to-firms-hoping-2021-is-when-sec-finally-says-yes.

Retirement Income Planning—The Critical Path You Can't Afford to Miss

Like a critical life-saving operation where every move must be perfect and every minute counts, crafting and maintaining a retirement plan entails some of the most important decisions you will ever make.

Properly done, this has never been a simple or intuitive process. In the storm-wracked second quarter of the twenty-first century, it can make rocket science seems like child's play.

So as we go through our retirement planning paces, beware: garden-variety financial planners and advisors—most with little education but big commission-sales ambitions for your dough—and slick websites by the carload offer retirement plans and calculators, for cheap, or even for free. These tend to be overly simplistic, ignore critical factors and risks, and are designed to attract and profit from your assets. Many if not most are disguised sales schemes in financial plan clothing. You need be careful, and you need know what a proper plan smells like in order to protect yourself.

This is complex stuff! My Ph.D. is in financial and *retirement* planning, and even I've just scratched the surface. My wonderful dissertation chair Wade Pfau—himself a Princeton Ph.D. whose own chair (or at least committee member) was the renowned Alan Blinder, former Fed Vice Chairman—has devoted his academic life to retirement research. He is probably the pre-eminent researcher in this area, probably having passed the 100 published scholarly study mark by now.

It should go without saying that what we do toward or past the end of our earning years has a grave finality to it, since we typically won't be able to

J. Camarda et al., *The Financial Storm Warning for Investors*, https://doi.org/10.1007/978-3-030-77271-0_19

make more money to replace that lost to poor decisions, or avoidable taxes, nor have the time to work a few more years and forgo withdrawals and wait on a couple of market cycles to make up lost ground. Getting retirement planning right can give us all the income we need for a satisfying lifestyle, with adequate reserves against the risks of higher healthcare costs and long-term care, and to leave a nice inheritance to the people or causes that we care about. But you must model taxes, inflation, changing stage-of-life expenses, and many other moving parts accurately. Getting it wrong can yield a life of misery and even a shortened one if we can't afford to pay for the drugs, operations, and other care we may need.

This chapter could alert you to danger areas that you or your advisors have overlooked and brighten your future. If so, I am overjoyed to have helped you and your family.

There are lots of big dangers in retirement planning that don't seem to get much media play, so I want to emphasize a couple before getting into other pitfalls.

The first is so-called longevity risk, the risk of living longer than expected or assets can support. Lifespans have gone way up—far past our parents'—and it is likely medical technology will give those who can afford it another quantum leap soon. The risk of running out of money has never been more acute, and the conservative approach is to consider a much longer life expectancy than may seem reasonable to you.

The second is cognitive risk, the irritating truth that our brains just don't function as well as we age. "Old timer's disease" does not necessarily mean Alzheimer's or other forms of dementia. Cognitive declines occur even as part of the healthy aging process, which is probably not good for financial and investment decision making. Recent studies have shown a steady decline in financial decisions quality after 65 or so, perversely with an increase in financial decisions making confidence! In other words, older folks can have rock-solid confidence in horrible, self-destructive decisions and stubbornly cling to them even as they go sliding down the ladder. Note this well, ye swaggering, blustering, cocksure gaffers! And listen to your wives!

Competent advice rocks, folks, but common "advice" is corrosive! Learn to discern the difference in the advisors chapter, coming right up in just one jiffy!

You hear a lot of fin-marketing blather about "what's your number?" When most folks worry about retirement, the biggest concern seems to be having enough money to sustain their current lifestyle. Will my assets be sufficient to supplement income sources like pensions and Social Security? Will I outlive my money? Will my investment returns keep up with inflation?

And so on. Those are all good questions and finding out "your number" is very important. Seems simple, but of course is devilishly complex in the real world.

But what the heck is your "number?"

Think of retirement planning as a cash flow equation.

On the left side, we have your number—the pile of capital you need to pay for a luxurious and hedonistic retirement lifestyle.

On the right side, we have a decade's long stream of credits and debits—investment returns, consumption distributions, taxes, the stealth debit of inflation, and whatever residue you wish to leave dear junior and darling daughters. It's a really messy, complex discounted cash flow calculation, heavily dependent on various assumptions and in need of regular recalculation as the world, and your situation and objectives change through time. A simple heuristic like the old 4% Bengen Rule dramatically understates the complexity—and the risks of running out of money.

To get a good result, you can't do it simple-minded, and you can't do it one-and-done. It's hard, confounding, and high maintenance. But that beats the dickens out of getting it wrong and running out of money, eh, guv'nor?

So let's take a hard look at some oft-overlooked but very real and hazardous dangers that most people face in retirement, but usually don't think about, often until it is too late. Sadly, many if not most financial advisors overlook them as well.

Pretending inflation will be benign is a big one. As propounded in Part I, price inflation has been quite tame in the US since the mid-80s, and many people have almost forgot about it. But back in the 70s, when inflation was raging, it was a major factor in every financial decision, and devastating for those on a fixed income. Call it the once and future swoon. Because we've gotten spoiled by relatively low inflation era beginning in the 80s, most of us don't factor rising prices into our financial planning. If inflation gets "real" again, as many predict, the whole retirement savings game could change for the hit-the-fan worse.

Going forward, ignoring the impact of inflation is probably a big mistake. The massive worldwide stimulus in the wake of the COVID Recession may drive inflation to dangerous levels in the US, as well as much of the rest of the world—eventually. This could be truly ugly given the trillions in stimulus money it will have to soak up.

In an inflationary environment, "safe" investments like bank accounts, bonds, and fixed annuities can spell disaster, dropping in real value, and paying an interest rate that never seems to keep up with rising prices, especially after taxes. That means that every year you have less and less money even if you don't spend a dime! After escalating taxes are considered, you can really get hammered like Thor's faux brother.

Another confounding factor is that the overall "official" inflation rate might not be your particular inflation rate. Assuming you believe the CPI to begin with. For instance, the cost of health care is expected to continue to rise much faster than other items, and this is particularly true for long-term care. Also, if you are hoping to help a grandchild with college expenses, know that college costs have a history of rising over twice as fast as most other costs.

If the predicted mega-inflation comes to pass, the risk is that you may not be able to continue living your current lifestyle becomes profound. In fact, it is possible you could run out of money just trying to keep up with what is bare-bones necessary, let alone comfortable. So, how can you guard against inflation-driven purchasing power erosion? Consider reducing your exposure to investments that lose real value during inflationary periods. Instead, invest in things with anti-inflationary properties or you could find yourself getting further behind instead of ahead. Equity investments—typically stocks, real estate, and small businesses—are often considered to fit this bill. We shared much more specific detail, and more than a few caveats, in the investments chapter.

Not to harp eternal on the coming tax timebomb, but remember that this is probably the biggest danger you face! The tax timebomb is twofold, the nation's and yours. No matter what side of the political fence you are on, you probably believe that government spending cannot continue on its present pace at the current tax revenue levels. Even in the unlikely event that fiscal curmudgeons regain control and actually cut spending, it is unlikely it will be reduced enough to trim the deficit, not to mention paying down the national debt. Part of the solution is highly likely going to be higher taxes. If you, fat cat you, are someone who is precariously balanced at the upper end of the affluence ladder, you are likely to one of the ones paying more taxes, whether you're working or retired. Long before the advent of the crushing fiscal strains of the 2008 Great Recession and the ten years later COVID and the nouveau-social programs trends of recent years, the country has been facing down a budget crisis of colossal proportions. Ever since the beginning of Social Security, America's been ticking down to a day of reckoning, and the Great Society programs like Medicare/Medicaid and the 2008 economic blowout have quickened the pace. Recall from Part I: the math is simple— when Social Security was born, the retired population was a relatively small fraction of the whole, life expectancy was short, so retirement benefits were not paid for long, and there were plenty of workers paying FICA taxes into the system to fund benefits. In the near-century since, all of these trends have reversed—fewer workers paying, more retirees drawing, and people living and collecting far longer than FDR ever dreamed. Back then, the retirement age was 62, life expectancy was 63, and the intent was not to provide a pension but a retirement supplement for the Depression-impoverished and the relative few who lived longer than expected. It has ballooned since. Add the costs of the financial meltdown, a black swan pandemic, and expanding new social programs, and the country is running short in a very big, and very fast, way, so big that many think it likely that US Treasury bonds will lose their prized zero-risk credit rating. I emphasize once again that this is not intended as political commentary, but as economic analysis. Regardless of how one feels about the underlying reasons, it is the numbers that matter, and they are grim.

If you are rich enough to care about what's in this book, you will prob-ably—many would argue necessarily—be targeted as a high-value pocket to fund America's mushrooming deficits. What's worse, IRAs, annuities, and other "retirement" assets have some of the highest tax burdens of any invest-ment asset—and are taxed at the highest ordinary income rates, which are likely to go sharply higher. Too many people fail to plan for taxes in their retirement spending. That can be a serious mistake. As I have written exten-sively on throughout the book, poor tax planning is probably the biggest impediment to wealth accumulation facing many well-off Americans. This goes double in retirement, when every penny can become more precious, and disappear twice as fast. Many assets have different tax treatments (capital gains vs. ordinary income, expedited and heightened taxation of mutual funds vs. ETF's, max-bracket and additional excise tax exposure in annuities and IRAs, tax-hammer LIFO (last in first out) annuity tax rules, max-bracket on interest vs. lower rate on dividends, etc.) and it is very common to see the wrong types of investments in the wrong sort of accounts, such as stocks and other capital gains assets in IRAs, which can double or more the effective tax rate. Paying attention to lining up account type and asset type tax treatment has been called asset location planning, but is often overlooked by investors and their advisors. Such asset location and withdrawal location planning can make a huge difference, with getting this right said to be over 3% or more a year in "free" extra returns.[1] On a million dollar nest egg, that could be over $30,000 more a year to spend! Other mistakes include not harvesting capital losses to offset taxable gains, not planning other income around Social Secu-rity tax issues, ballooning the amount in Social Security benefits forgone due to higher taxation, and so on.

Enough! Let those with ears, hear. Let those with eyes, go back and reread the tax control chapters. Time to move on.

Another common punji-stick pit is the malady of irrational investing, which seems to be endemic in the human condition. I can't tell you how often I've heard clients say "I want the maximum return, but I don't want to take any risk." The only guarantee in a proposition like that is disaster. To be smart, thou shalt not be shooting for any moons, or be hiding under any mattresses.

Sadly in our experience most retirees—and near-retirees—tend to take either too much risk or not enough. Both can lead to disaster. Too-little risk—the stuff-it-under-the-mattress mentality, focusing on CDs, bank accounts, bonds, guaranteed annuities, and the like—will nearly certainly not produce enough of a return to offset taxes and inflation, let alone generate enough income to keep principal intact long enough to fund an extended lifetime, unless you are so overfunded that returns don't matter. The fact that interest rates have been nearly at zero for years is very well-known to readers. On the other hand, taking too much risk can lead to obvious heartbreak as money is lost on unwise investments—as was evident in the 2008 meltdown, the many dips since, and maybe the Great Mother Bear Market coming up around the next bend. If you have to fund your retirement from a bear-market-crushed reduced "principal" amount, you can be setting yourself up for hardship and further risky behavior—and nearly depleted funds far too early in retirement.

Want to audition for "greetings, Wal-Mart shoppers?"

Oh they don't do that anymore?

Whether too little or too much risk, both paths can lead to shrunken assets and constrained lifestyles. What is particularly dangerous about each of these mindsets is that they seem perfectly reasonable to those who adopt them. Mattress-stuffers believe that this is the only safe, responsible way to protect their money and are oblivious to the rich returns that could otherwise be attained. The moon-shooters never seem to recognize their folly, thinking their bets are prudent. Then they crap out, and roll again. At least until the money's gone.

The nature of human thinking seems to sometimes guide us to the land of make believe. Some of us can't help believing, say, that $1,000,000 (a million dollars!) should be more than enough to provide $100,000 in inflation-adjusted after-tax spending income, even if we begin at 60 and have a realistic joint life expectancy to age 90, making for a 30-year-payout period! Sadly, the steady near-guaranteed average return to make this true is about 14%, which in nearly every imaginable scenario is hopelessly optimistic—those that believe in such numbers are almost sure to crash and burn.

We see this kind of wishful thinking pretty regularly in practice, especially for those who don't have baseline retirement income flooring (we will discuss flooring in a bit) like from pensions or other sources to give them a concrete budget anchor point to ground their thinking.

In many cases, pie-in-the-sky expectations are a recipe for disaster. Retirees risk blowing through their money and winding up dependent on children or government programs at a time when they will have no ability to do anything about it! As a reality check, the prognosis for government assistance is not good as we get deeper into the twenty-first century (already nearly 1/5th over!), with lots of gloom and doom for Social Security, Medicare, and other programs, forecasts that have festered for 50 years or more, with no political gumption to solve the problem even back when it seemed solvable.

Remember Part I?

Poor investment planning and product choices are another huge problem we consistently see in retirement planning, and one of the biggest dangers to retirees' happily ever-afters. Many investors' portfolios are riddled with high hidden costs and fees, and take far more risk than the investors—and probably even their advisors—seem to appreciate. This is, especially true where annuities are used, but also quite a problem for stock, bond, and mutual fund/ETF investors.

And when life insurance is hawked as a retirement "investment," Katy, bar the get screwed door! The abuse in this area can be astonishing! Just today, I met a couple in their mid-to-late 60s who said they'd been hustled into plowing a cool $4 M into life policies they did not need and which cost them big. They were duped into pulling nearly $2 M out of IRAs prematurely to pay the premiums. Taxes were nose-bleed. Push a million in tax alone. This kind of predatory "practice," particularly in the senior space, is far more widespread than consumers, and even the regulators, generally appreciate.

Much of the problem may rest with the relationship many investors have with their advisors, many of whom—probably the majority—are not generally required to put clients' interests before their own. Or even be trained to know what they are doing. In the example above, the client said the life agent (whose commission was probably 7 figures) actually drew a toilet on a whiteboard and claimed leaving the money in the IRA (instead of buying life insurance) was the same as flushing it down! The agent's advice? Cash out the IRAs, pay $800K in avoidable tax, and put the shrunken reside—plus way more besides—into the policies. (Which they did, by the way. As I proof this months later, I am happy to report we were able to get all of their money back—a feat the life insurance litigation attorneys we consulted early in the process said would be impossible. Not to brag too much, but without the concentrated fire my team's expertise brought to bear, they would have been stuck watching the policies tick down to worthless instead of getting a refund of their several millions of dollars.)

According to an extensive government[2] (GAO) study, these advisor short-comings are not widely known even among very astute investors, who believe they can rely on investments salespeople as fiduciary advisors when this is not really the case. The problem is compounded by the disclosure rules, which may satisfy legal disclaimer requirements, but rely on documents like prospectuses which are so complicated that many investors may feel overwhelmed and avoid reading them to get information on risks, costs, and other concern areas. In many cases, an investor may wind up owning a basket of investment products selected more to satisfy the compensation needs of the advisor than the investors' retirement funding needs. When risks and costs go up, retirement income security can really go down, with unfortunate or disastrous consequences. This is an area where a deep Portfolio Stress Test can help clarify. Such can provide suggestions that may help you reduce portfolio costs and risks, and more closely align your portfolio with your retirement income needs—perhaps while there's still time to right your boat and get through retirement comfortably.

Another big risk is ignoring your spouse's need for long-term care. There's been lots of discussion about long-term care in recent years, and for good reason. This is a very important and expensive issue, especially when we consider the possibility that you will live a long time, without a spouse and maybe in failing health, perhaps sadly (I pray not!) lost in a brain cloud. You should review your own needs in this regard, but my emphasis here is not your care, but on your spouse's needs. Here are the facts: As long as Medicaid lasts in its current guise, it will pay for decent long-term care for those who need it. But the catch is that "needing it" means that your joint assets have been spent down to the poverty level. That means that you—and only you—are responsible for the costs of your spouse's care until the money's nearly gone. What if you need care and are forced to blow your wad to pay for it? Not much left for healthy spouse to live off. Ditto if spouse needs care and consumes the wad. That could leave you without adequate funds to support yourself, and could even push you toward the poverty line, whether you need care or not. Take note: Existing Medicaid laws require most couples' assets to be completely drained before paying for long-term care. Given the current debt issues in the United States, it is likely these laws will get even tougher and that even thin cats with a few cans of tuna left will be deemed fat and unworthy. Run the math using sophisticated retirement planning software to see if you need to buy crazy expensive insurance to deal with this, or if your number can carry the weight with all the other demands on its broad shoulders. The time to plan is now, before the dice break the wrong way and before your retirement dreams are potentially shattered. Trust me, she shall haunt! You thought your spouse is tough now? Wait until the shining!

While we are touching on marital duress, forget not the devastation of mature divorce! In the "best" of times, divorce is expensive. Without proper planning, divorce can completely devastate retirement plans for one or both spouses, especially if it happens late in life. Depending on the settlement, one spouse can become almost destitute, and even with fair divisions of assets and alimony, resources can be stretched too thin to allow either divorcée much comfort. To make matters worse, the laws of most states require that a spouse at most receive only 1/3 of the other spouse's assets when that spouse dies, and one never knows if one's spouse's last will and testament leave everything to them, since there is no requirement that this document be shown to the other spouse, or even made known to them. As was once said, one never knows, do one?

Fortunately, while your marriage is still happy—or at least civil—this risk can be controlled quite easily as part of your estate planning, by using irrevocable beneficiaries and trust provisions and the like, to craft an effective post-nuptial agreement. By entwining your children's interests (whether yours, theirs, or both of yours) into this structure, you can make this seem far less self-serving, although the protections will benefit your spouse as well as you. Obviously, the time to do this is when all is well and both parties are amenable—and still alive! Once storm clouds gather, it can be more difficult. If divorce does threaten, be sure to engage the advice of a good divorce planner or attorney early on—the emotional gumbo that usually accompanies a failing relationship is sure to obscure one's judgment. Many who have cut deals without professional assistance come to deeply regret their generosity later, when it is too late to change things—or recover income that may be desperately needed for retirement.

Another concern is presented by "single-life-only" pension payouts. Usually when someone takes a pension, they choose from a variety of payout options, and the monthly amount depends on the option taken. For instance, a plan that pays so long as I live only will net a larger monthly payment than one that pays as long as me or my spouse are alive. The longer the life expectancy, the smaller the annual payout, and the life expectancy of two people is longer than for either alone. One that pays x for my life and ½ x ("joint and 50% survivor") to my spouse for her life if I die will have a monthly amount somewhere between the single life only and joint and 100% survivor options. In many instances, we see pensions based on single life only selected because it paid the "most," without enough thought given to the consequences to the survivor if the pensioner dies first. In many cases, this represents the lion's share of the couple's income, and the consequences can be devastating if the spouse with the pension dies.

For many couples, this issue is a very big deal. If one of you has a pension and has not yet made the election, plan long and hard with a competent, unbiased advisor working the numbers. In many cases, you will be better off taking a lower monthly income but getting survivor benefits. If your pension is already paying out, you probably can't change the payout option. In this case, you will want to earmark some assets to provide a rainy day fund to guard against the day the pension may stop. Think and calculate twice before buying "pensionmax" life insurance for this. Costs for insurance late in life can be astronomical—"shorter of breath and one day closer to death,"[3] don't you know—and shoveling in expensive premiums for a policy that may blow up before you do can make matters much worse. The goal is to make sure the assets are large enough to fund the survivor's lifestyle from that point—or make adjustments while both spouses are living using the cold retirement equations a skillful planner can crank out. Since in many cases, the female has the longer life expectancy, and the male the larger pension, the risk of sharp income curtailment to the widow is quite severe—and should be very carefully addressed in portfolio and other asset planning. Another reason to do the right thing and forestall the haunting.

A flipside danger to not having a clear retirement income plan is a kind of spending paralysis that afflicts some people, whose unrealistic expectations trick them into believing they don't have enough money, instead of plenty for whatever they want. Not sure of a safe spending rate, they spend far too little and live far too poorly, and so undermine the retirement lifestyle they have saved their whole lives for. Watch out for this. While you live, let you live!

Another retirement trap is ignoring home equity. As you have no doubt heard for decades, home ownership is the biggest investment many Americans make. It may even be true for you, gentle, and well-heeled reader. Unfortunately, real estate is fairly rigid and illiquid, and most people go to their deaths never unlocking this sometimes very large pool of resources that otherwise could have lifted their income, lifestyle, and safety margin.

This can be really huge for you. While there are many ways to skin this cat, the three most basic are:

1. Sell your home and find somewhere cost-effective to rent. If you can live with moving, the numbers may work so well that your spendable income jumps dramatically. You would also save on taxes, repairs, and breaking

your back to keep the place up. You may find a more suitable abode to age in place, with a single level, grab bars, and what not. This also makes eventual transition to an extended care facility smoother if it becomes necessary.

2. If you love your house and won't consider moving, you may want to use a home equity line of credit, with which you are no doubt familiar already. Downsides are interest rate risk (these are usually not fixed rate so when rates go up your costs do too), tightened rules post-2008 which may make these loan products harder to get and live with, and foreclosure risk—they may actually expect you to pay the money back sooner than is convenient, and if you (or your heirs) don't the house is toast.

3. Reverse mortgages still have a pretty bad hangover reputation, but actually have evolved into fairly good products. While too tangential for me to get into here, the main points are you don't have to pay the money back during your lifetime, you can't be forced to move, and come payoff time if the house can't be sold for what is owed, the government, not your heirs, eat it. While I personally think this is bad tax policy for the country, I think it is very good for you and you should jump on it if this sort of program works for you in boosting income, converting home equity into assets to invest elsewhere or payoff other pesky debt, or just set up a line of credit safety margin facility for you. With rates still low, this could be a real bonanza. If you consider this, shop carefully—still lots of abuse in the banking sector!

Social Security claiming decisions—when and how you take your benefits—can be one of the most bewildering and error-prone choices retirees make, and once done, there is usually no going back to fix mistakes. Since the old "file and suspend" "loophole" has been closed, I won't give you indigestion telling you about it, but hats off to those readers who had the foresight and good advice to grab the "free money" before the door closed, in some cases producing hundreds of thousands of dollars in additional benefits. A big mistake for many remains taking benefits too early—as soon as available, or not before reaching full retirement age, or even later depending on your fact pattern. If you expect to live a normal life expectancy, you may be leaving lots of money on the table by starting early since total payouts to you could be much less than waiting, and getting a bigger check even for a shorter period of years. Not coordinating with your spouse's claiming strategy is another potentially costly pitfall, as are divorcees not claiming benefits, and not carefully planning job income around Social Security tax traps. Another mistake we see is not checking for errors in the Social Security credit record—it is not uncommon to see government mistakes on past earnings that slash benefits unless corrected. Find a sharp and honest planner (there are bound to be two or three in the country!) to do a detailed Social Security claiming strategy analysis to help guide you toward the best decisions in your personal circumstances, and try to get ahead of this complex, error-prone area. As the tax vise tightens, remember your benefits will likely be sliced and diced and stealth-taxed into a grease spot. Still, plan carefully to stack the grease high as you can.

Another pitfall can be not building an income floor. By income floor I mean a baseline, dependable or guaranteed, paycheck-style income like from a pension, Social Security, or the right kind of annuity (and there are so many wrong kinds of annuities that are abusively sold that you should check out the classes at fweibook.org and request my report *The Unvarnished Truth about Annuities* (email me at drjeff@camarda.com for a copy before keeping any annuities you now have, or God forbid, writing any checks for new ones). The floor can also come from bond ladders if and when you can get decent interest (which also goes double for annuities), dependable rental property, side businesses, or other steady sources that you can count on. It can also come from a cash or very conservative investment pool or "bucket" that is intended to be methodically consumed to provide regular paycheck-like payments.

Unless you have a floor, you are at risk of pulling funds out of variable assets like the stock market or mutual funds in the wrong amounts or at the wrong times, exacerbating the odds of running out of money or underfunding your retirement lifestyle. If instead you have a steady income stream to meet life's basic expenses, you have more control over "extras" spending decisions, and a better chance of smoothing consumption and having your money last and provide a satisfying lifestyle regardless of how long you live.

Building a floor requires some careful thought—typically you want to convert some growth assets into flooring security, which inevitably involves tradeoffs. You give up the home run for the single, but both aspects are important. Convert too much to dependable income flooring, and you limit the growth you may need to offset higher costs later in life, slowly choking as income covers less and less lifestyle cost, and hurt the opportunity to pass money on to your heirs. But if you don't convert enough, you may be forced to sell growth assets at losses at the worst possible time, perhaps dangerously thwarting your wealth trajectory, and setting yourself up to run out of money before you run out of life.

As in so many things, balance is the key. Unfortunately for retirement planning, getting a clear picture on what balance looks like can be complicated and confusing, both to investors and to many advisors. Probably in no other area can high-end financial planning software, in the hands of a skilled and objective practitioner, be more valuable in averting disaster. Not the vidiot come-on retirement income apps used to hawk product, but real professional grade software. And again, beware that buying bonds (and fixed and immediate income annuities) during periods of low interest rates (like now!) comes with lots of purchasing power risk—so be extra careful!

You want to be sure to sidestep the guardianship sinkhole! Avoiding dependence on our children ranks as one of retirees' very worst fears. No one wants to be a financial burden on their children, especially when so many young families are struggling to achieve financial security themselves. But what retirees should fear more than dependency is guardianship.

Guardianship is where a court appoints someone else to take the legal responsibility to manage your assets and make decisions for you. Unless you have planned to avoid guardianship, it can become required if you ever get to the point where you cannot manage your affairs, typically from cognitive ailments like Alzheimer's, or other disabling accidents or conditions. Guardianship is a big problem for many reasons. The procedure is expensive and demeaning, requiring that you be proven legally incompetent, often while you are forced to look on. Once you are stripped of power and responsibility for your own affairs and the guardianship is in place, the appointed guardian (selected by a judge—not you or your family!) is tightly managed by the court. This can be the judge's idiot cousin, instead of your Harvard Law-trained attorney daughter. This in itself costs an amazing amount of money and hassle for you and your dependents. In short, guardianship is a thoroughly unpleasant and needlessly expensive mess.

Without proper planning, guardianship is a very easy mess to fall into. Fortunately, it can easily be avoided with common estate planning devices such as powers of attorney and living trusts. As discussed in the estate planning chapters, living trusts are far superior because they give you more flexibility and precision in controlling your estate and can help protect your heirs from lawsuits and other financial predators. Living trusts are also much more acceptable to banks, brokerages, and other custodians of your money; powers of attorney can often be rejected by asset custodians, who in the worst cases must be sued to recognize them, which can take a long time, during which you may be very uncomfortable. Much of the reason for this is the huge extent of financial fraud inflicted on seniors, most usually by family members. Living trusts not only allow for much more effective estate planning, but can save their cost many, many times over by avoiding needless probate fees and loss of control.

Watch out for the Catch 22 of a long, healthy life. Most of us want to live a long time, or at least as long as we feel good and take pleasure from life. Modern times are a fortunate time to feel this way, as lifestyle changes and rapidly advancing medical technology have extended life expectancies far beyond even those dreamed by science fiction writers just a few decades ago. Unfortunately, the dark flipside of this happy fact is that today's retirees need a much larger stockpile of funds to support long payout periods. The unforgiving equations of time and money yield the uncomfortable truth that many of us may not have saved enough, or invested profitably enough, to provide for a comfortable lifestyle for the long years of an extended retirement, even before the high costs of medical treatments to extend life even further are considered. Many investors—and most advisors who serve them—haven't properly prepared to build and manage a nest egg that might have to last 35 or more years from retirement. The pile of capital needs to pay for a retirement lasting from age 65 to one's early 70s is one thing—one can easily plan on consuming a measured amount of principal each year to accomplish this in style. It is quite another to plan the cash flow for a retirement stretching into one's 80s, 90s, or even beyond. In this case, consuming principal could be devastating; the longer the payout period, the more dependent retires are on just living off just the "interest" or other investment returns. As many of you have noticed, getting dependable returns without risk has become extremely challenging since 2007, the recent shazam COVID pop notwithstanding in the long haul. It gets even more challenging when the trends toward increasing taxes and reduced Social Security are considered, on top of the inevitable bear market. Since you will probably live much longer than any of your ancestors, you may well face the risk of running out of money with many years of life left. The time to plan for this is now! It begins with a sober assessment of what you can safely accomplish in terms of lifestyle budget over your realistic life expectancy. Critical factors are prudent risk control, meaningful investment returns, and hard-nosed tax control, along with serious countermeasures against the other risks highlighted in this chapter.

Let's leave you with a final pleasant thought. For many retirees, lifestyle change and enhanced healthcare costs are inevitable. Your personal health and genetic data (and your spouse's) can shed a lot of light on what's in store for you, but in the end you never know. Typically, retirement progresses slowly from an active recreation and travel phases, into a more sedentarily one, with higher health and prescription costs, and possibly with home health care, home modification, long-term care, and nursing home care later in life.

Budgeting for all these phases and other pesky considerations be extremely complex, frustrating, and uncertain. From my long and extensive professional practice, I can tell you I have only very rarely seen it done, even for those served by high-and-mighty, never-inexpensive, chest-thumping financial planners, certified, or otherwise.

But the alternative—ignoring the inevitable constellation of swirling changes and just assuming the money will work out—can be disastrous. This is another area where quality software (and again be careful to distinguish this from sales pitch software designed to drive commission sales) in the hands of someone who knows what they're doing and cares about doing a good job can really make a difference. Drill down. Do a *thorough* analysis, and review often!

Alright, enough, already! Chill, y'all. See ya in the next chapter, for sure, and in a fweibook.org class I hope!

Notes

1. Blanchett, David. "Alpha, Beta, and Now...Gamma." *The Journal of Retirement* 1, no. 2 (2013): 29–45.

    Accessed February 9, 2021.https://www.mstarbridgehouse.com/wp-content/themes/morningstar/resources/AlphaBetaandNowGamma.pdf.
2. United States Government Accountability Office, "Consumer Finance: Regulatory Coverage Generally Exists for Financial Planners, but Consumer Protection Issues Remain" (2011). https://www.gao.gov/new.items/d11235.pdf.
3. Pink Floyd, "Breath." Recorded 1972–1973. Track 2 on *The Dark Side of the Moon*. Harvest Records.

The Holy Grail…Screening for Smart Advisors You Can Trust

The Cartalk© guys used to gleefully zing about their law firm, the venerable Dewey, Cheatem, and Howe. Once upon a time, back in my dewy-eyed youth, I came up with a gag name I liked better, Badger, Hound, Fleece, and Dodge.

Now that I've got a few decades in the financial business, I often find such besmirches more applicable to financial advisors, than to lawyers (except for lawyers that are also financial advisors!).

This area is probably my biggest peeve, but I won't let myself get started. At least not too much. I'm actually a platitudes-spouting, award-winning academic researcher specializing in advisor education, ethics, and professionalism, but I'll cut through the ivory tower hoowy and try to just give you what you need to be a smarter consumer.

The financial advisor "profession" has some hair on it, no mistake. Licensure can be relatively easy to obtain, and true professional regulation is absent.

Many consumers may feel like Diogenes, endlessly casting a light in the fruitless search for an honest man. Finding a good advisor is needle-in-a-haystack hard.

For one thing, there is no profession of financial planning or financial advisory, as I demonstrated in one of my early academic papers.[1] There is no uniform regulation like in medicine or law. There's scattershot oversight of sales industries for insurance agents and stockbrokers, but nothing comparable to an AMA, Boards of Accountancy or attorneys' Bars. There is no

© The Author(s), under exclusive license to Springer Nature
Switzerland AG 2021
J. Camarda et al., *The Financial Storm Warning for Investors*,
https://doi.org/10.1007/978-3-030-77271-0_20

standardized, minimum body of professional knowledge, nor rigorous testing, vetting, and certification. Most importantly, there is no effective requirement to probe client needs and always put them first.

Nearly, anyone can call themselves a financial advisor. Regulatory restrictions on the term are scant or non-existent. Pretty much the same for terms like financial planner and investment advisor—these are technically under the purview of the SEC, but hardly anyone (including, sadly, the SEC!) pays much attention.

So you'll find this field a hot, scantly regulated, Wild-West stew of life insurance agents, bank tellers, stockbrokers, CPAs, real estate promoters, lawyers, CFP®s, and assorted other players, often looking good in a suit, but with differences in the depth of training and fiduciary obligations well-neigh indistinguishable to the general public, even the really rich and smart ones.

How bad is it? Let me give you some detail from my own career experience. Here's a snippet from my yute (misspelling courtesy of *My Cousin Vinny*).

"You now have a license to steal." Those were the words of the Wall Street branch manager to his rookie who'd just passed the Series 7 stockbroker's exam. I heard them at the huge broker training center where I was learning to cold call with the rest of the rookies. It was 1984. I was 27. I had a degree in chemistry but no training in investments besides the scant week I'd spent studying to pass my own Series 7. This was the "really hard" full-service stockbroker's exam, mind you, not the far simpler Series 6. This "study" mostly consisted of memorizing the answers to the hundreds of "practice" test questions they gave me, many of which I later saw on the exam. In my personal testing experience and in coaching employees to pass exams, memorization of practice exam questions—not deep study or exercises—seemed to be the ticket. This continues to the present day.

Once licensed I really had no idea what I was doing. But I was misty-eyed and trusting and very hopeful to support my new family with this job. Despite the "license to steal" quip—which most of us took as good-natured jocularity, but sadly took a darker view years later as we came to figure out the racket—I was very proud of myself. Look at me, an unemployed chemist and a week later, I'm a STOCKBROKER! My only jobs before this were pickin' antiques in college and selling home improvements door to door. Being a stockbroker—they call themselves financial advisors, as do life insurance salesmen, now—did then and still now signals a level of professionalism and social prestige not entirely consistent with the low bar needed to attain it.

I go here to demonstrate that the American financial advisory industry was and remains amorphous and lacking professional standardization and regulation. There are few guideposts to assess advisor quality, and risks to consumer welfare abound. Some 91% of investment advisors operate on conflicted sales commission licenses, though many if not most market themselves as fiduciaries. Again, this has become my special area of scholarly study. One of my early (award-winning) papers found that advisor misconduct was strongly associated with life insurance licensure, having both fiduciary and non-fiduciary commission licenses ("two-hats"—prone to switching when least expected), and, ahem, being male. In a new paper I just finished with my research team, we studied misconduct patterns among virtually all some-650,000 commission investment advisors in the United States. These are the stockbroker types licensed to sell securities, and this is the biggest data pool of advisors amenable to study. Their official term is "registered representatives." Misconduct—complaints, suspensions, fines, settlements, etc.—is public record for these advisors. Without going too deep into the academic weeds, we found elevated misconduct associated with high significance for two major categories which you may find interesting and probably alarming. I call these categories "badges" because advisors often tout them to get clients, and consumers may believe they indicate higher quality. They send signals of implied quality. Paradoxically, what we found was sharply higher misconduct associated with registered representatives who are: (1) Fiduciary investment advisors (two hats) or (2) Certified Financial Planners. Somewhat surprisingly—and quite encouragingly!—two-hat CFP®s showed lower misconduct, and commission-only CFP®s sharply higher misconduct (sigh).

It went way *down* for registered reps who are Chartered Financial Analysts (CFA®s).

Of course, there's lots more nuance and shades to this, and if you are really interested in the detail, drop me a line and I'll send you the paper. Not all fiduciaries or CFP®s are bad, of course. This is mostly an outlier effect, where most are OK but some are so bad they taint the barrel, and telling the difference can be devilishly difficult for the untrained. The major point is you *have to check*—you can't blithely assume a signal or badge like fiduciary or CFP® equates to quality, honest advice. Far too many sharks— a distinct minority but with 600K+ advisors still far to many—wear these badges and will use them to try to get your trust and your money. The kind of regression analysis used in the study, by the way, does not find relations— it finds correlations, a whole "nother kettle of fish." It is smoking gun stuff, not dead-to-rights evidence. But it provides very useful information on the probabilities of encountering an advisor with a history of misconduct, and in many cases serial misconduct. Again, bad actor odds go way up for two-hat nonCFP®s and for commission-only CFP®s. The new paper goes on to propose policy changes that will help consumers easily flag problem advisors, and I sure hope the regulators are paying attention.

So for a consumer litmus test, again hear this. The two most popular badges of advisory quality—being a fiduciary and the Certified Financial Planner mark—mask an alarming number of misrepresentative or downright abusive advisors. Primary findings? Having a record of misconduct is far more common than most investors imagine.

Consumers relying *just* on the CFP® (a bucket that includes all the single hat commission-only folks) or fiduciary claim may actually have a *higher* risk of putting themselves exactly where they hoped not to be—in the clutches of an advisor more prone to consumer abuse. Of course, there is much more to it than that, but people tend to rely on badges or labels or signals to save time and make decisions, which in advisor selection can be counterintuitive and dangerous.

Let's delve a bit more into the fiduciary and CFP® badges, since these tend to be the more popular consumer signals.

Many investors have finally gotten savvy to fiduciary and know that it means advisors who must put clients first. Not necessarily smart, but "honest." Or at least legally required to put clients first. While this seems pretty black and white, it's not as easy as it looks and still leaves room for lots of investor abuse. Getting a "real" fiduciary who's not covertly selling you expensive commission products can be a real challenge, but getting this right can be critically important, and literally could cost hundreds of thousands—or millions—in wasted family wealth, if got wrong.

Determining the difference between fiduciaries is fast and easy if you know how, but many consumers may not know how to conduct this important background check.

Advisors who claim to be fiduciaries can be of three sorts: (1) those that simply lie about it to get you to buy a high-commission, poorly disclosed product, (2) those who are actually dedicated, exclusive fiduciaries legally required to put you first, and—here's the squishy, dangerous part—(3) advisors who have both fiduciary investment advice licenses, and commission investment sales licenses, a condition known as "dual registration" regarding securities licenses. I call these "two-hats." For detailed instructions on sorting this out, Google my *Forbes* article on this called *When Fiduciary's Really A Four-Letter Word*.

Life insurance is an entirely different and much more opaque situation. Unlike securities licenses which are Federally administered, insurance is state regulated and much murkier and harder to get agent misconduct or other information. No organized database exists like the BrokerCheck we're about to discuss, which was the source of data in the above-referenced study. To that end, an adviser can be a bona fide securities fiduciary—without being a registered representative securities commission sales agent—but still a gun-slingin' out for blood life insurance commission sales agent. There is no easy way to check on the insurance licensure besides trolling the many states' license sites, or reading the hard-to-find fine print on the advisors website. In my humble view this is a major consumer protection flaw and a national misconduct database really should be built. Remember that even if an advisor is a securities fiduciary without a securities commission license, they can still have an insurance commission license, and the commissions on life insurance and annuity products tend to be not only hard to spot but out of the park huge. Annuities, since you probably don't know, are a form of life insurance. A pitch to beware of: "oh, yah! I'm a fiduciary. This insurance/annuity is the prefect retirement plan for you. Commissions? You don't need to worry about that! You pay no commission! I'm paid directly by the company..." Unfortunately the commission comes right out of your wealth, but in such a devious way you may not notice for years...if ever.

Sure gets murky!

Securities commission sales agents—again, we used to call them stockbrokers—are regulated by FINRA (Financial Industry Regulatory Authority) and typically have sales licenses like Series 6s or 7s. They are officially called registered representatives (RRs) and are sales agents of "broker/dealers," companies who deal in investment securities for a profit. They make money by taking (sometimes hard to spot) commissions and markups on investments. If you remember that the dealer means the same as in car dealer, you get the point. Most folks don't expect car sales reps to look out for their best interests, and registered reps are generally no different. It is perfectly fine, from a regulatory standpoint, for them to sell products that make more money for the advisor at the expense of consumers' wealth health. Perfectly legal, but not well-understood by most consumers.

Fiduciary investment advisors—officially "investment advisor representatives "(IARs) work for Registered Investment Advisors (RIAs) and have a legal obligation to put you first. RIAs are regulated by the SEC and actually comprise a whole different industry than broker/dealers.

Two-hat dual registered folks are licensed both by FINRA as non-fiduciary commission sales agents and by the SEC as fiduciary IARs. Dual registration—and I'm being charitable here—can make for confused advisors who may forget what hat they're wearing, and maybe sell a high-commission product to a consumer who mistakenly believes—or even is allowed or led to believe—that the advisor is acting as an IAR fiduciary. These are the smoking gun blokes we found sharply higher misconduct for. Maybe because consumers can become hopelessly confused, remembering only that the advisor once told them they were a fiduciary, and they just believed and trusted that, instead of questioning every recommendation to see if it was a product pitch, or reading the reams of disclosure documents that broker/dealers rely on to manage their liability.

Clearly, dual registration can expensively blur the line between what's best for the advisor and what's best for the consumer. Not surprisingly, repeated academic research[2] has found that in Florida, at least, dual registration is associated with significantly higher levels of advisor misconduct, like fines, license suspensions, client complaints, settlements, and so on. My recent national study confirmed this with a vengence.

It's not hard to imagine why, since such dual registration confusion can breed situations like the following true story, in this case, a retired lady using a large broker/dealer. The investor believed the advisor was a fee-only fiduciary who did not sell on commission and who put the investor's interests first. When I looked at her statements, I found a big-commission annuity. She insisted I call the "advisor" to clear the air. When asked, here's how the rap went. "Yes, I'm a fiduciary…Yes, I always put the client first…Yes, I only charge fees, no commissions!" When I challenged him about the million-dollar annuity found on his statement—an annuity that was showing no growth, had hard-to-find internal costs of some 6%/$60K a year, and which had generated an estimated commission of some $80,000 to him, over lunch—his response was—I kid you not—"well, except for *that*."

As you know by now, situations like this are actually encountered quite frequently by me in practice and clearly have the potential to be quite detrimental to a client's wealth.

This is a really big deal, since much if not most of the financial services industry remain in a buyer-beware stance, with "advisors" who can maximize their commissions perfectly legally, at the expense of investors' families' long-term wealth health. Where consumers believe advisors are putting consumers first, but advisors are legally free to line their own pockets at consumers' expense, the potential for massive consumer harm is enhanced.

This is not to say that fine, completely ethical work isn't routinely conducted by commission brokers and life agents who also hold fiduciary licenses and who remain cognizant of their respective duties. But the conflicts of interests are severe, the cheese keeps moving in the investments game, and many consumers may prefer to just skip the extra work and risk of using the these "two-hat" dually registered advisors when seeking fiduciary advice. In our recent study, we found these two-hat commission and fiduciary license advisors to be associated with four times the general misconduct, and nearly five times the advisor-related misconduct, as the entire study population. The whole CFP® bucket, including the "good" two-hats? Over seven times, and over ten times, respectively. Those are big-time betas (tobit regression coefficients, actually), baby! By contrast, CFA®s showed less than one-tenth of the misconduct as the whole population, which means around one hundredth CFP®s. The lesson here? CFA® is a fairly reliable signal to avoid misconduct. For CFP®s—whose misconduct probability at 77% is about 3x that of CFA®s—you simply MUST dig deeper. Though I stress that most are "clean" and the bad apples spoil the statistical barrel, the fact that some 22% show documented misconduct—some quite egregious—requires you dig deep. The badge really tells you nothing on its own.

Things *appear* to have improved a bit lately, though some fear it's more illusion than reality. There has been much ballyhoo recently about the new Regulation BI, for Best Interest. In a nutshell, or at least a ten-gallon hat, BI goes like this here. The advisor must act in the best interest of the consumer, and not put the interests of the firm first. Sounds great, until you realize this duty can be satisfied merely by disclosing that the advisor is acting as a commission agent for a brokerage firm, what fees and costs are, detail on offered products and strategies, and detail on conflicts of interests. All this can be satisfied by sending you more paper you won't read. The advisor needs to be able to show they exercised "reasonable diligence, care, and skill" in making the recommendation and has a "reasonable basis" to believe the recommendation in your best interest. The firm needs to flag and control conflicts that would put the firm first and control sales contests and bonuses that favor one particular product.[3] All this sounds very nice, but I can tell you from experience as a once gun-toting stock slinger that they are all pretty easy to dance around, to comply with the letter of the reg and still make gobs of money selling stuff that costs consumers far more than alternatives. One finance professor[4] has gone so far as to call BI "the greatest securities fraud in history..." explaining that "...now, brokers have begun advertising that they act in the best interest of their customers, who are going to believe that means they represent the customer, when in fact that's not the case."

A thorn by any other name still cuts as deep, and the spilt blood still spells buyer beware.

Next, let's take a tour of CFP® land. I warn you this will be a long segment, and you may just want to skim it. The reason I give you so much detail is because it's such a weird and counterintuitive situation that hiring a CFP®

may put you worse risk than using a non-CFP®. The words "certified financial planner" and the major marketing muscle behind the CFP® send an entirely different "highest standard" message.

Besides fiduciary, consumers typically rely on the CFP® letters as in indicator of advisor quality. My ongoing research over many years indicates CFP® may not be a reliable quality signal and consumers who rely on it may not get what they expect.[5] As the new national study discovered, having a CFP® was the biggest factor associated with reported misconduct. As noted, this ranged from seven to ten times that of the entire studied advisor population, depending on the misconduct measure. These findings were extremely statistically significant, all at the ***/1%/p < 0.01 value. These are major numbers in nerd-ville.

The CFP® long ago surpassed the CPA as the most-recognized financial credential,[6] and with sustained marketing, could soon top the CPA as the most trusted designation[7] as well. That's no accident. The CFP Board has spent a *lot* on advertising, with a recent annual budget pushing $12 M.[8] "The CFP Board now has spent more than $10 million a year for almost a decade promoting that the CFP® marks are the 'gold standard' when it comes to financial planning advice,"[9] according to respected industry blogger Michael Kitces.

Such trust, at least in some cases, may be severely misplaced.

Before I get into this, let it be known I think the CFP Board is the likeliest option to professionalize an industry desperately in need of it. It is well-organized, has great infrastructure and resources, and is widely known and respected. But for that to happen, I think it must endure pretty fundamental change. To work well, it needs to be converted from a tax-free non-profit to an actual professional membership organization overseen by its members. Many folks—including probably many if not most CFP®s—don't know that CFP Board is not a membership organization but instead a trademark licensing operation set up as a charity. Bizarre but true![10] Unlike professional organizations like the American Medical Association, the American Bar Association, or the American Institute of CPAs, the CFP Board is actually organized not as a professional membership group or professional regulator, but as a tax-free *charity*. It is run not by CFP®s but rather by long-tenured non-CFP® staff and a Board whose directors have short service terms, unlike staff. CFP®s who pay for the trademark license are not vetted or governed by peer review. They have no vote in the election or selection of executives or directors. They have no real say in formulating policy. In short, CFP Board is not run by CFP®s.

In a nutshell, CFP Board is an autocracy, controlled by a tight and perpetual inner circle. The largest component of the charity's cash flow comes from renting the right to use the CFP® brand.[11] The cash flow is robust. With over 80,000 CFP® licensees and counting, annual dues[12] generate nearly $30,000,000 a year to the 501(c)(3) non-profit. There have been persistent concerns CFP Board is more focused on growing its license base and revenue stream than enforcing quality financial planning. "There's much more interest in growing the number of CFP®s than there is in vetting them to protect the public," said a former CFP Board executive. A big chunk of these trademark license fees goes to support advertising to promote the CFP® brand and generate sales leads for CFP®s.[13]

It is a rich organization. For 2018, the last year I could find online, the CFP Board tax return listed[14] revenue of about $40 M and net assets of about $30 M. Despite its resources, the Board for a long time seems to have struggled to police its licensees, while at the same time, touting its troops as being "thoroughly vetted" and representing the "highest standard" of financial advice.[15]

A 2012 *Wall Street Journal* piece[16] reported a CFP® found to have been charging over 5% a year in fees plus taking commissions while claiming to be a fiduciary acting in the client's best interests. Multiple complaints were filed with CFP Board, that got "lost," and ultimately the client received a letter that no public action would be taken against this CFP®.

A year later, the *Journal* reported[17] hundreds of CFP®s improperly listed as fee-only on the CFP Board site who actually worked for commission brokerages like Morgan Stanley, UBS, Merrill Lynch, Raymond James, and others, noting "up to 11% of certified financial planners who work at big firms call themselves 'fee only' when, by definition, they can't be." While the Board publicly denied knowledge of the misrepresentation, one of its Disciplinary and Ethics Commissioners is on the record[18] as saying the Board had known about this "forever," and a commission CFP® is on the record as saying such rules don't "really apply to me" at Merrill Lynch. In the wake of the *Journal* piece, the Board did not sanction such CFP®s but rather issued broad amnesty.[19]

Press reports of ethical challenges have continued over the years. In 2019, the financial advisory world was rocked by the *Wall Street Journal* report[20] that thousands of CFP®s, nearly ten percent of Certified Financial Planners, promoted as clean on the CFP Board's "find a planner website," actually were not clean but had public records of misconduct ranging from customer complaints to crimes. Red flags include thousands of client disputes, fines, and suspensions, and including over a hundred felony charges or convictions. While the Board "boasts of its high standards and has touted its directory of professionals as a place where people can find a screened, skilled and trustworthy financial planner," in reality "what they won't find there is any indication that thousands of the planners bearing the board's seal of approval have had customer complaints or faced criminal or regulatory problems – often directly related to their work with clients," according to the *Journal* report. Regarding CFP Board's "thoroughly vetted" claim, the Journal reported it "has been presenting more than 6,300 planners (as clean that were not) ... more than 5,000 have faced formal complaints from their clients over investment recommendations or sales practices, and hundreds have been disciplined by regulators or left firms amid allegations of misconduct. At least 140 faced or currently face felony charges..."

Board CEO Kevin Keller has been quoted as saying "our primary goal is to keep certificants out of trouble" when pressed on why "actually enforcing standards" is not a priority.[21]

In the wake of the 2019 *Journal* exposé, in December of 2019, CFP Board appointed a task force which found "systemic, longstanding, governance-level weaknesses" which would "inevitably result in... a recurrence" if the Board failed to act. The Board accepted some but not all of the task force's recommendations.

As part of my team's most recent national academic study, in September of 2020, we reviewed the CFP Board site postings for the 151 CFP®s with the worst misconduct scores in our research. Of these, 138 (91%) were actively certified, and 126 (83%) were listed as in good standing (without CFP Board discipline). For the 25 with the very worst scores, we compiled a summary of disclosure events. Of these 25, 19 were actively certified, with 16 listed as in good standing. Of the worst CFP® offenders, 84% of certificants were shown as clean on the Board's site. One of these had 9 disclosure events over 16 years, including multiple large settlements, and a 60-day suspension of an insurance sales license, but showed up as clean as a CFP® licensee branded as "thoroughly vetted" and practicing to "the highest standard."

It appears the Board is moving, perhaps glacially, toward improving oversight and flagging bad apples, though it clearly suffers thousands of bad apples to still taint the barrel. Those of you not thoroughly exhausted by the preceding and who want more, Google my *Forbes* article called *America's Broken Financial Advisor Promise—What's Wrong with the CFP Board & Why You'd Better Check Twice Before Trusting a Certified Financial Planner.*

In any event, do these facts mean you should not consider an advisor claiming to be a fiduciary, or sporting the CFP® badge? Of course not! Many quality, ethical, caring planners fit this mold. But the sad reality is you have to dig much deeper, and can't just rely on the CFP® badge.

So what, dear and probably thoroughly bewildered reader, should you look for in a top-notch advisor?

As hopefully your stroll through this book has demonstrated, wealth management practiced well is a complex and arcane art.

To help you decide for yourself how to evaluate potential advisors, I'll start with the sort of checklist I'd give my kids or a beloved aunt, and then share some sense of how I run things in my own practice in case my model seems appealing to you. Mine is unique so far as I know—and I have looked!—but surely others have figured out what I have, though they may be very hard to find.

As you sift through this, consider what you may want from a planner. I see tremendous synergy in the family office approach—combining tax, estate, asset protection, business and real estate management, investments, accounting, retirement funding, insurance and risk control, and on and on. To me, this is the only sensible way to do wealth management. Put it all together and things seem to work much smoother and more efficiently together.

As bemoaned throughout the book, in a field every bit as complicated as rocket science or law, I am still astounded that the only regulatory requirements to "practice" are very basic licenses which can be acquired by those of average intelligence in only a few weekends of study without any background in finance or even a clean criminal history. These basic licenses are all the vast majority of advisors have, and I think it's a shame that this is the case and that most investors can't tell the difference.

Financial advice is one of the most mystifying services consumers purchase. In a field which has evolved to become as complex as medicine, it remains very difficult to tell the difference between highly trained, ethical, and effective advisors and charming salespeople who may or may not be able to effectively grow and protect your family's wealth. Hopefully, this chapter will help to clear the mystery and share some easy guidelines to help determine which advisor might best suit your needs, and whether your existing advisor makes the grade, or if you should consider replacing them. I believe there are eight critical factors, all of which I would want my family to have in a trusted and wise advisor.

1. Do they put you—or themselves—first?

2. How expert are they? Most sound like they are sharp, but are they actually highly trained and educated in wealth planning? What are their credentials? What proofs of education and expertise can they offer? Are they very well versed in all the major wealth disciplines to effectively quarterback your fortune and help dodge idiot advice from others?

3. Probably most importantly, are they tax savvy to conserve your wealth? Remember the status quo that many if not most tax advisors are not nearly as well versed in this extremely complicated area as you need them to be. Beyond this, do they *hate* needless tax? Far too many don't!

4. Is compensation clear and fair? Do they charge fees only? Have you done your due diligence to smoke out securities, insurance, and other commission licenses, and be satisfied these won't bite you when your guard is down?

5. Do they render deep advice and continuous planning or just sell products? You need an ongoing guide to steer you around the shoals and keep on course toward the gold. Be wary of the bait and switch, with promises of undying service that get forgot the moment the commission check is cashed…or only remembered when it's time to flip your products and convert more of your wealth into commission dollars.

6. How severe and obvious are conflicts of interest? Learn how to sniff these out, and read, read, read all the disclosure! This is the complex, boring stuff in fine print buried in the back of the package or the bowels of the website. They don't want you to see it. But it's there for legal reasons, like to point out when you complain—"well, all that was disclosed before you hired us." Bite the bullet and read it first!

7. Is there a record of misconduct? Is there regulatory disciplinary history? If they have insurance license, check out the record in the states of licensure. Look them up on BrokerCheck. Check with the BBB. Search their name and firm by googling "XXXX complaints." Look at Google reviews. Be a detective *before* you have lost big dollars.

8. Is there robust, third party recognition of excellence? Making lists like *Barron's* and *Forbes* is nice and says something, but I can tell you from having been on these for years they are not holy writ. Client references can help, but can be cherry picked. Being in the press because your advice is newsworthy is good, because the reporters will grill and fact-check you a bit. Beware badges of sales production like the Million Dollar Round Table (MDRT) that don't speak to expertise or advisory quality. And surly beware all the "best selling authors" who really just pay to put their names on a ghostwritten, cookie cutter book.

All these can be critical to getting excellent advice. The absence of even one of these factors can compromise the best quality and even lead to financial missteps or even disaster.

At the risk of being redundant, fiduciaries are legally required to put your interests ahead of their own, and to have a sound basis for all of the advice they give you. "Suitability" standard advisors—and this includes the vast majority of stockbrokers (even with the new BI twist), bank reps, insurance agents, financial planners, and others who use the term advisor (and all these last lot are not even BI-bound)—typically do not! While Reg BI (for "best interest") improves this somewhat, it still falls far short of an actual fiduciary standard and only applies to securities licensees. Non-fiduciary practice is a big reason to doubly beware life insurance/annuities sales folks pitching fixed insurance products (which include all the new equity index wonders). Most consumers don't know the difference between real fiduciaries and fair-weather ones, and most "advisors" are happy to let investors think their interests are first when really they are not. Make sure the advisor is acting in a fiduciary capacity on all the advice they give you—and get it in writing! And remember—two-hat part-time fiduciaries that also have sales licenses showed the highest rates of misconduct, right after CFP®s. You want a "pure" fiduciary to improve your odds.

Here's a neat trick. It's a Fiduciary Oath based on the one in my firm's brochure, that you can put into an email and ask the advisor to sign. If they won't sign something like this, your coal-mine canary just died! Do not use them! And make sure you tell them you need to email a signed copy to their compliance department—and copy you so you know they did—just to make sure you have something to rely on if they mislead you. If they promise to do this but never get around to it, BEWARE!

I Will ALWAYS put you first

(Enter firm name) _____represents it is an SEC Registered Investment

Advisor that believes in placing your best interests first. Therefore, we are proud to commit to the following six fiduciary principles regarding your investment planning:

1. _____ **will always exercise its best efforts to put your best interests first, above its own and its employees.**
2. _____ **will act with care and prudence, and with the skill, care, diligence, and good judgment of an accountable professional.**

3. _____ will seek to minimize your costs, not take compensation in any form on investment recommendations, and to clearly openly, and simply disclose how it gets paid on your behalf.
4. _____ will NOT accept commissions or other compensation besides fees for our securities investment management services.
5. _____ never intentionally mislead you and will provide conspicuous, clear, written, complete full and fair disclosure of all pertinent information of which it is aware. We will strive to tell you the whole truth as we know it, and not just parts that may serve our agenda.
6. _____ will seek to avoid conflicts of interest. We will fully disclose and fairly disclose any conflicts that we discover.

Advisor _____

Firm Affiliation _____

Date _____

Signature _____

Also, you want to be crystal clear on what you pay!

Sadly, most investors don't know how they pay their advisors, and many can even make it look like they work for free. Everybody loves free stuff. Even when clients know they must be paying something, the human mind will discount what is not obvious, and let itself believe things are better or cheaper than they are. Make no mistake, however: financial advisors usually make a lot of money. Even when you see a "reasonable" fee of 1% or less, there can be much higher additional costs that are hard to spot and rarely talked about by advisors. Some common products—I'm talking dastardly annuities here—may charge as much as 5% a year or more in fees that are nearly completely hidden, but perform no better than index funds costing less than 0.2% a year. This is important! The difference in wealth after 20 years with an average return of 7% and a 0.2% fee starting with $500,000 is over one million dollars, but gets shaved to less than half with 5% in hard to spot fees! (end value of $1,864,000 vs $743,000). And remember the legal disclosure— getting stacks and stacks of small print so intimidating and legalese-complex that few people ever read it, and fewer still understand it—often satisfies the liability requirements for a buyer-beware marketplace, but leaves consumers almost completely uninformed, yet happy, flush, and unaware their knickers have fallen to their ankles.

I am regularly astonished by how little people seem to understand about the true costs they pay in brokerage accounts and insurance products. They don't read the fine print and rely on some advisor's assurances that it is very inexpensive or even free—and in most cases, the advisor themselves probably does not know or understand the various ways the client is paying. Many sadly—and I hang my head in shame to have once been counted among them—know one number only—the commission payout.

Getting the full picture can be very difficult, and most investors don't have the time, inclination, or resources to do the research. To protect yourself demand a statement in writing of the various fees, costs, commissions, markups/markdowns, charges, insurance assessments, and other items that may be dragging your wealth down. Don't accept a box full of disclosure documents—demand a simple one-page explanation of everything you pay and be very suspicious of those who give you excuses instead of real information.

Beware of buying financial planning, but getting sold products. This is still far too common, and probably still the industry status quo. More and more, consumers are interested in financial planning. They are looking for solid, objective, and fiduciary advice. At the same time, the financial/investments industry remains dominated by companies driven by investment and insurance products profits. Advisors and their firms know consumers are hungry for advice and will typically pitch planning as a way to sell products, sometimes even generating elaborate, colorful financial plans and other (often boilerplate) documents. Unfortunately, in too many cases, such plans and planning are cunningly designed sales pitches, intended to promote an understated (or even hidden) product sales agenda.

In many cases, this can be worse than no planning at all, for two big reasons. First, the plan recommendations may be for high-compensation products the planner wants to sell, but which are not the best vehicles to target the consumer's actual financial goals. Remember non-fiduciaries are allowed to look out for themselves, not you, first, and BI lets brokers' disclosure wash most of this commission hair invisibly away. Second, if a "plan" is really a sales proposal (and I caution you that far, far too many are—and this can be really hard to tell!), it is very unlikely that the advisor will monitor and manage it for you. Once the commission is paid, the plan is likely to be forgotten, or only paid lip service without real updates and analysis. I see this all the time, but am still astonished by consumers who believe that "oh, Mr. Advisor is managing that for us" when it is clear that (a) they are not properly trained or even licensed to do so—and the legal authority—and liability!—for actual management rests with the client, not the advisor!—read that fine print, mate! and (b) there may have been no changes in 10 years or more, or, worse, commission-driven changes that do not relate to the plan at all. This is really sad, but true. I constantly see investment "plans" that are still deployed exactly as specified on the original now-yellowed paper application filled out eons ago.

I caution you that telling this can be very tough. It almost seems that the financial industry has carefully cultivated an illusion of service and clients-first duty which does not exist, in order to lull consumers into beliefs and decisions that profit Big Financial instead of consumers. As suggested above, your best defense is to get it in writing. Get a signed document of exactly what planning services will be performed, and when, and what you will pay. A good time to do this would be when you get the fiduciary compensation declaration we talked about.

You want to work hard to avoid fatal conflicts of interest! Conflicts of interest are inevitable. Couples have them. We even have them in our own heads all the time (ice cream? or exercise?)! The key is to try to minimize them so your interests and those of your advisor are reasonably aligned. Before you can minimize, you must recognize. That means do lots of digging and thinking. A good start is to insist on someone who pledges to act as a fiduciary for you—and make sure that what you hire them to do is what you actually need to advance your financial goals! What I call fatal conflicts occur when (a) the advisor does not have an obligation to put you first, and can legally make as much money on you—at your expense—as they can by convincing you to buy products you are allowed to believe are best for you, and (b) the advisor actually pushes the most profitable products on you to maximize their compensation, often at the request or demand of their employer (which, by the way, is who they owe a fiduciary duty to, not you). BI notwithstanding, some brokers will still find ways to make juicy, hard to spot markups on bonds, and some life agents will still sell "tax free" life insurance and guaranteed-return annuities, both loaded to the gills with hard to spot fees and cash out penalty charges (surrender charges are basically back-end load commissions, in case you did not know). Sociopath advisors do this with glee. Dumbass ones actually think they are serving you and still—Shazam!—make tons of money. These last sort can be the most dangerous, since they believe in free money. But there is none—that big commission comes out of your pocket—there is no other possible source. That's why I prefer the fee-only route to manage investments in my shop, and why we went that way way back in the 1990s. Fees are transparent, and we have no agenda to push one investment over another, since we only get paid by clients, not product vendors. Even this does not completely avoid conflicts! But it sure gets them out in the open, and I think mitigates them better than any other system I know. Most importantly, clients know exactly what they pay and can easily judge if they think they get fair value.

Another common error is not checking up on the advisor. We all like to work with people we like and trust. But the untrained look just as nice in a suit as those who have studied for years, and Bernie Madoff was no doubt very charming, indeed. You need to run a background check. Fortunately, this is pretty easy since FINRA and the SEC maintain an integrated site called BrokerCheck (http://brokercheck.finra.org/), and because many (though not all) financial advisors are registered with FINRA or the SEC. If they are not licensed by one of these, they are probably not licensed to sell or advise on securities, and that itself can be a red flag. It can mean they only sell fixed life insurance products, like those alluring equity index annuities that promise stock-market returns but a guarantee of no losses! Of course there is much more to it, but these stock-sounding "investments" are not regulated by FINRA or the SEC. No SEC/FINRA licenses can also mean they are shilling God-alone knows what. Steer clear.

Not all disclosures are causes for concern. For instance, I have one on mine (from around 1989, by golly!) showing registration in Michigan administratively revoked for failure to pay some $15.00 to "renew" a state registration I had never applied for or even knew about. Others—like the one below I pulled for an investor who asked for a portfolio stress test—are more troubling. This was for the investor's advisor at the time of the stress test:

activities occurred which led to the complaint:	
Allegations:	ACCOUNT RELATED-NEGLIGENCE; MISREPRESENTATION; BRCH OF FIDUCIARY DT; MISREPRESENTATION
Product type:	
Alleged damages:	$265,159.00
Additional information	

This is regarding a client complaint for negligence, misrepresentation, breach of fiduciary duty, and a claim for the return of over a quarter million dollars lost as a result of the broker's transgressions. This particular broker had several similar other disclosures, but remains employed. A groundbreaking academic study led by my pal Mark Egan (now at Harvard) found such misconduct is widespread.[22] More than one in ten stockbrokers have a disciplinary mark on their public records, and many prominent broker-dealers appear to "specialize in misconduct," according to the study. If you want to look up the firms with the worst track records per Mark's paper, go here: https://www.nber.org/papers/w22050. I'd give you the names myself, but I don't want to make my editor blush. This was "the first large-scale study that provides evidence documenting the extent of misconduct of financial advisors and advisory firms," said Mark. He found a high rate of disciplinary actions in the industry and that 44% of financial advisors who are fired for misconduct find new jobs in the industry within a year. "Why are some firms willing to hire advisors who were fired following misconduct?"[23] The study's conclusion? Because these ethically challenged producers are *earners*. Then can *sell*.

So better check it out yourself! BTW, these screens would not have popped that Madoff was a crook. A telltale would have been that his firm took custody—you made the check out to Madoff Investments, not your account at TD Ameritrade like how we and other reputable advisors do it. Bernie pocketed your dough and made up whatever he wanted on the Madoff statements. We've used Vanguard, Fidelity, and Schwab in the past. No, we don't work for them or take pay from them. We use them as safe places to keep clients' accounts custodied in clients' names. Beware any other arrangement!

Hopefully by now, I've impressed you to the point where you won't deal with the poorly trained, compensation-ally conflicted, or duties-muddled! You know I think it's a shame how very quick and easy it is to become a financial "advisor." Just having a government license means nothing in terms of deep knowledge.

So what sort of training credentials to look for in an expert advisor? My thoughts on what a "real" profession will shed some light.

To my mind, to do achieve true mastery across all important wealth disciplines, one must tread a long and difficult education path, as I have. Of course, I am an admitted outlier, and many advisors probably won't have the lifelong passion and commitment to do what I have done. For these reasons, I am probably not the best role model, and for a real, trusted profession to emerge, it is probably too much to ask others train themselves as I have.

I think the first basic step on the long road to financial expertise is the Certified Financial Planner™ (CFP®) or the Chartered Financial Consultant® (ChFC®). Despite my issues with CFP Board, their credential, and the education it represents, is valuable. That said, it is basic, undergraduate level training, not advanced expertise. It is a gateway, not a destination, credential. Typically, it represents a single undergrad class each in investments, insurance, retirement, estate, tax, and financial planning.[24] A degree is not required. Both it and the ChFC® can be self-study. As undergraduate degree programs in financial planning have emerged, I think such a degree and CFP® certification is an excellent foundation on which to begin advanced learning. To *begin*.

I emphasize these are not the be-all, end-all, but just the very basic exposure to fundamentals which must be refined and internalized with later, more advanced study. Getting wealth management education is not yet akin to going to medical school, but should be. One of my passions is to professionalize the planning trade to the medical professional level, and perhaps I will succeed.

This is not an easy mission. Commission sales of investment and insurance products are big, big business. A real problem is lack of Federal oversight of life insurance and annuities licensure and sales, and very powerful lobbying forces have succeeded in keeping it that way. This may be such an intractable problem that a true profession never emerges. Reduced transparency makes for easier sales. When New York recently imposed a rule requiring insurance companies to provide consumers cost-comparison information between commission annuities and their fee-only, fiduciary analogs, several companies instead chose to suspend sales of the less profitable fee products in order to avoid the requirement.[25]

While countries like Australia, the U.K., India, Norway, Finland, and Denmark have long banned commissions on the sale of investment products in order to reduce conflicts and protect the public, such a goal may be effectively illusionary given the US political system and the remarkable lobbying might of Big Financial.

What is, perhaps, more attainable is codification, professionalization, and regulation of financial planners/advisors. They should be distinguished from vendors in a way that pharmaceutical sales reps are from physicians. The Wild West application of these terms is confusing and damaging to consumers.

In my view, state regulation of advice is a critical issue and realistic goal. There are some things government does really well, and professional regulation is one of them. The CPA, MD/DO, attorney, and other state-regulated professional models work reasonably well, and far better than the financial advisory chaos. While the national Financial Planning Association supports state regulation,[26] perhaps not surprisingly, CFP Board is strongly opposed[27] to such a model, which clearly could wreak havoc with its own revenue machine, and, perhaps, often alleged (and denied) quasi-regulatory ambitions. As I said when Barron's interviewed me on advisor professionalism,[28] "professions are institutionalized, overseen, and enforced by government. The profession exists to serve society. The government grants monopoly power to qualifying professionals, and only they may practice. ... To practice as a medical doctor you need to be...licensed (or) you commit a crime. Ultimately, I see a real profession developing along these lines, regulated by a state analog to a Medical Association or Bar, requiring at least a Master's degree and maybe a practitioners doctorate called Wealth Doctor or something like that."

But I'm not holding my breath. In the meanwhile, smart consumers will want someone who is very extensively trained in multiple areas to help coordinate the extremely complex decisions you face to make the best financial moves. Having completed myself the CFP®, ChFC®, CLU®, CFA®, CFS®, BCM™, and EA, along with a masters and Ph.D. in financial planning, another masters in tax law cooking, and numerous programs and studies in technical analysis, asset protection, real estate, and all kinds of other stuff I can't remember right now, I still feel I've barely scratched the surface.

It is defiantly worth finding someone who can quarterback the many wealth disciplines for you. Most of the time, consumers—and their many fair-weather advisors—are "lost in space." Collaboration is minimal, advisors are territorial and mistrustful of each other, and clients don't know who to trust or whose advice to take. Often, of course, each advisor's own level of skill is less than optimal, but there is no overarching wealth manager who might point that out and clang the alarms.

If you want someone truly expert, you want someone with that kind of advanced, multidisciplinary background in study. We are rare indeed. In fact, I'm not aware of any others with this sort of skill set, but surely they are out there, at least a few, if you look hard and ask the right questions. At a minimum, I would want someone who has a CFP®/ChFC® (either), a masters in financial planning, a CFA®/CMT® (either) and an EA (not CPA) tax credential; the EA is all tax, the CPA is mostly accounting, not tax. Some (a minority in my view) CPAs are tax masters, but unless you are one yourself you probably won't be able to judge and pick. A clean misconduct record goes without saying, and I would quiz the advisor about personal tax strategies and net worth—if they can't do it for themselves, what kind of job would they do for you? I would also quiz them on the major concepts in this book, and if they fall short, insist they read the book and sign up for my classes at fweibook.org.

Finding top shelf advice is hard, but it's worth the effort. I mean, it's worth millions...or more! You simply have too much on the line to get bad, incomplete, or abusive advice.

On a final note, I would not necessarily rule out an advisor who takes insurance commissions. Probably not as a financial advisor, but at least to buy cheap term insurance from. Yes, there is much abuse in the life insurance space, and you must be wary. Wery, wery, wherery! (sic). But unlike the investments world where cheap, non-commission alternatives abound and are pretty universally superior to commission brethren, the insurance world—particularly the life and health insurance world—ain't like that. There's limited choice low-load (read low commission) and not much no-load. The product spectrum for commissionable products remains far, far broader than for products geared toward fee-only advisors. Perhaps this is because there are so few qualified fee-only insurance advisors, and the market is just too tiny to interest insurance companies in product development and promotion. For instance, I bet most agents and advisors are not even aware that fee-only/no commission insurance licenses—like the one I currently hold in Florida—exist. This license, by the way, prohibits commissions, and I think that's just perfect. And it's virtually unknown despite being around pushing a decade. It's called Unaffiliated Insurance Agent (UIA or UA), for those acting as "independent consultant ...analyzing or abstracting insurance policies...advice or counseling...for a fee... prohibited from being affiliated with an insurer..."[29] or taking commissions. But a problem with this model is for those consumers for whom a commissionable product is better, getting objective advice costs a fee, but they still pay a commission—so they pay twice. So I flip flop on this. In the end, I think you are safer having a fiduciary advisor—even at additional fee cost—direct your purchase of insurance products, rather than relying on the commission-slinger alone. Just too much risk.

Anyway, thanks for suffering this very long diatribe of a chapter, and all of my peeves and rants about the hair on the advisory profession! Hopefully we have armed you with a razor or two to trim misleading pitches and better protect yourselves, and make better wealth decisions for you and your family.

To atone, the next and final wrap-up chapter is right around the page! I promise to make it short, sweet, and pithy and deliver an energizing game plan to put you to happy work, getting richer and safer, and to dance between the raindrops of the gathering mega wealth storm!

Notes

1. Camarda, Jeff M. "Why Financial Advisors Have Yet to Leap the Professionalism Bar." *Journal of Personal Finance* 17, no. 1 (2018): 33–42.
2. Camarda, Jeff, Inga Chira, and Pieter de Jong. (2018). "Who is Less Likely to Be Involved in Financial Advisor Misconduct?" *Journal of Wealth Management* 21, no. 2 (2018): 85–96; Camarda, Jeff M. "Relation between Financial Advisory Designations and FINRA Misconduct." *Financial Services Review* 26, (2017): 271–290.

3. https://www.barrons.com/articles/a-quick-summary-of-the-secs-reg-bi-515638 32062.

4. https://www.barrons.com/articles/critic-calls-reg-bi-a-fraud-51561404290.

5. Camarda, Jeff J. "America's Broken Financial Advisor Promise—What's Wrong with the CFP Board & Why You'd Better Check Twice Before Trusting a Certified Financial Planner." *Forbes*, September 23, 2019. https://www.forbes.com/sites/jeffcamarda/2019/09/23/americas-broken-financial-advisor-promisewhats-wrong-with-the-cfp-board-why-youd-better-check-twice-before-trusting-a-certified-financial-planner/?sh=fea0ca737123.

6. Kitces, Michael. "Consumers Now Prefer Their Financial Planner To Have CFP® Certification Over A CPA License." *Nerd's Eye View* (blog). *Kitces.com*, July 20, 2015. https://www.kitces.com/blog/cfp-board-public-awareness-campaign-making-significant-brand-progress-as-consumers-prefer-cfp-to-cpa-for-financial-planning/.

7. Hood, Daniel. "Trust is Just the Beginning for Accountants." *Accounting Today*, March 4, 2019. https://www.accountingtoday.com/opinion/trust-is-just-the-beginning-for-accountants.

8. Schoeff Jr., Mark. "CFP Board to Launch New Round of ads to Build Public Awareness of Designation." *Investment News*, August 28, 2018. https://www.investmentnews.com/article/20180828/FREE/180829927/cfp-board-to-launch-new-round-of-ads-to-build-public-awareness-of.

9. Kitces, Michael. "Is The CFP Board Finally Ready To Enforce The Standards Its Public Awareness Campaign Promotes?" *Nerd's Eye View* (blog). *Kitces.com*, August 8, 2019. https://www.kitces.com/blog/is-the-cfp-board-finally-ready-to-enforce-the-standards-its-public-awareness-campaign-promotes/.

10. ProPublica. "Certified Financial Planner Board of Standards Inc: Form 990 for period ending December 2018." https://www.wsj.com/articles/looking-for-a-financial-planner-the-go-to-website-often-omits-red-flags-11564428708.

11. Ibid., 9.

12. "CFP® Certification Renewal Policies." *CFP Board of Standards*. https://www.cfp.net/for-cfp-professionals/certification-renewal/renewal-policies.

13. CFP Board of Standards. "Plan With Confidence. Partner With A CFP® Professional." https://www.letsmakeaplan.org/?utm_source=LMAP&utm_medium=header&utm_content=homepage&utm_campaign=header&utm_source=LMAP&utm_medium=header&utm_content=homepage&utm_campaign=header.

14. ProPublica. "Certified Financial Planner Board of Standards Inc: Form 990 for period ending December 2018." https://www.wsj.com/articles/looking-for-a-financial-planner-the-go-to-website-often-omits-red-flags-11564428708.

15. Zweig, Jason, and Andrea Fuller. "Looking for a Financial Planner? The Go-To Website Often Omits Red Flags." *The Wall Street Journal*, July 30, 2019. https://www.wsj.com/articles/looking-for-a-financial-planner-the-go-to-website-often-omits-red-flags-11564428708.

16. Roth, Alan S. "Is the Fiduciary Standard a Joke?" *The Wall Street Journal*, September 12, 2012. https://blogs.wsj.com/totalreturn/2012/09/12/is-the-fid uciary-standard-a-joke/.

17. Zweig, Jason. "'Fee-Only' Financial Advisers Who Don't Charge Fees Alone." *The Wall Street Journal*, September 20, 2013. https://www.wsj.com/articles/fee only-financial-advisers-who-dont-charge-fees-alone-1379714516.

18. Marsh, Ann. "CFP Board Allows Wirehouse Advisors to Call Themselves Fee-Only on Its Website." *FinancialPlanning.com*, September 19, 2013. https://www.financial-planning.com/news/cfp-board-allows-wirehouse-advisors-to-call-themselves-fee-only-on-its-website.

19. Marsh, Ann. "CFP Board Offers Broad Amnesty to Rule-Breaking Advisors." *FinancialPlanning.com*, September 24, 2013. https://www.financial-planning.com/news/cfp-board-offers-broad-amnesty-to-rule-breaking-advisors.

20. ProPublica. "Certified Financial Planner Board of Standards Inc: Form 990 for period ending December 2018." https://www.wsj.com/articles/looking-for-a-fin ancial-planner-the-go-to-website-often-omits-red-flags-11564428708.

21. Roth, Alan S. "The CFP Board 'Inexcusably' Protects Certificants at Expense of the Public." *FinancialPlanning.com*, August 2, 2019. https://www.financial-planning.com/opinion/the-cfp-board-inexcusably-protects-its-own-members-at-expense-of-the-public.

22. Egan, Mark, Gregor Matvos, and Amit Seru. "The Market for Financial Adviser Misconduct." *Journal of Political Economy* 127, no. 1 (2019): 233–295.

23. Braswell, Mason and Jed Horowitz. "Wells, UBS, OpCo Named in Scathing Report on Broker Misconduct." *AdvisorHub.com*, February 29, 2016. https://advisorhub.com/wells-ubs-opco-named-in-scathing-report-on-broker-miscon duct/.

24. Alabama A&M University. "Family Financial Planning Certificate Program." https://www.aamu.edu/academics/colleges/agricultural-life-natural-sciences/dep artments/family-consumer-science/_documents/fcs-am-fact-sheet.pdf.

25. Iacurci, Greg. "Jackson National suspends fee-based annuity sales in New York due to best-interest rule." *Investment News*, September 3, 2019. https://www.investmentnews.com/article/20190903/FREE/190909989/jackson-national-suspends-fee-based-annuity-sales-in-new-york-due-to?X-IgnoreUserAgent=1.

26. Schoeff Jr., Mark. "FPA splits with CFP Board over state regulation of financial planners." *Investment News*, September 28, 2018. https://www.investmentnews.com/article/20180928/FREE/180929914/fpa-splits-with-cfp-board-over-state-regulation-of-financial-planners.

27. "CFP Board Opposes State Regulation." *Forbes*, September 24, 2018. https://www.barrons.com/articles/cfp-board-opposes-state-regulation-1537810877.

28. Camarda, Jeff M. "Barron's Asks Jeff About His Designations & Misconduct Research." *Camarda Wealth Advisory Group*, December 5, 2018. https://www.camarda.com/camarda-again-interviewed-by-barrons/

29. https://goldcoastschools.com/news/i-have-a-florida-insurance-license-but-i-am-not-appointed-with-any-company-what-should-i-do/.

It's Your Wealth Ship, Captain!

Well, my merry pirates, it sure has been a wide-eyed cruise.

Part I seems a distant shore, and its stormy clime has no doubt softened in memory to an unpleasant yet poorly recalled blur, a mere hint of a stench, and perhaps to "not to worry!" rationalization.

Don't slip down that greasy gangplank!

Let's recall, for the nonce, that remote and shifting terrain.

We trudged through the momentous US government debt crisis and staggered through the perhaps worst stresses on states and local governments in living memory, if not ever. We cried over the looming implosions of Social Security and Medicare, then openly wept that whatever social welfare benefits that might survive the crisis would, alas, fall short of saving even a gnawed morsel to such fat cats as read this book. Worst, our own dwindling morsels stand to be raided to fuel the unquenchable redistribution fires.

We suggested that the COVID bailouts and the trend toward expanding social welfare would exacerbate this train wreck, and lamented that these conditions were perfect drivers for both massive tax increases and vicious inflation, even as a caring new administration keeps open the Fed money spigots, and romances a totally Blue Congress into more and more spending packages billed at a couple of *trillion* a pop. A trillion, as you recall, goes something like this here: $1,000,000,000,000.00.

We basked in the oxymoronic dilemma of a stock market foaming at the ticker even as COVID scorched the world and the likelihood that the bear will have his due in due time. And if all that were not frightening enough,

© The Author(s), under exclusive license to Springer Nature Switzerland AG 2021
J. Camarda et al., *The Financial Storm Warning for Investors*,
https://doi.org/10.1007/978-3-030-77271-0_21

we dwelt on the rise of Great China and the Age of the Machine, and the needle-in-a-haystack challenge of finding a smart and honest advisor to help parse through all this mess.

Search well, my oft-invoked Diogenes! Lest your wealth liver be eternally gobbled by birds of dollar prey, a slaughtered fat-cat Prometheus for the great redistribution age!

Figuring just how deep a personal fix you're in with all this mess going on is a complex problem for sure. Please forgive us for trotting you through the seven circles of your looming financial hell, but without a bead on the landscape it's awfully hard to plot the safest path through the she-hite blathering through the fan, and get you to the happy land you want to settle in.

In Part II, we offered the golden keys to the promised land of prosperity. We explained why and how taxes are financial acid and gave smart and uncommon tips on avoiding various sorts, with emphasis on the big wealth killers of income and estate taxes. You got deep insight on key elements of erudite estate planning, and solid information on asset protection barriers to keep financial predators from your booty. We reviewed the supreme importance of methodical and enlightened retirement planning and gave you sumptuous food for investment thought in the post-COVID stock bubble era, as the fires of inflation kindle anew, to potentially firestorm proportions. Finally, we spent a lot of time uncovering the veritable minefield that comprises the financial advisor marketplace these days, pointing out the profound ethical, regulatory, and educational shortcomings of this, ah, "profession," and gave you some sharp pointers on trying to find a good one.

Honest, smart, hard-working, and educated ain't easy to find, but we gave you the hallmarks to judge. What's more, there's a worksheet and scorecard in the appendix that can help you with this screening process.

Throughout the book, I tried hard not to proselytize and pitch to attract you as a potential client for my investment, estate, tax, etc., businesses. We do family office/comprehensive wealth management for families across the country, as I am sure you have figured out by now. But the book is motivated by my deep passion to help families build and keep wealth. It is not intended as a marketing tool, though if you have an interest and think we could be a fit I am happy to talk to you.

More importantly, I want to emphasize that you—yes you!—must commit to ongoing financial education. You need it to smoke out charlatan financial advisors, and you need to fill in the inevitable gaps in expertise of any trustworthy advisors you are lucky to find. I certainly don't know everything, and though I study from here to the grave I never will. That said, I am regularly astonished by the huge gulfs in expertise I encounter in the rare "good" advisors I encounter. They may be great with investments, tax (sadly very, very rare even in tax *specialists*) estate, financial planning, and so on, but are usually one-trick specialists clueless in other areas. Not to thump my chest too much, but advisors like me are most rare. I say once again that so far as I know, there are no others with my bandwidth of expertise. Surely some must exist—o golly I hope and pray so!—but are so rare as to be Holy Grails for those searching.

One of my many missions is to clone myself by teaching the expert systems I've developed to my expanding advisor team, both in my expanding firm and as affiliates. Those advisors reading this book or taking it for CE who resonate with my philosophy and ethical compass—which I am confident I have made remarkably clear—are encouraged to reach out to explore a working relationship. I can think of no better mentorship opportunity for bright, ethical, and ambitious advisors than throwing in with the lot of us.

All readers are encouraged to take classes at our Family Wealth Education Institute, free to readers by going to fweibook.org.

And you, dear consumer, must learn enough to find domain experts and stitch together a quarterbacked team with the disciplines you need. To do that competently you need enough knowledge to screen out the incompetent.

You have made a GREAT start by reading this book. I hope you keep it and refer to it often. But there is so much more to prudent family wealth management I didn't get into here. This book has a specific purpose. I needed to stay on point and avoid waxing encyclopedic lest my kind and lovely editor excoriate me; I am already nearly twenty thousand words over target and my skin trembles at the risk of her wrath. Perhaps I will do more books on other areas, and hope you will find and read them if I do.

In the meanwhile, I encourage you to take advantage of the education I regularly produce and "publish" on the internet. I make it available free for readers of this book at fweibook.org.

One of my passions is for the Family Wealth Education Institute I founded with my wife and business partner Kim. Once again, FWEI—we call it "fee-wee"—sponsors a vast and growing series of webinar-type online classes and other education on a very wide range of financial and wealth topics. I teach many of these myself, and try real hard—real, real hard—to make them punchy, fun, entertaining, and clear. That clear part's real important. You need to understand the why and the how without too much effort, or it won't do you any good. I am told by many that I succeed on all these counts, and that the video classes are fun, clear, and effective.

So I encourage you to check them out. Do it now before you shut the book and forget about it. Readers can access the entire catalog of on-demand courses at **fweibook.org.** You will also get alerts of upcoming new and live classes when you register. I tend to crank out new classes frequently. Check them out, have fun, learn a lot, teach your advisors something, and keep them honest! And please, share the resource with your family and friends.

So my friends, we come to the end of the rainbow! I hope you enjoyed our journey across the yellow brick road. You must remember: It's your money and your ship. No one will ever care as much about your pot of gold as you do, as much as you *must*. So scan the horizon, pick up the sextant (or GPS!), and study the charts. Even if you hire a helmsman, you are captain. It's your ship! Only you are responsible to see that your ship carries you safely across the tempestuous ocean of life, to gently deposit you on the bright, distant shore at the end of your days, with a clear map to the chest of gold you seek to leave your heirs. You alone, skipper. Enjoy and steer well the journey, or be lost in the waves in a leaky lifeboat, calling for help in the darkling, mocking night, as the sharks circle, the waves build, the wind howls, and the skies pour forth the biting rain. Plot your course well, keep sharp your skills, and good sailing!

Advisor Report Card

The following information can be used in several ways. The first section is a quickly read overview and will help you form an overall impression of your—or a prospective—advisor's comparative score. Section two applies the concepts to specific questions, with numerical scores that will produce an overall "grade." While either section can be used independently, reading section one, and then completing section two, will produce the highest quality judgment of your advisor's value as a professional to you.

Section One

- **Disclosure** Does your advisor tell you—*and* put in writing—everything you need to know to make an informed decision? Do you feel you understand costs, fees, risks, and conflicts of interest adequately?
- **Objectivity** Do you feel that your advisor makes recommendations purely in your best interest? Do you wonder if recommendations are made to benefit the advisor more than you?
- **Stand-Behind** If misunderstandings or outright mistakes have occurred, does your advisor accept responsibility and make things right without cost or attempt to assign blame to you? Have mistakes and lack of accountability cost you money?

© The Editor(s) (if applicable) and The Author(s), under exclusive
license to Springer Nature Switzerland AG 2021
J. Camarda et al., *The Financial Storm Warning for Investors,*
https://doi.org/10.1007/978-3-030-77271-0

- **Disciplinary History** Has your advisor—or their employer—had complaints from clients or action from regulators? This information is typically found at BrokerCheck. Have you checked? Does there seem to be a pattern of problems?
- **Portfolio Turnover** Do changes—or pleas to change—seem to occur frequently and for reasons you believe due more to commissions than prudent management? Do you suspect your portfolio is managed to target *your* wealth objectives, or for some other agenda?
- **Employer Turnover** Has your advisor moved around a lot, frequently finding greener pastures, and asking you to come along for the ride, producing extra work and expense for you? Do these changes impress you as being more for your or their benefit?
- **Proprietary Products** Does your advisor frequently suggest that their employers'—or a collection from brands that their employer seems to favor—products are best in an unusually high number of instances? Do you wonder if these products are recommended because they are really best for you, or if because they are more profitable for your advisor and their employer?
- **Reporting Clarity** Do your statements clearly show you how much money you make or lose, clearly showing effects of cash flows, and disclosing all fees and expenses? Do they tie all your accounts together in one easy, informative format? After reading them, do you *know*, or instead grab a calculator, scratch your head, and just hope for the best?
- **Credible Answers** When you ask questions, do you get easy-to-understand answers that make sense, and your advisor is willing to put in writing and will actually deliver? Or are the answers so convoluted that you question their understanding, or willingness to be completely forthcoming?
- **Wealth Management Simplification** Does your advisor have the skill and concern for what is best for you in order to consider recommendations that are coordinated with your overall life objectives—considering estate, retirement, college, tax, investment, risk-management, and special items of interest to you—instead of focusing on their own particular business interests?
- **Contact frequency/quality** Does your advisor reliably stay in touch to update you with important information affecting your situation, remind you of how important your relationship is, and stay apprised of changes in your life so as to constantly upgrade the advice they render to help you adapt to changing needs?
- **Life Simplification** Does your advisor's service help to simplify your life—maximizing your wealth and at the same time freeing you to spend less time

worrying? Does it seem the strategies optimize your assets for your goals and dreams? Overall, do you feel they help you work less, and gain more?

- **Risk and Suitability** Does your portfolio seem to be a good fit for you, or is it too risky—go down too much in bad markets—or too conservative—not make enough of a return to satisfy you—for your needs and disposition? How well matched are recommendations with your situation?

- **Service Speed and Accuracy** Are your instructions quickly executed, with error rates approaching zero? Are your calls returned promptly—in a day or less? When you request information, do you get what you want fast and without hassle, in a format that understandably answers your questions?

- **Investment Performance** Does your portfolio seem to show the kind of profit you expect? Does it consistently meet or exceed market indexes without excessive risk? Do you know if you've done as well as clients of the best professional money managers?

- **Risk Control** Is your portfolio structured to control risk, so that pieces balance and it is unlikely that everything will go down at the same time, such as a tech-heavy account in the early 2000s? Has your advisor explained the risk control techniques to your satisfaction, and have they proved effective by protecting your money in down markets?

- **Service Commitment** Do you know to what scope of service your advisor is committed, both legally and professionally? Have you purchased an investment *product* with no required ongoing service (other, perhaps, than lip service), or have you engaged for ongoing *service* of your investment needs? If there is service, is it described in a contract or agreement with your advisor? Does it require regular, ongoing reviews of your situation and portfolio? How frequently? With what degree of rigor?

- **Fiduciary Capacity** Does your advisor accept fiduciary allegiance to you? This means they accept legal liability to always act in your best interest, and be driven by your needs over their own pay or their employer's directives. Have they put in writing that they are fiduciaries acting solely in your best interest?

- **"Pure" or "Incidental" Advisor?** Is your advisor a "pure" registered investment advisor, whose only business is advice, or an "incidental" advisor, such as a brokerage house, bank, or insurance company, whose advice is "incidental" to their sale of products? Incidental advisors are exempt under the SEC's "Merrill Lynch Rule" from fiduciary accountability to you for their recommendations; "pure" advisors are fully liable for their advice.

- **Cost to Terminate** Are there significant costs to you if you decide to do something else with the money? Are "redemption fees," "surrender charges," "back-end loads," account termination fees, or sales commissions imposed if you decide to get out?

- **Compensation** What you pay is critical, but frequently poorly communicated to clients by advisors. The most common, in order of prevalence, are *commission* (sales agent for employer paid to sell you product, duty to employer, not you); *fee-based* (sales agent paid commission by employer for product sales and to collect fees for service, conflicted duty but mostly to employer, not you); and fee-only (only compensation is fees paid by you, duty is to you only as fiduciary). The compensation structure tells you a lot about the duty (or lack) to you and bears close examination. If confused, in doubt, or overwhelmed by material, request (and insist on receiving) a simple one-page letter describing the compensation structure and duty to you.

- **Total Product Costs** Today's investment products can be extremely complex, with many embedded costs that are not easy for clients (or even investment reps, who may care more about figuring their commissions than the costs to you) to ferret out and understand. Be sure you receive detailed disclosure on all costs, including compensation, product costs (including surrender charges, market value adjustments, trading charges, management, and other expenses). If unsure (and most investors should be) request (and insist on receiving) a simple one-page letter describing all costs and charges, at product, distribution, and liquidation levels.

- **Credentials** The financial world is extremely involved, and, like most professional endeavors, demands extended study for proficiency. While no panacea, professional educational credentials demonstrate at least an attempt at mastery. Look for advanced academic degrees in finance (or the somewhat less pertinent disciplines of economics, business, or accounting), or worthy professional designations like CFP®, ChFC, PFS, or CFA®.

- **Clear, simple answers to questions** This is a great litmus test that is often overlooked. There is nothing in investments that cannot be simply explained to the layperson of average intelligence, so that the concept is understood. When you ask questions, do you get reasonable, easy to grasp answers? Or are the responses hopelessly technical or mystifying? If the answers are not clear, it means one of only two things, neither good: the adviser does not know the answer, or knows but does not want to tell you.

- **References** The experience of other of the advisor's clients offers a rare window on what you can expect. Is the advisor willing to give you the names and numbers of more than a few "pet" clients willing to speak off the record of their experience with the advisor? While the SEC's "no testimonials" rule may inhibit firms from advertising that they offer references, those that make them available will give some to you if you remember to ask.

- **Clarity of duty** What, exactly, are you getting when you engage the advisor? Is there a clearly described set of functions you can rely on them to deliver? Or a loose expectation that they will make recommendations or sell products when the opportunity presents itself? Financial services are usually expensive, even if the costs are not clear, as is often the case. Do you know exactly what you are buying, even if unclear as to what you are paying?

Section Two

Disclosure

Does your advisor tell you—*and* put in writing—everything you need to know to make informed decisions?

2—All fees, costs, any conflicts, and what I get for what I pay is clear
1—Some attempts made but still unclear on costs, duties, and conflicts
0—This information not forthcoming or intentionally concealed

Do you understand costs, fees, risks, and conflicts of interest adequately?

2—Yes—it is well and frequently explained
1—Think so but really not sure
0—No, or suspect hidden costs/conflicts that I should know about

Objectivity

Do you *know* that your advisor makes recommendations purely in your best interest?

2—Have no doubt
1—Hope so but sometimes wonder if there's a commission motive
0—Think they care more about their pay than my best interests

Do you wonder if recommendations are made to benefit the advisor more than you?

2—No, my advisor's incentive matches my interests
1—Sometimes wonder

0—Believe so

Accountability

If misunderstandings or outright mistakes have occurred, does your advisor accept responsibility and make things right without cost or attempt to assign blame to you?

2—I'm made whole quickly & advisor even points out his mistakes
1—Advisor makes good but it's like pulling teeth
0—Does not acknowledge or correct mistakes

Do you wonder if mistakes and lack of accountability have cost you money?

2—No
1—Yes
0—It clearly has

Disciplinary History

Has your advisor—or your advisor's employer—had complaints from clients or action from regulators? (For companies, this information is typically found in news stories. For individual advisors/reps/planners, you can check by name at nasdr.com and myflorida.com.) Reports of problems should be a major concern

2—No complaints or disciplinary history
1—A few complaints
0—Pattern of problems

Portfolio Turnover

Does your advisor make changes to your portfolio—or urge you to change—for reasons you believe are due more to commissions than prudent management?

2—Never—changes well-reasoned and for my good
1—Sometimes calls seem more for sales than management
0—Believe all changes suggested mostly to benefit advisor

Do you suspect your portfolio is managed to advance some agenda other than your own?

2—No
1—Not sure
0—Think my advisor and their employer come first

Employer Turnover
Does your advisor change affiliations to find greener pastures and ask you to come along for the ride, producing extra work and expense for you?

2—Never
1—At least once
0—Several times or more

Do you believe these changes are more for your advisor's benefit than yours?

2—No
1—Not sure
0—Think my advisor's career and income come first

Proprietary Products
Does your advisor suggest that products offered by his or her employers—or a collection of products from brands that the employer seems to favor—are best for you in an unusually high number of instances?

2—Always
1—Sometimes
0—Never

Do you wonder if these products are recommended because they are really best for you or because they are more profitable for your advisor and his or her employer?

2—Always
1—Sometimes
0—Never

Reporting Clarity
Do your statements clearly show you how much money you make or lose, clearly showing effects of cash flows, and disclosing all fees and expenses?

2—Always
1—Sometimes
0—Never

After reading them, do you *know* the status of your accounts, or instead grab a calculator, scratch your head, and just hope for the best?

2—Always
1—Sometimes
0—Never

Credible Answers

When you ask questions, do you get easy-to-understand answers that make sense, and is your advisor willing to put these answers in writing and actually deliver? Or are the answers to your questions so convoluted that you question your advisor's understanding or willingness to be completely forthcoming?

2—Get clear answers nearly always
1—Sometimes get credible answers
0—Never get straight answers

Wealth Management Simplification

Does your advisor exhibit the skill and concern for your best interests that allow him or her to consider recommendations that are coordinated with your overall life objectives, such as estate, retirement, college, tax, investment, risk-management, and special items of interest to you?

2—Knows me well, knows what they're doing, takes care of me
1—Sometimes tries to optimize my "big picture"
0—Does not seem to know or care what is best overall for me

Contact frequency/quality

Does your advisor call and/or meet with you frequently to update you with important information affecting your situation, remind you of how important your relationship is, and stay apprised of changes in your life so as to constantly help you adapt to changing needs?

2—Frequent, quality contact designed to serve, not sell
1—Occasional contact *besides* sales calls
0—Contact infrequent or rare or pure "sales" calls

Life Simplification
Does your advisor's service help to simplify your life—maximizing your wealth and at the same time freeing you to spend less time worrying?

2—My advisor makes my financial life very easy to deal with
1—Financial life is complicated but manageable
0—I get lots of confusing statements, but little quality info or help

Does it seem that your advisor's strategies optimize your assets for your goals and dreams?

2—My advisor's actions track my goals specifically
1—There are some efforts to have recommendations pace goals
0—My goals are not asked about or are not followed

Overall, do you feel your advisor helps you work less and gain more?

2—Strongly agree
1—Somewhat agree
0—No

Risk and Suitability
Does your advisor take the time to get to know you—and keep up with your changing situation—and make recommendations that seem well suited to who you are and what you want?

2—Always
1—Sometimes or not sure
0—Never

Do investments recommended seem too risky (bigger losses) or too conservative (insufficient returns) than you want, need, and can afford?

2—Great risk/return match for me
1—Spotty match or not sure
0—Poor match

Have losses occurred that seemed much out of proportion to what you were led to expect, or allowed to believe?

2—Never—risks were clearly explained and understood
1—Sometimes
0—I am/was sometimes shocked by the difference between my expectations and what happened

Does your overall portfolio seem to be well balanced with the pieces complementing each other, or does your account seem more like it contains a number unrelated individual investments, which rise and fall on their own instead of as part of a well-engineered whole?

2—Portfolio seems well integrated
1—Spotty structure or not sure
0—No apparent (or explained) relationship between components

Service Speed and Accuracy
Are your calls returned within one day?

2—Always
1—Sometimes
0—Never

Are questions quickly answered to your satisfaction?

2—Always get straight answers
1—Sometimes clear, sometimes not
0—Never—all I get is jargon or smoke

Are your instructions executed promptly, without excessive cost or error?

2—Always
1—Sometimes
0—Never

Investment Performance
Does your portfolio seem to grow in line with your expectations, and at least pace market averages after all costs and expenses?

2—Yes, and I know it
1—Not sure

0—Pretty sure it does not

Do you believe your return matches that of the best available money managers?

2—Yes, and I know it
1—Not sure
0—Pretty sure it does not

Do you receive transparent reporting that lets you compare—without confusion—your returns to established indexes?

2—Yes, and I know it
1—Not sure
0—Pretty sure it does not

Risk Control

Do you know if your portfolio employs risk control, and if so, has your advisor explained the techniques so that you understand and believe them?

2—Yes
1—Not sure
0—No

The proof is in the pudding. During down markets, have your accounts held up better than you expected from the media, and heard from your friends? Did you sleep better knowing that it was unlikely you would suffer big losses?

2—Yes, my portfolio's been very stable
1—Not sure
0—It's been a roller coaster, and sometimes I don't want to look

Service Commitment

Have you purchased products, like mutual funds, annuities, or stocks or bonds that seem to receive very little attention once the sale has been completed?

2—No, my portfolio gets regular attention and management

1—Not sure

0—Yes, past sales receive little attention (except to sell something else)

Do you *know*—as opposed to *hope* or *believe*—to what scope of service your advisor is committed, both legally and professionally?

2—Yes

1—Not sure

0—No

Have you purchased an investment *product* with no required ongoing service or have you engaged for ongoing *service* of your investment needs?

2—*Sure*, it is pure service (fee-only)

1—Not sure

0—Products, or products and service (fee-*based*)

Have you received a written statement describing the services you have purchased and are entitled to receive?

2—Yes

1—Not sure

0—No

Are you receiving detailed, regular, useful reviews that help pace financial changes to your life changes?

2—Yes: frequent, detailed, substantive

1—Occasional reviews with some sales pressure

0—Never, or haphazard, or only for sales purposes

Fiduciary Capacity

Does your advisor accept fiduciary liability that they are liable that the advice they render to you is purely in your best interest?

2—Yes, they have made a point of telling me this

1—Not sure

0—No

Have they put in writing that you have received that they are fiduciaries acting solely in your best interest?

2—Yes, and have it in writing
1—Not sure
0—No

"Pure" or "Incidental" Advisor?

Is your advisor a "pure" registered investment advisor, fully liable for its advice, or an "incidental" advisor, such as a brokerage house, bank, or insurance company, whose advice is "incidental" under the Merrill Lynch Rule to their sale of products, and for which they are not accountable for acting in my best interest?

2—Pure, fee-only advisor
1—Not sure
0—Broker, bank rep, or insurance company agent (Merrill Lynch Rule)

Prudent Expert

Does your advisor adhere to the very highest legal standard for financial advice? Do they give you the same advice at the same cost that an investment expert would take for themselves? Have they (or will they) put it in writing that they accept legal liability for this standard?

2—Yes, and have it in writing
1—Not sure
0—No

Cost to Terminate

Are there significant costs to you if you decide to do something else with the money, such as "redemption fees," "surrender charges," "back-end loads," account termination fees, or sales commissions? Or does the advisor make it easy and pleasant to leave if you feel you no longer wish to purchase their service?

2—No cost, actually will receive unused fee refund
1—Not sure
0—They seem to make it expensive to leave

Compensation

Do you understand clearly what you pay, and what you get for it? Are compensation costs now, and later, carefully explained to you, and do you feel comfortable that they are fair for what you get?

2—Yes, clear and fair, and have it in writing
1—Not sure
0—No, and somewhat uncomfortable

What is the compensation structure?

2—Fee-only, fully disclosed fiduciary
1—Commission only or not sure
0—Fee-based

Do you have it in writing?

2—Yes, have it in writing
1—Not sure
0—No, or have asked but not received

Total Product Costs

Today's investment products can be extremely complex, with many embedded costs that are not clear. Have you received detailed disclosure on all costs, including compensation, product, distribution, and liquidation costs? Do you fairly understand them?

2—Yes, clear and fair
1—Not sure
0—No

Have all costs been fully explained in writing to you, in a simple, one-page document?

2—Yes, have it in writing
1—Not sure
0—No

Clear, simple answers to questions

This is a great litmus test. If answers are not clear, it means one of only two things, neither good: the adviser does not know the answer, or knows but does not want to tell you. When you ask questions, do you get reasonable, easy to grasp answers?

2—Always clear answers
1—Sometimes clear, sometimes not
0—Rarely or never

References The experience of other of the advisor's clients offers a rare window on what you can expect. Is the advisor willing to give you the names and numbers of more than a few "pet" clients willing to speak off the record of their experience with the advisor?

2—Yes
1—Not sure
0—No

Clarity of duty What, exactly, are you getting when you engage the advisor? Is there a clearly described set of functions you can rely on them to deliver? Or a loose expectation that they will make recommendations or sell products when the opportunity presents itself? Financial services are usually expensive, even if the costs are not clear, as is often the case. Do you know exactly what you are buying, even if unclear as to what you are paying?

2—Yes, advisor's duty is clear, in writing, and what I want
1—Not sure
0—No

Scoring Section Two

Scoring is simple. Just add the point total from your answers (count twice to be sure!) and divide by 51. Read your advisor's report card grade below, along with the opinion for the grade.

A—2.0 Excellent!—You seem to be in good hands. Congratulations!
B—1.6–2.0 Good. —You would probably benefit from a second opinion, if only to fine-tune an apparently decent program.
C—1.2–1.6 Fair.—Shop around.
D—0.8–1.2 Red flag.—Attention required. Interview others.
F—less than 0.8—Immediate action seems prudent.

Index